W9-BCF-154

# MINDTOOLS

## Computers in the Classroom

MINDTOOLS FOR CRITICAL THINKING

David H. Jonassen
*Pennsylvania State University*

Merrill, an imprint of
Prentice Hall
Englewood Cliffs, New Jersey . Columbus, Ohio

**Library of Congress Cataloging-in-Publication Data**

Jonassen, David H.
    Computers in the classroom : mindtools for critical thinking /
        David H. Jonassen
        p.  cm.
    Includes bibliographical references and index.
    ISBN 0-02-361191-X
    1. Computer-assisted instruction. 2. Critical thinking—Study and
    teaching.   I. Title.
LB1028.5.J612 1996                                         94-43081
371.3'34—dc20                                                  CIP


Editor: Debra A. Stollenwerk
Production Editor: Patricia A. Skidmore
Text Designer: STELLARViSIONS
Production Manager: Pamela D. Bennett
Electronic Text Management: Marilyn Wilson Phelps, Matthew Williams, Jane Lopez,
    Karen L. Bretz
This book was set in New Baskerville and Swiss by Prentice Hall and was printed and
bound by R.R. Donnelley & Sons. The cover was printed by Phoenix Color Corp.

 © 1996 by Prentice-Hall, Inc.
A Simon & Schuster Company
Englewood Cliffs, New Jersey 07632

Printed in the United States of America

10 9 8 7 6 5 4 3 2 1

ISBN: 0-02-361191-X

Prentice-Hall International (UK) Limited, *London*
Prentice-Hall of Australia Pty. Limited, *Sydney*
Prentice-Hall of Canada, Inc., *Toronto*
Prentice-Hall Hispanoamericana, S. A., *Mexico*
Prentice-Hall of India Private Limited, *New Delhi*
Prentice-Hall of Japan, Inc., *Tokyo*
Simon & Schuster Asia Pte. Ltd., *Singapore*
Editora Prentice-Hall do Brasil, Ltda., *Rio de Janeiro*

*To Rose Marie*

# MINDTOOLS

# Preface

The term *Mindtool* represents a concept, not a real entity. You cannot find advertisements for Mindtools. Rather, a Mindtool is a way of using a computer application program to engage learners in constructive, higher-order, critical thinking about the subjects they are studying. Although nearly any computer application program has the potential of being used as a Mindtool, not all are effective in amplifying learners' thinking.

This book presents a rationale for using Mindtools (Part 1), in-depth discussions of the individual Mindtools and their use (Parts 2 and 3), and suggestions for teaching with Mindtools and evaluating learning outcomes (Part 4). Part 1 consists of Chapters 1 and 2. In Chapter 1, I present the rationale for Mindtools and contrast them with other, more traditional uses of computers in schools. In Chapter 2, I describe the outcome of using computer applications as Mindtools: critical thinking. Critical thinking skills represent ways to think about the content one is studying, and Mindtools provide alternative ways of thinking about and representing ideas.

The Mindtools are described in Parts 2 and 3. The ones described in Part 2—databases (Chapter 3), spreadsheets (Chapter 4), semantic networking (Chapter 5), expert systems (Chapter 6), computer-mediated communication (Chapter 7), and multimedia and hypermedia (Chapter 8)—are powerful knowledge representation tools. The tools described in Part 3—computer programming (Chapter 9) and microworlds (Chapter 10)—are missing some of the knowledge representation components that the ones in Part 2 possess, so I refer to them as quasi-Mindtools. In these eight chapters, each Mindtool is described in depth and is evaluated in terms of the critical thinking skills it supports.

Because this book is designed as a handbook to be accessed, used, and experimented with, the chapters in Parts 2 and 3 share the same structure and features, which are intended to facilitate access to the ideas and experimentation with them. Each chapter provides examples of how the applications can be used as Mindtools, descriptions of how to use them as Mindtools, and suggestions for how to foster collaboration among learners who are using them. These chapters suggest software to use and also assess the learning outcomes from using each Mindtool. The focus of this book is practical, with an emphasis on experimentation.

Finally, in Part 4 I discuss some of the challenges to implementing Mindtools in classrooms, including the new roles for teachers that the use of Mindtools will require (Chapter 11) and the different types of assessment that Mindtools support (Chapter 12).

Mindtools represent an alternative application of computers in schools. They do not represent the only way computers can or should be used, nor are they the latest technological panacea correcting the intellectual ills of our schools. They are tools for engaging learners in constructive, higher-order thinking about the subjects they are studying, for extending learning outcomes and expectations beyond recall, and for helping learners become self-directed, critical thinkers. For teachers who wish to nurture these skills in their students, Mindtools are powerful and effective.

## Acknowledgments

I would like to acknowledge the help of many people, including the designers and developers of the many tools I describe in this book. They have advanced computing and thinking more than they know. I also want to express my thanks to the many students who have tested out many of the ideas, methods, and beliefs described here.

In addition, I would like to thank the reviewers of this book: David J. Ayersman, West Virginia University; Margorie A. Cambre, The Ohio State University; Richard A. Cornell, University of Central Florida; Thomas A. Drazdowski, King's College; Gary Ellerman, Radford University; Richard C. Forcier, Western Oregon State College; Kathleen M. Holmes, The University of North Texas; Mark A. Horney, University of Oregon; James D. Lehman, Purdue University; James Lockard, Northern Illinois University; Gary Marchionini, University of Maryland; Margaret L. Niess, Oregon State University; Sharon E. Smaldino, University of Northern Iowa; and Robert Tennyson, University of Minnesota.

Authoring is a bittersweet experience, aided in Chapter 2 by Rita Schnittgrund, in Chapter 6 by Scott Grabinger, and in Chapter 12 by Mark Davidson. I also appreciate the ideas, files, and screen dumps contributed by Richard Lehrer, Elliot Soloway, Robert Beichner, and Kathy Spoehr.

Many people, including Mauri Collins, Scott Grabinger, Peggy Cole, and Jim Lockhard, have provided insightful editorial commentary on the book. I cannot hold them responsible for the ideas contained herein, only for helping me to clarify those ideas. Last, and certainly not least, I gratefully acknowledge the impetus and support provided by my friend, colleague, and co-editor of *Cognitive Tools for Learning*, Piet Kommers, who helped me start this book during a difficult time in my life.

*David H. Jonassen*

# MINDTOOLS

# Contents

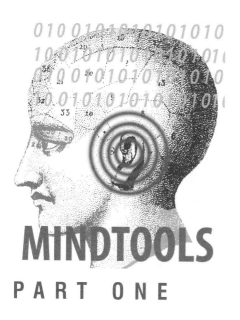

# MINDTOOLS

## PART ONE

# What Are Mindtools?
# What Do They Do?

· · · · · · · · · · · · · · · · · · · · · · · · · · · · · · · · · · · · · · · · · · · · · · · · · · · ·

Using computers as Mindtools requires a change of thinking about how computers should be used in schools. In Part 1 of this book I lay the conceptual foundation for using computers as Mindtools, providing theoretical, pedagogical, and practical reasons why using computers as Mindtools represents an important change in computer applications. Part 1 consists of two chapters:

**Chapter 1**   Learning *from*, Learning *about*, and Learning *with* Computing: A Rationale for Mindtools

**Chapter 2**   Using Mindtools to Develop Critical Thinking and Foster Collaboration in Schools

In Chapter 1, I present conceptual arguments for the use of Mindtools. After describing more traditional uses of computers in schools (learning *from* and learning *about* computers), I discuss educational and practical reasons why computers are better used as knowledge representation tools, that is, tools for thinking about the content being studied (learning *with* computers). I also provide some criteria for evaluating the usefulness of any computer application as a Mindtool.

1

In Chapter 2, I describe the primary intellectual reason for using computers as Mindtools: they engage students in critical thinking. I then provide some background on critical thinking, which is defined as a set of critical, creative, and complex thinking skills. These skills are used throughout most of the rest of the book to evaluate the mental outcomes of using each of the Mindtools described in chapters 3 though 10. In the latter part of Chapter 2, I describe yet another reason for using computers as Mindtools: they foster collaboration among students. Mindtools are best used collaboratively, and they provide opportunities for students to share ideas and build knowledge bases that represent their interpretations of the ideas being studied.

In Part 1, I present arguments that Mindtools represent new and alternative ways for using computers in education to engage students in critical thinking while they represent the content being studied and their knowledge of it. Mindtools are knowledge representation tools for thinking.

# CHAPTER 1

# Learning *from,* Learning *about,* and Learning *with* Computing: *A Rationale for Mindtools*

## Introduction

This book is about using computers to support education and learning. In it I recommend a significant departure from traditional approaches to using computers in schools. I promote the idea of using selected application programs as cognitive tools (which I call Mindtools) for engaging and enhancing thinking in learners. How are Mindtools a departure from traditional applications? I do not believe that students learn from computers—which has been a traditional assumption of many computer applications—but rather that students learn from thinking in meaningful ways. Some of the best thinking results when students try to represent what they know. Thinking is engaged by different learning activities, which can be embedded in the tasks and functional requirements of computer applications.

Mindtools, therefore, are computer applications that require students to think in meaningful ways in order to use the application to represent what they know. I argue that students cannot use the applications described in this book without thinking critically (engaging the mind). I also argue that the most appropriate use of the computer is as a cognitive tool for accessing information and interpreting and organizing personal knowledge. Just as carpenters cannot work effectively without a proper set of tools to help them assemble wood and construct furniture or houses, students cannot work effectively at thinking without access to a set of intellectual tools to help them assemble and construct knowledge. The recommendation of this book is that they use Mindtools.

The primary distinction between traditional computer learning applications and Mindtools is best expressed by Salomon, Perkins, and Globerson (1991), who speak of the effects *of* computer technology versus the effects *with* computer technology. The former refers to the effects *of* computers on the learner, as if the learner has no input into the process. The latter refers to the effects of the learner entering into an intellectual partnership *with* the computer. Learning with Mindtools depends "on the mindful engagement of learners in the tasks afforded by these tools," which raises the "possibility of qualitatively upgrading the performance of the joint system of learner plus technology" (Salomon et al., 1989, p. 4). In other words, when students work with computer technology, instead of being controlled by it, they enhance the capabilities of the computer, and the computer enhances their thinking and learning. The result of this partnership is that the whole of learning becomes greater than the sum of its parts. Carpenters use their tools to build things; the tools do not control the carpenter. Similarly, computers should be used as tools for helping learners build knowledge; they should not control the learner.

The purpose of this chapter is to lay the conceptual foundation for using the various Mindtools described in chapters 3 through 10. I will begin by briefly describing some traditional applications of computers for learning—learning *from* computers and learning *about* computers—and the shortcomings of these approaches. Next I will promote the idea of learning *with* computers—that is, using computers as cognitive tools—and justify that application with several theoretical, educational, and practical rationales.

## Learning *from* Computing: Computer-Assisted Instruction

Until recently, a primary use of computers in schools was to deliver computer-assisted instruction (CAI), including drill and practice, tutorials, and, on a very limited scale, intelligent tutors. CAI represents learning *from* computers, where the computer is programmed to teach the student, to direct the activities of the learner toward the acquisition of prespecified knowledge or skills.

### Drill and Practice

Throughout the 1970s and much of the 1980s, the most prominent form of CAI was drill-and-practice programs. These electronic ditto sheets presented problems—most commonly mathematical problems—for learners to solve. Learners would enter their answer and receive feedback about the accuracy of their response, often receiving graphic rewards (smiley faces, explosions, or other distractions to learning) for correct answers. Drills were based on the behaviorist notions of reinforcement of stimulus-response associations. The reward (visual distraction) enhanced the likelihood that learners would make a particular response when presented with a specific stimulus. More complicated drill-and-practice strategies, consisting of large item pools, placement algorithms, mastery learning, and review strategies, overcame some of the learning limitations of simple drill-and-practice programs. Unfortunately, the behaviorist principles underlying drill and practice are unable to account for, let alone foster, the complex thinking required for intellectual tasks such as problem solving, transfer of those skills to novel situations, verbal learning, and originality.

The best rationale for the use of drill-and-practice applications was automaticity (Merrill et al., 1986). In order to learn complex, higher-order skills, the argument goes, it is necessary for learners to first be able to perform the lower-level subskills automatically. So, practicing these subskills on a computer enables learners to gain automaticity. This assumption about learning is questioned by the contemporary learning theories described later in this chapter.

The thousands of drill programs that were made available to educators were easy for publishers to produce, and they satisfied the demand that teachers be innovative and use computers. The irony of their existence and use was that they replicated one of the oldest and most meaningless forms of learning, rote drill and practice. While drill programs did help some remedial learners who needed practice, they were not the most effective way to use powerful computer technologies.

## Tutorials

The monolithic nature of drill-and-practice programs gave rise to tutorials, which sought to respond to individual differences in learning by providing remedial instruction when learners' responses were incorrect. The archetypal tutorial would present some information in text or graphics and then ask the learners a question to assess their comprehension of what had been displayed. The student would respond, most often in multiple-choice format, and the tutorial software would compare the student's response with the correct answer. Correct responses were rewarded, while incorrect responses resulted in the presentation of remedial instruction. Sometimes the remediation strategies were fairly sophisticated, with the software providing instruction geared to the nature of the student's error. The program would then branch to alternative forms of instruction. Following the remediation, the program typically presented the problem again, affording the student another opportunity to respond correctly.

Tutorials consisted of sequences of these presentation-response-feedback cycles. Many tutorials also provided orienting strategies, such as objectives, advance organizers, overviews, summaries, and personalization (e.g., responding to the learner by name). More modern tutorials adapted to learners' entry level of learning, allowed learners to select the amount and form of instruction they preferred, or advised them about how much instruction they needed.

The inherent limitation of tutorials is that every form of learner response and appropriate instruction has to be anticipated and programmed. Anyone who has taught students realizes that it is impossible to anticipate how every student or even most students will interpret instruction. The other weakness of tutorials, according to learning theories described later in this chapter, is that they do not allow learners to construct their own meaning but rather seek to map a single interpretation of the world onto what students know. Students are not encouraged or even able to determine what is important, reflect on and assess what they know, or construct any personal meaning for what they study. What they too often acquire from tutorials is "inert" knowledge.

## Intelligent Tutoring Systems

The most sophisticated form of CAI is an intelligent tutoring system (ITS), sometimes referred to as intelligent CAI. ITSs were developed throughout the 1980s and 1990s by artificial intelligence (AI) researchers to teach problem solving and procedural knowledge in a variety of domains. What ITSs add to tutorials is intelligence in the form of student models, expert models, and tutorial models. Expert models describe the thoughts or strategies that an expert would use to solve a problem. How the student performs while trying to solve the problem in the ITS is compared with the expert model. When discrepancies occur, the student model is thought to have bugs in it, and the tutorial model diagnoses the problem and provides appropriate remedial instruction. ITSs have more intelligence in them than traditional tutorials and so can respond more sensitively to learners' misinterpretations.

Although ITSs are more powerful than traditional tutorials, there are many problems with the expert/student modeling procedures used in them. For example, Derry and LaJoie (1993) claim that the student model cannot possibly specify all of the ways that students may go about trying to solve a problem. And providing "canned" text as feedback cannot possibly offer the same sensitivity as a good human tutor. More important is the issue of whether tutorials should be engaged in intelligent diagnosis, because many educators believe that the most important goal of education is that students learn how to reflect on and diagnose their own performance. Students should be encouraged to become "reflective practitioners" (Schön, 1983). Derry and LaJoie also note that good ITSs are technically difficult to implement, often costing millions of dollars to develop. There are relatively few intelligent tutors available, and most are used in universities; virtually none have seen widespread use in public schools. Finally, the student modeling methods most commonly applied to tutors are useful only for diagnosing a particular type of procedural knowledge. ITSs resemble powerful instructional devices that benefit most, I argue, the professionals who develop them. Like Derry and LaJoie, I argue that limited instructional resources are better spent on *un*intelligent computer applications (to be discussed later).

## Learning *about* Computing: Computer Literacy

In the 1980s, when educators were grappling with the implications of microcomputers for education, most felt that it was important for learners to learn *about* computers. Definitions of computer literacy were developed to guide the use of computers in schools. Most of the early definitions included programming, often using BASIC (see Chapter 9 for a more detailed description). Later, educators developed more meaningful definitions of computer literacy, such as "the skills and knowledge needed by all citizens to survive and thrive in a society that is dependent on technology for handling information and solving complex problems" (Hunter, 1983, p. 9). Although computer literacy experts such as Luehrmann (1982) stressed that, beyond verbal awareness of computer components, computer literacy is the ability to do something constructive with the computer, what too many students learned on the way to becoming computer literate was how to memorize the parts of a computer. Learning to do something meaningful with computers is the subject of this book and is described in the next section.

For a number of reasons, computer literacy is no longer a major issue in schools. First, many more students are able to use computers (most play computer games and use a variety of word-processing and application programs) without instruction in schools, in part because computers are more available and easier to use. Many students have computers in their homes, and most are exposed to computers at an early age in preschools and elementary schools.

Second, the de-emphasis on computer literacy has resulted from discovering that learners do not have to understand the computer in order to use it productively. Computers are intellectual tools and, like most tools, should support the desired functionality in an efficient, comprehensible way. Clearly, skill with most tools relies on experience using it to accomplish real-world tasks. However, students generally do not need to study a tool—especially one as powerful as a computer—in order to understand how to use it. Contemporary software better uses the computational power of the computer to make the tools friendly or even transparent. Have you ever taken a course in telephone or automatic teller machine literacy? No, yet you can use telephones and automatic teller machines, which are controlled by sophisticated networks of computers, to place telephone calls or retrieve cash from your account. The trend in software transparency will only continue to improve software interfaces, making computer literacy even more unnecessary. Touch-sensitive and WIMP (*w*indowed, *i*con, *m*ouse-driven, *p*ull-down menus) interfaces of today will be replaced in the relatively near future with voice-activated interfaces that require little or no computer-literacy skills.

The third reason for the de-emphasis on computer literacy is that most of the applications or skills that students learned about did not support the educational goals of schools. Tools are really useful only if they help you perform a task you need or want to perform. Millions of students in the United States were forced to acquire computer-related skills and knowledge that had no relevance to them and did not support meaningful learning goals.

Another common problem with computer literacy is the "strong belief that vocabulary implies knowledge" (Bork, 1985, p. 34). It is a mistake to believe that if students memorize the parts and functions of computers and software, then they will understand and be able to use them. The following questions (from a test given to my fifth-grade daughter when she was learning about computers in school) are typical of those that are still asked of students.

| | | |
|---|---|---|
| _____ | 1. bug | A. programs for computers |
| _____ | 2. programmer | B. a mistake in a program |
| _____ | 3. software | C. like a typewriter |
| _____ | 4. CPU | D. person who writes games |
| _____ | 5. printer | E. the brain of a computer |

_____     Storage is where the information is saved. (True or False)
_____     A floppy disk is a piece of hardware. (True or False)

Unfortunately, it is much easier to assess vocabulary than thinking, so computer literacy remains largely verbal information.

I am not arguing here that knowledge of computers is irrelevant. Some knowledge of any tool is required in order to use that tool. That is why I begin chapters 3 through 10 with brief summaries of the software to be used as Mindtools. However, knowledge of any tool is most meaningful if it is acquired in the context of learning how to effectively use that tool. Memorizing the parts of a computer or any other facts about computers is relatively meaningless if the computers are not used as tools. Understanding results from using, not memorizing.

In summary, learning about computing should be situated in the act of using the computer to do something that is useful, meaningful, and intellectually engaging. If the task consists of something that is relevant to the learners or important to their educational lives, students will learn and comprehend more about the computer than they will from memorizing definitions.

## Learning *with* Computing: Mindtools as Cognitive Tools for Learning

This book is about Mindtools—computer-based tools and learning environments that have been adapted or developed to function as intellectual partners with the learner in order to engage and facilitate critical thinking and higher-order learning. These tools include (but are not necessarily limited to) databases (Chapter 3), spreadsheets (Chapter 4), semantic networks (Chapter 5), expert systems (Chapter 6), computer conferencing (Chapter 7), multimedia and hypermedia construction (Chapter 8), computer programming (Chapter 9), and microworld learning environments (Chapter 10).

Tools are extensions of humans. Throughout our history, we have developed mechanical tools to facilitate physical work. The wheel and the lever provided humans with an enormous mechanical advantage. The industrial revolution added artificial sources of power to extend that advantage. The information revolution has further extended that advantage by extending the functionality and speed of tools. As Salomon (1993) points out, tools are not just implements, but also serve culturally defined purposes and require a skilled operator in order to function usefully.

Electronic technologies, including the computer, have provided multiple information-processing functions. Many of the software tools developed for computers serve functions beyond themselves. They can assume different purposes. This book is about developing and adapting computer-based tools as Mindtools to extend cognitive functioning during learning, to engage learners in cognitive operations while constructing knowledge that they would not otherwise have been capable of (Pea, 1985).

Mindtools are generalizable computer tools that are intended to engage and facilitate cognitive processing—hence cognitive tools (Kommers, Jonassen, & Mayes, 1992). Cognitive tools are both mental and computational devices that support, guide, and extend the thinking processes of their users (Derry, 1990). They are knowledge construction and facilitation tools that can be applied to a variety of subject-matter domains. I argue, first, that students cannot use these tools without thinking deeply about the content they are learning, and second, that if they choose to use these tools to help them learn, the tools will facilitate the learning and meaning-making processes.

As I discuss further in Chapter 2, applications function as Mindtools because they engage learners in critical thinking. They do this by modeling—in their functions—critical thinking skills. For example, learners cannot construct semantic nets (Chapter 5) or expert systems knowledge bases (Chapter 6) without analyzing and therefore thinking critically about the content they are studying. The tools scaffold meaningful thinking; they engage learners and support them once they are engaged. Mindtools (as shown in Figure 1.1) actively engage learners in creation of knowledge that reflects their comprehension and conception of the information rather than focusing on the presentation of objective knowledge.

Mindtools rely on students for ideas. When they develop databases, for example, students are constructing their own conceptualization of the organization of a content domain. Mindtools do not necessarily reduce information processing (that is, make a task easier); rather, their goal is to make effective use of the mental efforts of the learners. They are not "fingertip"

**Figure 1.1**
Learning processes of Mindtools

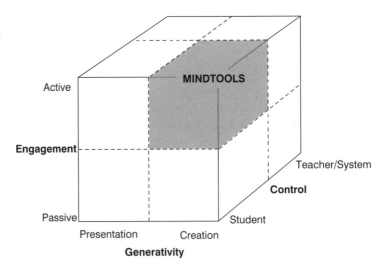

tools (Perkins, 1993) that learners use naturally, effortlessly, and effectively. In fact, Mindtools provide an environment and a vehicle that often require learners to think harder about the subject-matter domain being studied than they would have to think without the Mindtool. Learners are creators of knowledge rather than receivers of presentations. So Mindtools are cognitive reflection and amplification tools that help learners construct their own representations of a new content domain or revisit an old one.

# Why Use Mindtools?

## Theoretical Reasons for Using Mindtools

Mindtools foster constructive learning, in which learners construct their own knowledge rather than recall the knowledge of the teacher. Constructive learning, according to Simons (1993), is necessarily

- *active*—students process information meaningfully
- *cumulative*—all new learning builds on prior learning
- *integrative*—learners elaborate on new knowledge and interrelate it with their current knowledge
- *reflective*—learners consciously reflect on and assess what they know and need to learn
- *goal-directed* and *intentional*—learners subscribe to goals of learning

This definition sounds reasonable, but what do these attributes mean? How is active and cumulative knowledge construction different from regular learning, and why should Mindtools help?

### Knowledge Construction

Learning theory is in the midst of a revolution, in which researchers and theorists are arguing about what it means to know something and how we come to know it. The new theory that seeks to replace the old is *constructivism.* Constructivism is concerned with the process of how learners *construct* knowledge. How learners construct knowledge depends on what they already know, which depends on the kinds of experiences that they have had, how they have organized those experiences into knowledge structures, and the beliefs they use to interpret objects and events that they encounter in the world. Mindtools are tools for helping learners organize and represent what they know.

Constructivists claim that we construct our own reality through interpreting our experiences in the world. Reality does not exist completely in the "real" world. The teacher cannot map his or her interpretation onto the learner, because the two don't share a set of common experiences and interpretations. Rather, reality (or at least what we know and understand of reality) resides in the mind of each knower, who interprets the external world according to his or her own experiences, beliefs, and knowledge.

A common misinterpretation of constructivism suggests that if learners end up constructing their own individual knowledge representations, then intellectual chaos will result. If all learners have their own set of perceptions and beliefs, how can they share common representations? Constructivists believe this can occur through a process of social negotiation of meaning. Socially, we collaborate in determining the meaning of certain perceptions. For example, we socially agree on the meaning of a red traffic light, and society negotiates laws to solidify those interpretations. Social negotiation enables us to construct common interpretations of events and objects. Mindtools are media for collaboratively negotiating meaning. That process is required in order to build the kinds of knowledge representations provided by Mindtools.

Constructivist models of instruction strive to create environments in which learners actively construct their own knowledge, rather than recapitulating the teacher's interpretation of the world. In constructivist environments such as Mindtools, learners are actively engaged in interpreting the external world and reflecting on their interpretations. Active, constructive learning combats the occurrence of so-called "inert" knowledge (Cognition and Technology Group at Vanderbilt, 1992). If learners actively build their own interpretations of the world, they have more ownership of those thoughts, so those thoughts are less likely to degenerate over time. The foundations and implications of the constructivist debate can be investigated further (Jonassen, 1991; Duffy & Jonassen, 1992). The implication of the debate for this book is that Mindtools are constructivist knowledge construction tools.

## Reflective Thinking

Donald Norman (1993) distinguishes between two forms of thinking—experiential and reflective. *Experiential* thinking evolves from one's experiences with the world; it is reflexive and occurs automatically. You experience something in the world and react to it. *Reflective* thinking, on the other hand, requires deliberation. You encounter a situation, think about it, reflect on stored knowledge, make inferences about it, determine implications, and reason about it. Reflective thought is the careful, deliberate kind of thinking that helps us make sense of what we have experienced and what we know. It usually requires external support, such as books, computers, or other people. Computers support reflective thinking, Norman contends, when they enable users to compose new knowledge by adding new representations, modifying old ones, and comparing the two. Other conceptions of this idea are Donald Schön's (1983) "reflective practitioners" and the general idea of metacognitive thinking. Rather than merely absorbing what the teacher tells them, learners must reflect on what they know, assess that knowledge, and decide what it is they need to know. When learners perceive and declare an intention to learn, they learn those lessons much better.

Mindtools engage learners in these necessary reflections. Mindtools are a reflective use of technology. That is, using Mindtools necessarily engages learners in reflective thinking, which leads to knowledge construction.

## Constructionism

Papert (1990) distinguishes between *instructionism* and *constructionism.* Instructionism, the dominant method of teaching in schools, is based on the idea that students are passive receptacles for the information and knowledge that the teacher or the instructional media impart to them. Instructionism relies on the *sponge* method of teaching (Schank & Jona, 1991), where the goal of learners is to absorb what they are given until the examination, at which time the information is wrung out of them. The alternatives, Papert argues, are constructivism and constructionism.

> *The word with the v expresses the theory that knowledge is built by the learner, not supplied by the teacher. The word with the n expresses the further idea that this happens especially felicitously when the learner is engaged in the construction of something external or at least sharable . . . a sand castle, a machine, a computer program, a book. (Papert, 1990, p. 3)*

Constructivism and constructionism (perhaps an unnecessary distinction, since constructivism is a more generic concept and clearly supports the production of external products) both argue that learners should be constructors and producers of personal knowledge rather than receivers and repeaters of inert knowledge. When learners actively construct knowledge, it is more meaningful, applicable, and memorable.

# Educational Reasons for Using Mindtools

## Cognitive Processing Tools

In the past two decades, learning systems have become increasingly cognitively oriented, investing more intellectual responsibility and intentionality in learners. Designers of learning environments and instructional systems are engaging learners in more meaningful mental processing. The next logical step in this revolution is to invest additional responsibility in the learners for constructing knowledge. If this occurs, learners should become more self-reliant thinkers, better able to relate new information to existing knowledge and to apply that new knowledge in novel situations. Rather than designing learning systems that supplant the thinking of the learner, effective cognitive tools support meaningful thinking by performing lower-level operations that enable learners to generate and test hypotheses in meaningful problem-solving situations (Derry & LaJoie, 1993). Learning systems and environments that employ cognitive tools that perform in these ways represent a further step in the constructivistic direction of learner empowerment.

## (Un)intelligent Tools

Instructional systems, like computer-based instruction, too often try to do the thinking for learners, to act like tutors and guide learning. This is especially true in ITSs. These systems possess "intelligence" that they use to make instructional decisions about how much and what kind of instruction learners need. Derry and LaJoie (1993) argue that "the appropriate role for a computer system is not that of a teacher/expert, but rather, that of a mind-extension cognitive tool" (p. 5). Computers should be used as *un*intelligent tools, relying on the learner to provide the intelligence, not the computer. This means that planning, decision making, and self-regulation of learning are the responsibility of the learner, not the computer. However, computer systems can serve as powerful catalysts for facilitating these skills, assuming they are used in ways that promote reflection, discussion, and problem solving.

## Cognitive Partnership Tools

Cognitive technologies are tools that may be provided by any medium and that help learners transcend the limitations of their minds, such as limitations to memory, thinking, or problem solving (Pea, 1985). The most pervasive cognitive technology is language. Imagine trying to learn how to do something complex without the use of language. Language amplifies the thinking of the learner. Computers may also function as cognitive technologies for amplifying and reorganizing how learners think.

Unlike most other tools, computer tools can function as intellectual partners that share the cognitive burden of carrying out tasks (Salomon, 1993). When learners use computers as partners, they off-load some of the unproductive memorizing tasks to the computer, allowing learners to think more productively. Perkins (1993) claims that learning does not result from solitary, unsupported thinking by learners. So our goal should be to allocate to learners the cognitive responsibility for the processing that they do best while we allocate to the technology the processing that it does best.

For example, rather than focusing exclusively on how the computer screen presents information, we should also analyze what the learner is doing with the computer. Rather than using the limited capabilities of the computer to present information and judge learner responses (neither of which computers do well), while asking learners to memorize information and later recall it (which computers do with far greater speed and accuracy than humans), we should assign cognitive responsibility to the part of the learning system that does it best. Learners should be responsible for recognizing and judging patterns of information and then organizing it, while the computer system should perform calculations and store and retrieve information. When learners use cognitive tools as intellectual partners, their performance is enhanced, leaving some "cognitive residue" in the learners that will likely transfer in situations where they use the tool again (Salomon, 1993).

## Practical Reasons for Using Mindtools

There are also a number of practical rationales for using Mindtools that make their use in schools more feasible than other applications of computers.

### Shallow Pool of Software

The first practical reason for considering Mindtools is the lack of availability of traditional instructional software. Since the late 1970s, CAI has been available to support learning. Surveys have shown that approximately 85% of that software was either drill-and-practice or tutorial software that was designed to support rote learning. Even assuming that you wanted to use drills or tutorials, it is unlikely that you would be able find a program to drill the specific skill that was deficient. Despite the thousands of instructional programs that have been published, the sum still does not cover a fraction of the school curricula. There simply is no software available to teach in any significant way the bulk of subjects and skills taught in schools. Also, the difficulty of locating, selecting, previewing, and implementing each program, which typically covers only a single objective in the curriculum, is impossible for teachers and librarians. Mindtools require only a few, typically public domain, programs or software packages that are already available in schools. These application programs can be used across the curricula. That is, you can develop knowledge-oriented databases (see Chapter 3) in every math, science, social studies, literature, and health course taught in schools.

## Cost

The second practical rationale for using cognitive tools is cost. Each computer-based instructional program constructed by a separate software producer typically addresses only a single instructional objective or goal, or, at best, a set of related instructional goals. So, addressing a significant portion of the science curriculum would require many individual computer-based instructional programs. Most of these instructional programs—especially the higher quality ones—will cost well over $100 for a single-station license and several hundred dollars for a school-site license, so the cost of providing computer-based simulations or thought-provoking software for each school to cover even the science curriculum, for example, would likely be tens of thousands of dollars. Most of the software for engaging students with Mindtools is either already available in the schools or is available as public domain software.

## Efficiency

The third and related practical rationale for using cognitive tools is efficiency. Since Mindtools can be used across curricula—that is, in the sciences, social sciences, and humanities—to represent knowledge and content structures, and since the cost per application is so low, a great deal more of the curriculum could be affected by Mindtools than other currently available computer-based approaches to learning.

Not only do Mindtools provide cost efficiency, they also provide operating efficiencies. Each computer-based instructional program constructed by a separate software producer possesses a different set of outcomes and so involves different procedures for operating it and for providing related instructional activities. Learning the procedures for using each program requires the teacher to study the software and related instructional materials for each individual lesson. Having to adapt each instructional program to the needs and abilities of each class would not be an efficient use of teachers' time. Mindtools require the acquisition of a limited number of user skills that can be applied to the broad range of subject content. Mindtools simply represent a more efficient use of time.

# Evaluating Software as Mindtools

The software applications described in this book do not represent all of the possible Mindtools. New computer applications are being developed constantly, and many existing applications may be repurposed as Mindtools. In order to assess the potential of any application as a Mindtool, I will first distinguish Mindtools from productivity tools and then provide a set of criteria for evaluating the use of any application as a Mindtool.

## Mindtools versus Productivity Tools

Earlier in this chapter, I argued that learning *from* computers and learning *about* computers should be replaced by learning *with* computers. Learning *with* computers means using the computer as a tool to learn with. Computers are frequently used in schools and the workplace as tools to help students or workers produce work—as productivity tools. Using computers in this way involves computers as a medium for helping the user accomplish some task, making the user more productive. It is important to distinguish between Mindtools and productivity tools in order to explain why tools such as word-processing programs and paint programs were not included in this book as Mindtools.

Tools such as word-processing (the most commonly used) programs, graphics and paint programs, and computer-assisted design (CAD) programs have significantly enhanced the productivity of users. That is, they are powerful productivity tools and can make us more productive writers and artists. For example, most academics and writers have repressed their memories of the cumbersome nature of the writing process before word processors. Using even primitive (by today's standards) word processors like "Electric Pencil" on 8-kilobyte computers with cassette tape drives in the mid-1970s represented to me a revolution in the process of composition. Most of us believe that word processors have made all of us more efficient, effective, and productive writers. What is questionable is whether, as many advocates claim, word processors have made us *better* writers. In an unscientific study, Halio (1990) claimed that the use of more powerful and friendly Macintosh word processors by college students resulted in sloppier, simplistic, more banal, and grammatically incorrect compositions. The friendliness of the interface causes writers to perceive the computer more as a toy than as a tool, and this may arrest writing at an immature stage of development. Clearly, the ease of editing ideas makes us less careful during initial composition, but does that make us more *creative* writers? While Halio's findings have been widely criticized, I am not convinced that word processors significantly amplify the user's ability to write. They certainly facilitate the process—that is, writing is a conceptual talent that can be facilitated by productivity tools—but they do not necessarily amplify that process. I am not convinced that William Faulkner's novels or the characters in them would have been significantly enhanced had Faulkner used a word processor rather than his manual typewriter.

However, word processors, graphics and paint programs, and other productivity tools are not included in this book because I feel that they do not *significantly* restructure and amplify the thinking of the learner or the capabilities afforded by that thinking. Word processing does not restructure the task. It does not provide an alternative formalism for representing ideas. The formalism is language, which is the richest and most flexible yet complex formalism for representing knowledge. Word processing does not fundamentally change that representation process.

You may ask, then, Why include productivity tools such as databases and spreadsheets? They are also used most commonly as productivity tools. However, I believe that databases and spreadsheets, like the other applications described in this book, can also function as cognitive tools for enhancing, extending, amplifying, and restructuring the way learners think about content they are studying. These applications provide alternative conceptualizations of the content for the learner. They provide new formalisms for thinking. That makes them Mindtools.

Some will argue that the newer generations of idea-processing tools, which integrate note taking, outlining and structuring compositions, and drafting and proofing the text, are more powerful tools and can function as Mindtools. Examples of such programs are Writer's Toolkit (from the Scottish Educational Technology Council) and Writer's Assistant (Sharples, Goodlet, & Pemberton, 1992). While these are powerful tools for supporting the composition process, they only assist learners in using the composition formalism to represent their ideas. These programs do not restructure the knowledge representation process; in fact, they supplant much of the thinking that has traditionally been required to represent knowledge through composition.

As described before, Mindtools are intellectual partners that enhance the learner's ability to think. Although productivity tools significantly enhance production processes, they do not provide alternative ways of thinking. It may be possible for you to justify word processors, graphics, and CAD programs as Mindtools. In fact, I began writing chapters on word-processing and graphics programs more than once but could not justify their inclusion. In the next section I will present the critical attributes for my conception of Mindtools. I do not believe that word processors and graphics programs meet enough of those criteria to be included. Perhaps you can include word processors and graphics programs in *your* conception of Mindtools. A Mindtool is only a construct and not a real thing, so it is natural that our understandings of that construct may differ. If this is the case, I would encourage you to construct your own word-processing and graphics activities to supplement this text.

## Criteria for Evaluating Mindtools

In this final section, I will provide some criteria for assessing whether or not an application you encounter qualifies as a Mindtool. These are not absolute criteria, but rather indicators of "Mindtoolness." Each of the Mindtools described in this book will be evaluated using these criteria. The first three criteria are practical:

**1. *Computer-based.*** Doubtless there are many noncomputer applications that can function as Mindtools, but this book is about how to use computers more effectively as Mindtools.

**2. *Available applications.*** The software applications that are used as Mindtools are readily available, general computer applications. Good Mindtools may also function in ways that support other computing needs. For example, databases have a range of applications other than serving as a Mindtool, such as record keeping, scheduling, information access, and producing the index for this book.

**3. *Affordable.*** Additionally, Mindtools should be affordable. Most Mindtool applications are available in the public domain, as shareware, or from educational consortia, such as the Minnesota Educational Computing Consortium, that distribute software inexpensively. If not, they should be available from vendors at a reasonable cost.

The next six criteria are pedagogical and relate to the learning outcomes supported by Mindtools:

4. *Knowledge representation.* The application can be used to represent knowledge, what someone knows or how someone represents content or personal knowledge.

5. *Generalizable.* The application can be used to represent knowledge or content in different areas or subjects. Most Mindtools can be used in pure science (chemistry, physics, biology) or applied science (engineering) courses, math courses, literature courses, social science (psychology, sociology, political science) courses, philosophy courses, home economics and health, and even many physical education and recreation courses.

6. *Critical thinking.* Using Mindtools engages learners in critical thinking about their subject. That thinking is deeper, higher order, and/or more meaningful than memorizing and paraphrasing what someone else (the teacher or the textbook) said about the content.

7. *Transferable learning.* Using Mindtools results in the acquisition of generalizable, transferable skills that can facilitate thinking in various fields. This is different than number 5 above, which stated that Mindtools can be used in different subjects. This criterion suggests that critical thinking developed in the context of using Mindtools in science classes will transfer to (be applicable in) English classes.

8. *Simple, powerful formalism.* The formalism embedded in the Mindtool is a simple but powerful way of thinking. The thinking required to build knowledge bases or produce multimedia is deep. Expert systems require learners to think causally. If-then, cause-effect connections are not always obvious, but they are not that difficult to find when one searches for them in the appropriate way.

9. *Easily learnable.* The mental effort required to learn how to use the software should not exceed the benefits of thinking that result from it. The software should be learnable in one to two hours or less. The syntax and method for using the software should not be so formal and so difficult that it masks the mental goal of the system. You may want students to think causally about information in a knowledge domain, but if the system requires weeks of agonizing effort to learn, the benefits of thinking that way will be outweighed by the effort to learn the system.

## Conclusion

Mindtools are knowledge representation tools that use computer application programs such as databases, spreadsheets, semantic networks, expert systems, computer conferencing, multimedia and hypermedia, programming, and microworlds to engage learners in critical thinking. The process of using these tools as formalisms for representing the ideas being learned in personal knowledge bases represents an alternative approach to integrating computers in schools. Mindtools represent an effective and efficient way of integrating computers in schools. They can be used across the school curricula to engage learners in thinking deeply about the content they are studying. Mindtools are intellectual partners that facilitate knowledge construction and reflection by learners.

## References

Bork, A. M. (1985). *Personal computers for education.* New York: Harper & Row.

Cognition and Technology Group at Vanderbilt. (1992). Technology and the design of generative learning environments. In T. M. Duffy & D. H. Jonassen (Eds.), *Constructivism and the technology of instruction: A conversation.* Hillsdale, NJ: Lawrence Erlbaum Associates.

Derry, S. J. (1990). *Flexible cognitive tools for problem solving instruction.* Paper presented at the annual meeting of the American Educational Research Association, Boston, April 16–20.

Derry, S. J., & LaJoie, S. P. (1993). A middle camp for (un)intelligent instructional computing: An introduction. In S. P. LaJoie & S. J. Derry (Eds.), *Computers as cognitive tools.* Hillsdale, NJ: Lawrence Erlbaum Associates.

Duffy, T. M., & Jonassen, D. H. (Eds.). (1992). *Constructivism and the technology of instruction: A conversation.* Hillsdale, NJ: Lawrence Erlbaum Associates.

Halio, M. P. (1990). Student writing: Can the machine maim the message? *Academic Computing, 6*(1), 18–19.

Hunter, B. (1983). *My students use computers.* Reston, VA: Reston Publishing.

Jonassen, D. H. (1991). Objectivism vs. constructivism: Do we need a new paradigm? *Educational Technology: Research and Development, 39*(3), 5–14.

Kommers, P. A. M., Jonassen, D. H., & Mayes, T. M. (1992). *Cognitive tools for learning.* Heidelberg, Germany: Springer-Verlag.

Luehrmann, A. (1982, May/June). Computer literacy: What it is; why it is important. *Electronic Learning,* pp. 20–22.

Merrill, P. F., Tolman, M. N., Christensen, L., Hammons, K., Vincent, B. R., & Reynolds, P. L. (1986). *Computers in education.* Englewood Cliffs, NJ: Prentice-Hall.

Norman, D. A. (1993). *Things that make us smart: Defending human attributes in the age of the machine.* Reading, MA: Addison-Wesley.

Papert, S. (1990). Introduction. In I. Harel (Ed.), *Constructionist learning.* Boston: MIT Laboratory.

Pea, R. D. (1985). Beyond amplification: Using the computer to reorganize mental functioning. *Educational Psychologist, 20*(4), 167–182.

Perkins, D. N. (1993). Person-plus: A distributed view of thinking and learning. In G. Salomon (Ed.), *Distributed cognitions:* Psychological and educational considerations. Cambridge: Cambridge University Press.

Salomon, G. (1993). On the nature of pedagogic computer tools. The case of the writing partner. In S. P. LaJoie & S. J. Derry (Eds.), *Computers as cognitive tools.* Hillsdale, NJ: Lawrence Erlbaum Associates.

Salomon, G., Perkins, D. N., & Globerson, T. (1991). Partners in cognition: Extending human intelligence with intelligent technologies. *Educational Researcher, 20*(3), 2–9.

Schank, R. C., & Jona, M. Y. (1991). Empowering the student: New perspectives on the design of teaching systems. *The Journal of the Learning Sciences, 1*(1), 7–35.

Schön, D. (1983). *Educating the reflective practitioner: Toward a new design for teaching and learning in the professions.* San Francisco: Jossey-Bass.

Sharples, M., Goodlet, J., & Pemberton, L. (1992). Developing a Writer's Assistant. In J. Hartley (Ed.), *Technology and writing: Readings in the psychology of written communication.* London: Jessica Kingsley.

Simons, P. R. J. (1993). Constructive learning: The role of the learner. In T. Duffy, J. Lowyck, & D. Jonassen (Eds.), *Designing environments for constructive learning.* Heidelberg, Germany: Springer-Verlag.

# 2

# Using Mindtools to Develop Critical Thinking and Foster Collaboration in Schools

## Introduction: Conceptualizations of Thinking

Over the past few millennia, philosophers, theologians, and psychologists have developed many theories of thinking. They have developed a range of conceptions, from the simple disposition to behave in certain ways all the way to mysterious acts of sorcery. A detailed treatment of the evolution of thinking about thinking is beyond the scope of this book, so I will introduce the topic by briefly describing one of the more popular contemporary psychological conceptions of thinking, Gardner's "multiple intelligences."

Gardner and his colleagues examined the literature in cognitive capacities in individuals of all types in order to produce a theory of multiple intelligences (Gardner, 1983; Gardner & Hatch, 1989). This theory contends that there are seven different kinds of thinking, each with its characteristic use:

- *logico-mathematical*—using logical and numerical patterns and deductive reasoning; used by mathematicians, scientists, and logicians
- *linguistic*—sensitivity to sounds and meanings of words and language abilities; used by writers and literature teachers
- *musical*—sense of rhythm, pitch, and melody, and appreciation of musical expressions; used by musicians
- *spatial*—spatial memory and manipulating and transforming perceptions of visual objects; used by artists and architects
- *bodily-kinesthetic*—control of bodily movements and proprioceptive abilities; used by athletes and skilled artists

- *interpersonal*—understanding and dealing with the moods, temperaments, motivations, and behaviors of other people; used by counselors, social workers, and salespersons
- *intrapersonal*—understanding one's own feelings, motivations, needs, strengths, and weaknesses; used in guiding one's own behavior

Most individuals use most or all of these kinds of thinking, with varying levels of skill. And when we engage in complex learning tasks, we use combinations of these different kinds of thinking.

Since developing meaningful thinking through using computers is the focus of this book, and since my purpose is to contrast the thinking required by various computer tools, it will be necessary to settle on a single interpretation of what meaningful thinking should be in schools. Among the contemporary conceptions of thinking in schools, I believe that the concept of critical thinking (generalizable, higher-order thinking, such as logic, analyzing, planning, and inferring) is the most applied and therefore the most useful way to describe the outcomes of schooling and of Mindtools. Therefore, I will use critical thinking as the metric for comparing the effects of using Mindtools.

So, the primary hypothesis of this book is that using computer-based Mindtools necessarily engages learners in critical thinking about the topics being studied, which, in turn, results in better comprehension of the topics and the acquisition of useful learning skills. Each Mindtool described in the following chapters will be compared in terms of critical thinking skills, which I will describe in the following sections.

# Critical Thinking in Schools

## Traditional Models of Critical Thinking

Critical thinking as an issue emerged during the 1970s and 1980s as an antidote to reproductive, lower-order learning (Paul, 1992). Reproductive learning, resulting from the "sponge" method of learning as described in Chapter 1, leaves students with fragments of information that are not well connected or integrated: "What they have in their heads exists there like so many BBs in a bag." So Paul equates meaningful thinking with critical, logical thinking—"disciplined, self-directed thinking" (p. 9). Paul's elements of thought include the "ability to formulate, analyze and assess the

- problem or question at issue
- purpose or goal of thinking

- frame of reference or points of view involved
- assumptions made
- central concepts and ideas involved
- principles or theories used
- evidence, data, or reasons advanced (interpretations and claims made)
- inferences, reasoning, and lines of formulated thought, and
- implications and consequences that follow" (1992, p. 10).

Paul's conception of critical thinking, like most traditional models, regards it as "reflective thinking focused on deciding what to believe or do" (Ennis, 1989, p. 4), consisting of skills such as the following (Ennis, 1987):

- grasping the meaning of a statement
- judging whether there is ambiguity in a line of reasoning
- judging whether certain statements contradict each other
- judging whether a conclusion follows necessarily
- judging whether a statement is specific enough
- judging whether a statement is actually the application of certain principles
- judging whether an observation statement is reliable
- judging whether an inductive conclusion is warranted
- judging whether the problem has been identified
- judging whether something is an assumption
- judging whether a definition is adequate
- judging whether a statement made by an alleged expert is acceptable

According to Ennis, these skills occur in three dimensions: *logical* (judging the relationships between meanings of words and statements), *critical* (knowing the criteria for judging statements covered by the logical dimension), and *pragmatic* (considering the background or purpose of the judgment and the decision as to whether the statement is good enough for the purpose). So, the skill of judging the reliability of a statement, for example, involves judging whether a statement makes sense in terms of what it says, knowing the criteria for what make a statement reliable, and understanding the source of the statement and the context in which it is used. This is because critical skills are critical in different ways in different circumstances. Such a conception of critical thinking, like most of the traditional conceptions of critical thinking, is very logic-oriented. Traditional conceptions describe a restricted set of tasks that can be applied to ideas that already exist, but they do not account for generating original thoughts and ideas, which I believe must be the hallmark of any conception of critical thinking.

## Current Models of Critical Thinking

Walters (1990) describes the outcomes from traditional conceptions of critical thinking as the *vulcanization* of students. Vulcans, as exemplified by Spock in the television series *Star Trek,* are incapable of thinking or acting illogically. Spock's ability to stick to the evidence and draw logical conclusions made him unparalleled at problem solving and critical analysis. He never succumbed to prejudices, hidden agendas, or emotional confusion. He was the epitome of objectivity. However, he was also devoid of imagination, intuition, insight, and the capacity for metaphorical thinking. The literalness of his thinking made imaginative speculation and practical adaptability to novel situations impossible. His reasoning was reactive and not innovative. He was unable to suspend the rules of logic, even when his predicament required him to. Spock believed that logical thinking—or rationality—is good thinking.

Walters holds that there is a more holistic view of rationality, one that includes, along with the logical processes, intuition, imagination, conceptual creativity, and insight. He argues that much of the bandwagon effect of critical thinking assumes that critical thinking is logical thinking. Although Walters agrees that logical inference, critical analysis, and problem solving are fundamental elements of good thinking, they are practically useful only if they are supplemented by imagination, insight, and intuition, which he considers essential components of discovery. Concentrating only on logical thinking will produce Vulcans and not students who appreciate the multiple perspectives necessary for meaningful knowledge construction.

There are numerous other conceptions of critical thinking. Closer to the constructivist position I described in Chapter 1, Litecky (1992) defines critical thinking as "the active, mental effort to make meaning of our world by carefully examining thought in order to better understand content" (p. 83). Resnick and Klopfer (1987) also include aspects of thinking that are not included in traditional models of critical thinking. Rather than proffering a precise definition of higher-order thinking, they lists its key features:

- Higher-order thinking is *nonalgorithmic.* That is, the path of action is not fully specified in advance.
- Higher-order thinking tends to be *complex.* The total path is not visible (mentally speaking) from any single vantage point.

- Higher-order thinking often *yields multiple solutions,* each with costs and benefits, rather than a unique solution.
- Higher-order thinking involves *nuanced judgment and interpretation.*
- Higher-order thinking involves the application of *multiple criteria,* which sometimes conflict with one another.
- Higher-order thinking involves *self-regulation of the thinking process.* We do not recognize higher-order thinking in an individual who allows someone else to "calls the plays" at every step.
- Higher-order thinking involves *imposing meaning,* finding structure in apparent disorder.
- Higher-order thinking is *effortful.* There is considerable mental work involved in the kinds of elaborations and judgments required.

## Model of Complex Thinking

All of these conceptions are useful in helping us to understand the kinds of thinking that Mindtools engage. However, in order to compare and contrast the effects of using Mindtools, it is easier to use a single conception of critical thinking. Therefore, I have selected as a model one of the most comprehensive and useful models of critical thinking, the Integrated Thinking Model (Iowa Department of Education, 1989). It defines complex thinking skills as an interactive system, not a collection of separate skills. It also describes the various processes that are referred to as "thinking," and their relationships to each other. I will use this model to analyze and compare the effects of Mindtools discussed in this book.

This model has three basic components of complex thinking (see Figure 2.1): content/basic thinking, critical thinking, and creative thinking (the three circles surround the complex thinking core). Complex thinking includes the "goal-directed, multi-step, strategic processes, such as designing, decision making, and problem solving. This is the essential core of higher order thinking, the point at which thinking intersects with or impinges on action" (Iowa Department of Education, 1989, p. 7). It makes use of the other three types of thinking in order to produce some kind of outcome—a design, a decision, or a solution. I will discuss these three types of thinking in turn.

### Content/Basic Thinking

Content/basic thinking represents "the skills, attitudes, and dispositions required to learn accepted information—basic academic content, general knowledge, 'common sense,'—and to recall this information after it has

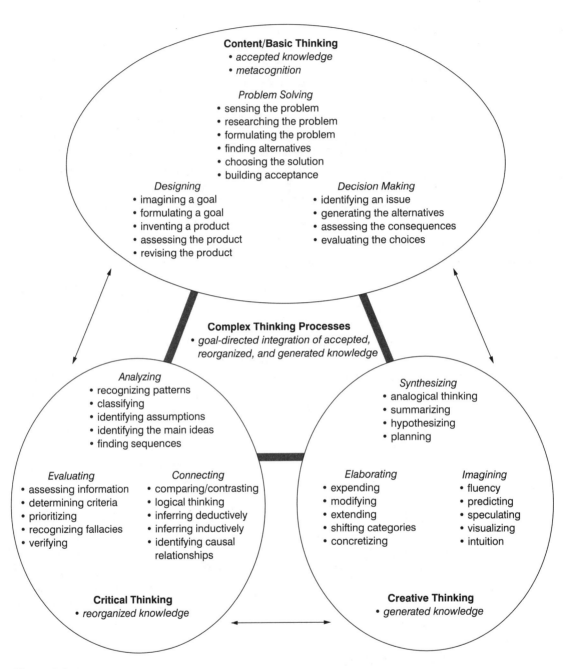

**Figure 2.1**
Integrated Thinking Model

been learned" (Iowa Department of Education, 1989, p. 7). Content/basic thinking thus includes the dual processes of learning and of retrieving what has been learned. Content/basic thinking describes traditional learning, except that it is important to note that this content-based knowledge is in constant interaction with critical, creative, and complex thinking because it is the knowledge base from which they operate. Since the hypothesis of this book is that Mindtools engage learners in critical thinking (which, in this model, consists of critical, creative, and complex thinking), I will focus exclusively on those thought processes in the analysis of each Mindtool.

## Critical Thinking

Critical thinking involves the dynamic reorganization of knowledge in meaningful and usable ways. It involves three general skills: evaluating, analyzing, and connecting.

*Evaluating* involves making judgments about something by measuring it against a standard. Evaluating is not expressing a personal attitude or feeling. It involves recognizing and using criteria in different instances. Recognizing criteria is important when criteria are unstated; otherwise, the learner is required to use a publicly available set of standards. It is also important that students be able to determine which criteria are appropriate. Evaluating information involves skills such as

- assessing information for its reliability and usefulness, and discriminating between relevant and irrelevant information (e.g., evaluating the meaningfulness of criticism of a film based on the ability of the critic; evaluating an historical account in terms of its accuracy)
- determining criteria for judging the merits of ideas or products by identifying relevant criteria and determining how and when they will be applied (e.g., developing an evaluation sheet for critiquing research studies; establishing evaluation guidelines for judging an art show)
- prioritizing a set of options according to their relevance or importance (e.g., ranking a set of interventions for solving a child's behavioral problem; rating a set of bonds for long-term gain)
- recognizing fallacies and errors in reasoning, such as vagueness, non sequiturs, and untruths (e.g., propaganda in political campaigns; sales pitches that promise more than they can deliver)
- verifying arguments and hypotheses through reality testing (e.g., solving proofs in geometry; checking the accuracy of arguments in court actions)

*Analyzing* involves separating a whole entity into its meaningful parts and understanding the interrelationships among those parts. Manipulating part/whole relationships helps learners understand the underlying organization of ideas. Analyzing knowledge domains involves skills such as

- recognizing patterns of organization (e.g., meter and rhyme schemes in poetry; arithmetic series)
- classifying objects into categories based on common attributes (e.g., sets in math, plant/animal classifications; economic, social, or political groups)
- identifying assumptions, stated or unstated, including suppositions and beliefs, that underlie positions (e.g., postulates in geometry; meaning in advertising campaigns)
- identifying the main or central ideas in text, data, or creations, and differentiating core ideas from supporting information (e.g., discovering the theme of a series of paintings; finding important arguments or themes in a passage or poem)
- finding sequences or consecutive order in sequentially organized information (e.g., determining sequences for preparing dishes in a meal; determining the order of operations in solving math problems).

*Connecting* involves determining or imposing relationships between the wholes that are being analyzed. Connecting compares and contrasts things or ideas, looks for cause-effect relationships, and links the elements together. Connecting builds on analyzing because it often compares wholes based on the parts that were analyzed. It involves skills such as

- comparing/contrasting similarities and differences between objects or events (e.g., comparing business plans; contrasting different phyla of animals in terms of locomotion)
- logical thinking, required to analyze or develop an argument, conclusion, or inference or provide support for assertions (e.g., evaluating the logic used in a geometric proof or a position paper in economics; using a method for determining an unknown element in chemistry)
- inferring deductively from generalizations or principles to instances (hypothetico-deductive or syllogistic reasoning) (e.g., proving theorems given a set of axioms; solving logic problems in philosophy)
- inferring a theory or principle inductively from data (e.g., developing a theory of animal behavior from observing animals in the wild; drawing conclusions from collections of data such as tables or charts)
- identifying causal relationships between events or objects and predicting possible effects (e.g., predicting the effects of a physics experiment; inferring the causes of social strife in a country)

## Creative Thinking

Creative thinking requires going beyond accepted knowledge to generate new knowledge. Many creative thinking skills are closely tied to critical thinking skills. Critical thinking makes sense out of information using more objective skills, such as analyzing and evaluating information using established, external criteria. Creative thinking, on the other hand, uses more personal and subjective skills in the creation of new knowledge, not the analysis of existing knowledge. That new knowledge may also be analyzed using critical skills, so the relationship between critical and creative thinking is dynamic. The major components of creative thinking are synthesizing, imagining, and elaborating.

*Synthesizing* involves skills such as

- thinking analogically, which involves creating and using metaphors and analogies to make information more understandable (e.g., creating characters to describe different chemicals or chemical groups; finding everyday occurrences to relate to fictional events in literature)
- summarizing main ideas in one's own words (e.g., summarizing the meaning of a story in English or foreign language; stating a personal method for solving math problems)
- hypothesizing about relationships between events and predicting outcomes (e.g., sampling classmates' attitudes about new laws and projecting their parents' beliefs; predicting the reaction of chemicals in a laboratory simulation)
- planning a process, including a step-by-step procedure for accomplishing activities (e.g., developing a new study sequence for improving course grades; developing a plan for completing a term paper)

Creative thinking also involves *imagining* processes, outcomes, and possibilities. It involves intuition and fluency of thinking, and often calls on students to visualize actions or objects. Visualization is a skill that some students will find difficult to develop because of individual differences in thinking abilities. Although imagining skills are not as concrete or easily taught as other skills, they are nonetheless important for generating new ideas. Imagining includes skills such as

- expressing ideas fluently or generating as many ideas as one can (e.g., thinking of things that are red and round; generating an adjective checklist to describe individuals in history lessons)
- predicting events or actions that are caused by a set of conditions (e.g., predicting the effects of new seat belt laws on traffic fatalities; predict-

ing the effects of healthier diets and exercise on body weights and fat counts)
- speculating and wondering about interesting possibilities, and solving "what if" questions without logical evaluation (e.g., speculating about the effects of a major earthquake in California; what if historical figures had known each other)
- visualizing, which involves creating mental images or mentally rehearsing actions (e.g., imagining yourself performing a double front flip in a diving class; imagining a battle between the immune system and an invading virus)
- intuition or hunches about ideas are powerful strategies that are impossible to teach but worth accepting, at least as hypotheses that can be tested using other skills (e.g., guessing the worth of a painting in an art class; predicting who will win an election).

Creative thinking also involves *elaborating on information*, that is, adding personal meaning to information by relating it to personal experiences or building on an idea. Elaborating includes skills such as

- expanding on information by adding details, examples, or other information (e.g., generating as many examples as possible of a concept such as "value"; developing a story around solving a type of math problem)
- modifying, refining, or changing ideas for different purposes (e.g., change a story line to have a sad ending rather than a happy one; modifying the form of a musical composition)
- extending ideas by applying them in a different context (e.g., treating science problems like military battles from history; translating experiences from one culture to another foreign culture)
- shifting categories of thinking by assuming a different point of view (e.g., changing from the role of a Democrat in a debate to that of a Republican; classifying food groups and nutritional values of typical meals from different countries)
- concretizing general ideas by giving examples and uses (e.g., writing a short poem in different meters; creating a voyage to the center of different atoms)

## Complex Thinking Skills

Finally, at the center of the Integrated Thinking Model are complex thinking skills. These thinking processes combine the content, critical, and creative thinking skills into larger, action-oriented processes. The three major types of complex thinking skills involve problem solving, designing, and decision making. These processes, each with a number of steps, are used in deciding whether, when, and where to use Mindtools. The Iowa Department of Education (1989) has described the critical and creative skills that are involved in each of these steps.

*Problem solving* involves systematically pursuing a goal, which is usually the solution of a problem that a situation presents. Problem solving is perhaps the most common complex skill. It includes the following steps and their related skills:

1. sensing the problem (intuition, visualizing, fluency, identifying assumptions)
2. researching the problem (assessing information, shifting categories, classifying, recognizing fallacies)
3. formulating the problem (summarizing, inferring, hypothesizing, concretizing, identifying main ideas)
4. finding alternatives (expanding, extending, modifying, predicting, fluency, speculating)
5. choosing the solution (assessing information, comparing/contrasting, determining criteria, prioritizing, verifying)
6. building acceptance (planning, fluency, shifting categories, inferring, identifying causal relationships, predicting)

*Designing* involves inventing or producing new products or ideas in some form, whether artistic, scientific, mechanical, or other. It involves analyzing a need and then planning and implementing a new product. Designing includes the following steps and their related skills:

1. imagining a goal (fluency, shifting categories, speculation, visualizing, intuition)
2. formulating a goal (visualizing, predicting, identifying causal relationships, recognizing patterns, hypothesizing, planning, logical reasoning)
3. inventing a product (fluency, planning, expanding, concretizing, shifting categories, analogical thinking, visualizing)
4. assessing the product (determining criteria, assessing information, comparing/contrasting, recognizing fallacies, verifying)
5. revising the product (expanding, extending, modifying)

*Decision making* involves selecting between alternatives in a rational, systematic way. Decision making includes awareness and manipulation of objective and subjective criteria. It involves the following steps and their related skills:

1. identifying an issue (identifying the main idea, recognizing patterns, identifying assumptions, recognizing fallacies)
2. generating alternatives (fluency, extending, shifting categories, hypothesizing, speculating, visualizing)
3. assessing the consequences (classifying, comparing/contrasting, determining criteria, identifying causal relationships, predicting, thinking analogically)
4. making a choice (summarizing, logical thinking, inferring, concretizing, intuition)
5. evaluating the choices (assessing information, verifying, intuition)

The Integrated Thinking Model from the Iowa Department of Education, described above, is probably the most comprehensive and rational model available for describing critical, creative, and complex thinking. Throughout the remainder of the book, each Mindtool will be described and evaluated in terms of the critical, creative, and complex thinking skills it engages and supports.

# Collaborating to Construct Knowledge

In Chapter 1, I stated that one of the educational rationales for using Mindtools is knowledge construction. Learners who construct their own representations will better comprehend and remember what they learn. One of the essential means for helping learners construct their own knowledge representations is collaboration (Jonassen, 1994). It is not necessary to construct knowledge in isolation. In fact, constructivists believe that social negotiation of knowledge is the purpose of collaboration. Groups of people can collaboratively build more meaningful knowledge than individuals alone. So it is with Mindtools. They are probably best used, in most circumstances, collaboratively. In fact, it is quite likely that cooperation will be *required* to use them, since they require learners to think in new ways. The skills of using Mindtools are new for many learners. So, in this chapter and throughout the book, I will describe reasons and methods for collaborating in the reflective knowledge construction that is engaged by using Mindtools.

It is therefore necessary to lay the foundation for collaborative use of Mindtools, to describe some of the assumptions that collaborative learning makes. Collaborative groups must cooperate. Cooperation is more than sharing the same space or assignment. In order for groups to cooperate, four elements must be present: positive interdependence (succeeding or failing together); face-to-face interaction; individual accountability (personal responsibility of each member); and interpersonal skills (Johnson & Johnson, 1987). In collaborative groups, learners must share a goal and a vision about how to reach that goal, and they must work together in order to attain that goal.

Collaboration is a method of learning that students too seldom use, especially when teachers insist on conveying their own interpretations of the world and holding each student personally and individually responsible for understanding (or at least remembering) those interpretations. Cooperation works because responsibility is spread out and because other group members support the performance of the group; both of these factors lead to increased motivation to perform (Slavin, 1983). In addition to improved achievement, cooperative learning leads to improved interpersonal relations among its members (Johnson & Johnson, 1987), which, in turn, improve the self-esteem of its members (Slavin, 1983).

You cannot assume that learners necessarily possess the skills needed to collaborate with other students, since they have seldom been required to collaborate, at least in formal educational settings (the literature on everyday thinking suggests that learners can collaborate effectively in solving real-world, everyday problems). They need to learn how to communicate, how to assume leadership, and how to deal with controversy when it arises. Johnson and Johnson (1987) identified many of the following skills as critical to collaborative efforts:

- clearly communicating ideas and feelings in the group
- stating complete and specific messages that convey needs and interpretations
- asking for and receiving concise feedback about how messages were received, that is, what the receiver understood from the message
- paraphrasing the content of a message without evaluating its content
- discerning and describing the feelings of the sender of the message
- negotiating the meaning of any message or information
- accepting, sharing with, and supporting the needs and wants of other members of the group
- taking action to ensure the completion of the group's responsibility, such as determining the required tasks and subtasks that need to be completed in order to achieve the group goal and delegating responsibility for those tasks to group members

- negotiating responsibility for completing required tasks or portions of tasks that lead to completion of the group problem
- accepting responsibility for completing the tasks or portions of the tasks assigned to each member
- learning how to argue ideas and positions and to not personalize those arguments
- clarifying differences of opinion or interpretation
- empathizing with the other members of the group

Implementing collaborative learning involves agreeing on and understanding each skill, practicing and receiving feedback on the use of each skill within the group, and using each skill consistently in learning situations. In order to accomplish these objectives, you must certainly be committed to cooperative and collaborative learning in the classroom.

## Collaborative Use of Mindtools

Because knowledge construction is facilitated by collaboration, and because the most important goal of Mindtools is knowledge construction, it is reasonable to conclude that classroom uses of Mindtools can certainly be enhanced by collaborative and cooperative efforts. This is true for a number of reasons.

First, the skills required to use Mindtools and the reasoning engaged by them are likely to be novel to most learners. Some may already be adept with some of the tools described in this book, though it is doubtful that any are familiar with all of them. The types of reasoning required to effectively use Mindtools are also likely to be novel to most learners. Since learning activities most often support memorization and repetition, using tools to represent personal interpretations is likely to be unusual, so having the support of group members will probably help.

Second, from a constructivist perspective, an important goal of this type of learning is for learners to recognize that there are multiple perspectives on any problem or idea. Their way of conceiving the world, like the teacher's, is not the only way people see things.

Third, most Mindtools result in the creation of large knowledge bases (the products of Mindtools that represent the learners' knowledge) of information, such as the databases, spreadsheets, multimedia programs, semantic nets, and rule bases that learners will produce. The larger these products are, the more meaningful they are likely to be for learners, who will be able to see the natural complexities of content. However, large knowledge bases require a lot of time and effort to research, conceive, and construct, and that time and effort will require collaborative efforts. An advantage of Mindtools is that they provide constrained environments in which learners can more readily identify their roles, practice them, and use them consistently while working on a knowledge construction project.

The following sequence of activities describes the processes that you, the teacher, need to accomplish in order to help form collaborative groups to use Mindtools. The sequence is a synthesis of research on collaborative learning. Each of the Mindtool chapters (3–10) relates how this sequence should be applied using the particular tools being described.

**1.** *Form the groups.* There are several types of group arrangements: heterogeneous ability groups, homogeneous ability groups, random groups, and interest groups. Heterogeneous groups are generally formed with a mixture of ability, gender, or race; that is, high achievers, middle achievers, and low achievers may be mixed on a team. Heterogeneous groups are often preferred because they produce the best opportunity for peer tutoring and support, better integrate the classes being mixed, and improve classroom management (Kagan, 1990). Homogeneous groups seek to group like-minded or similar-ability students together. Such students tend to bond and communicate more effectively, though the low-ability groups are often left at a significant learning disadvantage. Random groups contain members selected from the class at random. They provide variety in the groups, enable all members to acquire some leadership, and are perceived as more fair. They also produce greater incompatibilities and all of the problems entailed. Interest groups are self-selected, with class members deciding on the group's composition. This may lead to enhanced communication among members, which can be both good news and bad news. Occasionally, allowing learners to group themselves functions as a meaningful reward for their efforts.

Most researchers recommend heterogeneous grouping of students (Johnson & Johnson, 1987). However, collaborative use of Mindtools may not be best facilitated by grouping according to ability, achievement, and intelligence, which are the typical measures for stratifying learners. Rather, for Mindtool use, consider grouping according to cognitive controls. Cognitive controls are relatively stable learner traits that describe how learners interact with, perceive information from, and make sense of the world. There are a few related cognitive controls that will likely interact with and better predict effective Mindtool use, including field independence, cognitive flexibility, and cognitive complexity. They describe a general processing continuum of global versus analytic learners. These cognitive controls describe the ways that learners process information along the following continuum (Jonassen & Grabowski, 1993):

| **Global** | **Analytic** |
|---|---|
| uses given structure_____ | imposes own structure |
| externally directed_____ | internally directed |
| attentive to social cues_____ | inattentive to social cues |
| interpersonal_____ | intrapersonal |
| influenced by the salient features_____ | generates own hypotheses |
| factually oriented_____ | conceptually oriented |
| uses ideas as presented_____ | represents concepts through analysis |
| influenced by format/structure_____ | less affected by format/structure |
| nondiscriminating_____ | discriminating |
| concrete_____ | abstract |
| sensory_____ | intuitive |

Both global and analytic learners have strengths and weaknesses. Global individuals tend to be more socially oriented, better communicators, and more sensitive to others. Those attributes make them better group members. Analytics are better at analyzing and organizing content and seeing how it all fits together, but they also tend to be more introverted and so less adept at working in groups. By themselves, it is very likely that analytic learners will be much better able to learn to use most Mindtools. However, they would produce knowledge bases that represented only their points of view. So, for purposes of forming groups to use Mindtools, I recommend heterogeneously mixing global and analytic learners in groups. They will be able to complement and tutor each other. Communication skills may be more difficult to develop, because global and analytic learners comprehend the world so differently, but the differences in thinking should result in better productions and more learning for both groups.

**2. *Clarify the group goal.*** The specific goal of the group will depend somewhat on the Mindtool it is using. Generally the goal is to collaboratively develop some type of knowledge base using different representations. Certainly the content domain being represented needs to be negotiated, even within a specific subject class. For example, in a history class, what specific period in history or what countries should be represented? How will the content domain be limited or bounded? That is, not everything about a country can be represented, so what aspects will be emphasized? The content domain may be used in the first step to form groups. Students could be allowed to join groups based on the content being analyzed in that group.

**3. *Negotiate tasks and subtasks to be completed.*** Break down the required tasks and delegate them to various group members. This task may be modeled by the teacher the first few times it is required. These leadership skills should be delegated to the learners as soon as possible. Later, learners will understand the various roles involved in searching for information, analyzing it, constructing different parts of the knowledge base, and verifying the knowledge base. Which of these tasks can be delegated to individuals, and which should be accomplished in group brainstorming and problem-solving settings? These topics will be examined more thoroughly in each of the Mindtool chapters.

**4. *Monitor individual and group performance.*** As the individuals in the group are performing their assigned tasks, someone needs to keep track of their progress to ensure that all of the required information has been gathered and represented in the knowledge bases to support the group work when it is scheduled. These leadership skills need to be modeled by the teacher and then assigned to the students and coached by the teacher. Leadership skills may develop naturally in natural settings, but in formal school settings they need to be developed and practiced carefully to avoid conflicts.

**5. *Reconcile differences in interpretations or approaches to the goal.*** During the group settings, learners must negotiate differences of opinion or interpretation in the content or the nature of the task. The group goal negotiated in the second step should be used as the arbiter in deciding which interpretations to include in the group's product. This is the time when communication skills—such as asking for and receiving feedback, paraphrasing the content of individual messages without evaluating it, negotiating the meaning of any message or information, and accepting, sharing with, and supporting the needs and wants of other members of the group—are most important and where cooperation is most likely tested.

## Conclusion

In this chapter I provided descriptions of the outcomes—both intellectual (critical, creative, and complex thinking) and social (cooperation)—of using Mindtools. Critical thinking is the conceptual rationale for using Mindtools, and collaboration is an important means. It is obvious to those who have used the tools described in this book that they engage learners in critical thinking and cognitive learning strategies. The relevance of such outcomes in schooling cannot be doubted. Mindtools are cognitive tools that efficiently and effectively support deeper-level information processing, engage learners in knowledge construction, and basically require learners to think more. The remainder of this book will describe and illustrate Mindtools (Part 2) and quasi-Mindtools (Part 3) and provide specific advice on how to implement them, including recommendations on how to facilitate collaboration.

## References

Ennis, R. H. (1987). Critical thinking and the curriculum. In M. Heiman & J. Slomianko (Eds.), *Thinking skills instruction: Concepts and techniques.* Washington, DC: National Education Association.

Ennis, R. H. (1989). Critical thinking and subject specificity: Clarification and needed research. *Educational Researcher, 18*(3), 4–10.

Gardner, H. (1983). *Frames of mind.* New York: Basic Books.

Gardner, H., & Hatch, T. (1989). Multiple intelligences go to school: Educational implications of the theory of multiple intelligence. *Educational Researcher, 18*(11), 4–10.

Iowa Department of Education (1989). *A guide to developing higher order thinking across the curriculum.* Des Moines, IA: Department of Education. (ERIC Document Reproduction Service No. ED 306 550).

Johnson, D. W., & Johnson, R. T. (1987). *Learning together and learning alone: Cooperative, competitive, and individualistic learning.* Englewood Cliffs, NJ: Prentice-Hall.

Jonassen, D. H. (1994). Thinking technology: Toward a constructivist design model. *Educational Technology, 34*(4), 34–37.

Jonassen, D. H., & Grabowski, B. L. (1993). *Handbook of individual differences, learning, and instruction.* Hillsdale, NJ: Lawrence Erlbaum Associates.

Kagan, S. (1990). *Cooperative learning: Resources for teachers.* San Juan Capistrano, CA: Resources for Teachers.

Litecky, L. (1992). Great teaching, great learning: Classroom climate, innovative methods, and critical thinking. In C. A Barnes (Ed.), *Critical thinking: Educational imperative.* San Francisco: Jossey-Bass.

Paul, R. W. (1992). Critical thinking: What, why, and how. In C. A. Barnes (Ed.), *Critical thinking: Educational imperative.* San Francisco: Jossey-Bass.

Resnick, J. B., & Klopfer, L. E. (1987). Toward the thinking curriculum: An overview. In L. B. Resnick & L. E. Klopfer (Eds.), *Toward the thinking curriculum: Current cognitive research.* Association for Supervision and Curriculum Development in cooperation with the North Central Regional Educational Laboratory.

Slavin, R. E. (1983). *Cooperative learning.* New York: Longman.

Walters, K. S. (1990). Critical thinking, rationality, and the vulcanization of students, *Journal of Higher Education, 61*(4), 448–467.

# MINDTOOLS

**PART TWO**

# Learning with Computing: Developing Critical Thinking with Mindtools

Part 2 of this book describes the Mindtools that were rationalized in Part 1. This is the heart of the book. It includes the following chapters:

These tools are Mindtools, according to the definition in Chapter 1, because they fulfill each of these criteria:

1. They are computer-based applications.
2. They are readily available and generally applicable.
3. They are affordable—most are available as shareware, at a cost of less than $100, or are in the public domain.

4. They can be used to represent personal knowledge and content domains.
5. They are applicable to different content domains; that is, they can be used to analyze different kinds of content.
6. Using them to analyze and represent knowledge necessarily engages critical thinking in learners.
7. The knowledge acquired through using them is better comprehended and therefore more transferable.
8. The representational formalism each provides is a simple but powerful way of representing knowledge.
9. They are reasonably easy to learn, most requiring only 1 or 2 hours to acquire proficiency.

In Part 3 (chapters 9 and 10) I will describe other tools that possess most, but not all, of the characteristics of Mindtools listed above. I refer to them as "quasi-Mindtools."

All of the chapters in parts 2 and 3 are organized similarly. Each begins with a description of the application, followed by examples of products developed using it. Each Mindtool is analyzed for the kinds of critical thinking it engages and compared with other Mindtools that function in similar or complementary ways. A brief description of some of the commonly available application tools for Apple II, DOS, and Macintosh computers is presented. I then describe how to use these tools in classrooms, and identify the advantages and disadvantages of using these application as Mindtools.

Because chapters 3 through 10 follow the same pattern, you will find it easy to access the information in each chapter and to compare and contrast the Mindtools and the methods for using them. This book is designed to function as a handbook rather than a continuous body of prose, so, after reading chapters 1 and 2, you can investigate and try out the Mindtools in whatever sequence you prefer.

# 3

# Databases:
## *Structuring Content Domains*

## What Are Database Management Systems?

Database management systems (DBMSs) are computerized record-keeping systems. They were originally designed to replace paper-based information retrieval systems. They are, in effect, electronic filing cabinets that allow users to store information in an organized filing system and later retrieve that information, just as a secretary would store documents in organized filing drawers. The advantages offered by computerized information storage include compactness (several drawers full of paper information can be stored on a single floppy disk), speed of entering information into the system (directly via the keyboard, bar code readers, or scanners), faster and easier access to information in the system, and easier updating of information in the system. Information stored in DBMSs is more accessible and easier to keep up to date.

DBMSs consist of several components: the database, a file management system, database organization tools, and reporting (printing) functions. A database consists of one or more files, each of which contains information in the form of collections of records that are related to a content domain, event, or set of objects (e.g., an individual's account information). Each record in the database is divided into fields that describe the class or type of information contained therein. The same type of information for each record is stored in each field. For example, the address database in Figure 3.2 contains four records, each with information about a different individual. These records are systematically broken down into fields (subunits of each record) that define a common pattern of information. The database in Figure 3.2 contains six fields: one for the last name, one for the first

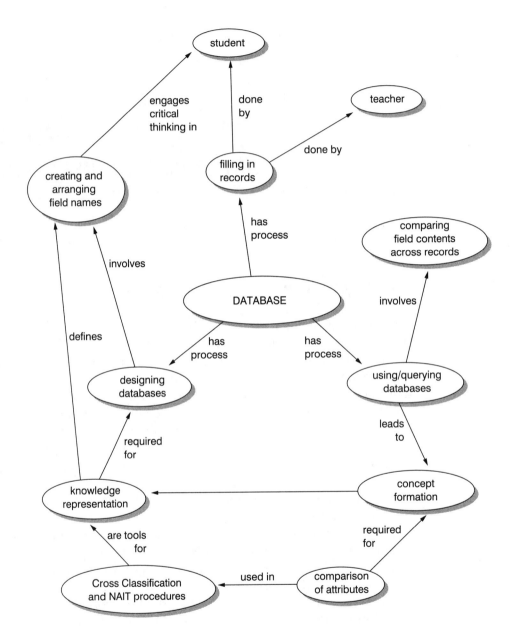

**Figure 3.1**
Databases as Mindtools

| Record | Field 1 Last Name | Field 2 First Name | Field 3 Address | Field 4 City | Field 5 State | Field 6 Zip |
|--------|-------------------|--------------------|-----------------|-------------|---------------|-------------|
| 1 | Smith | John | 123 Maple Dr. | Columbus | Ohio | 54211 |
| 2 | Buchanon | Peggy | 4700 Oglethorpe St. | Moose | Oregon | 90202 |
| 3 | Fernandez | Jose | 6325 Van Buren Blvd. | Los Angeles | California | 95543 |
| 4 | Richmond | Aletha | 321 Aspen Way | Craig | Colorado | 80437 |
| etc. | | | | | | |
| | | | | | | |

**Figure 3.2**
Database structure

name, one for the street address, one for the city, one for the state, and one for the zip code. The content and arrangement of each field is standardized within the records so that the computer will know which part of the record to search in order to locate a particular kind of information.

Database-manipulation tools permit the user to organize and reorganize the information in order to answer queries. The primary tools are searching, sorting, and retrieving information. For example, you can use the file management capability of the DBMS to create a file that contains the class schedule of each student in a school. You could save that file, access it, and change it to reflect changes in schedules using the file management and editing capabilities of the DBMS. For example, if a student were transferred to another class during fourth period, you would open the file, find the student's record in the database (by searching in the name field for that student's name), move across the record to the correct period, and change the information in the file.

The more important functions of DBMSs are the organization tools that will help you answer queries about students' schedules. The tool used more often is the search function, which allows you to search through the database to find specific information. For example, you may search on the name field for a particular student's name because you know that the student's record contains other information you need. For example, you could search through the name field for "Smith." Search capabilities vary with each system, although most allow you to tailor your search using different requests. You could search the name field, for example, for records that EQUALS Smith. Such a search request would show every record that contains the word "Smith" and nothing more. Searching using CON-

TAINS Smith would produce every record that has the letters SMITH in it, though there could be additional letters, such as in Smith*son* or Smith-*field*. EQUALS is obviously a much more limiting search term, so it would be used if you wanted to refine the search. For example, you could search the database for all students scheduled into Mr. Brown's social studies class during fourth period. This would be useful for printing grade sheets or interim reports.

Another common search feature is the NOT function. Searching a database field using NOT Smith would show every record in the database except those with Smith in the field. Most DBMSs support search methods that can search a date or number field for values greater than, equal to, or less than a particular value. Most DBMSs also permit you to identify multiple search criteria, that is, to search simultaneously on more than one field. For example, if you wanted to find all the Smiths in the eighth grade, you would make a search that identifies name field EQUALS Smith and grade EQUALS 8.

The other function that is important to the use of databases as Mindtools is the sort function, which enables you to rearrange the contents of the database in ascending or descending order according to one or more of the fields. For example, if you sorted on Field 1 Last Name in the database in Figure 3.2, then the order of the records would change, with Buchanon appearing first, followed by Fernandez, Richmond, and Smith. Essentially, DBMSs allow you to store information in an organized way and to locate or arrange the information in the database to help you answer queries about that information. The examples I gave to illustrate the DBMS features all use the data for administrative purposes (e.g., attendance, scheduling, student records). In order to use DBMSs as Mindtools, you will use the same functions to analyze and enter subject-matter content into databases, which you can then search and sort to answer specific questions about the content or to seek interrelationships and inferences among the subject content.

DBMSs also possess file management capabilities that allow you to create and define new database files. Once the data structure is defined, information can be entered into or deleted from the file. Any database file can be saved on a disk, deleted, copied, or saved under a new name. These file management functions enable the user to make permanent copies of the information in the database.

The ease, capacity, and speed with which these activities can be accomplished varies with the system. Many databases also possess security features and the capacity to integrate with other databases.

# Examples of Content Databases

I will present a number of content databases that have been constructed by teachers and students to reflect their knowledge of different content domains. The database in Figure 3.3 (only the data structure and a single record are illustrated) depicts thematic, stylistic, and syntactic information about British Romantic poems. The next example (Figure 3.4) is a simple database produced by an elementary class that includes socioeconomic statistics about different countries. In this example, students developed questions such as the following to ask each other about the contents of the databases (see How To Construct and Use Content Databases in Classrooms, later in this chapter):

1. What is the relationship between average income and literacy rate? Which country is different from the others with a high literacy rate? How will recent events affect that country?

| Poem | The World Is Too Much With Us | | Poet | Wordsworth | | Dates | 1770-1850 | | Form | Sonnet |

| Speaker – Listener | The Poet - himse | | Tone | exhorting; frustrated | | Eg of Tone | "Great God! I'd ra |

| Subject or Situation | The effect of our present world view. |

| Theme | Comparison between our present materialist world view and its effects on our character with ear |

| Sound Devices | alliteration (b) | | Rhyme Scheme | abca abca dedede | | Rhythm | iambic pentameter |

| Symbolism | none | | Comparative devices | metaphors: "we are out of tune"; allusion |

| Syntax Patterns | apostrophizing (Gre | | Frequent Diction I Imagery | images of nature: flower, leaves |

| Freedom Motif | reflected in desire for freedom from limitations of scientific world view |

| Innocence & Inner Child Motif | the innocent view of pagans is upheld as desirable |

| Importance of Nature Motif | reflected in our estrangement from natural world: "little we see in natur |

| Glory of the Common Man Motif | belief that Pagans lived better lives |

| Spiritual Values Motif | reflected in reaction against material values (getting, spending) and a time orie |

| Immediate & Individual Experience Motif | reflected in the importance of new individual experience |

**Figure 3.3**
Data structure for database on British Romantic poems

| name | population | GNP $bil | pop density | tvs per pers | infant mortality | defense budget | ave income | literacy |
|---|---|---|---|---|---|---|---|---|
| Australia | 16,646,000 | 220 | 5.4/sq. mi. | 1/2.0 | 8.1/1000 | 2.7% | $14,458 | 99% |
| Brazil | 153,771,000 | 313 | 47/sq. mi. | 1/4.0 | 67/1000 | .8% | $2,020 | 76% |
| Canada | 26,527,000 | 486 | 6/sq. mi. | 1/1.7 | 7.3/1000 | 2.0% | $13,000 | 99% |
| China | 1,130,065,000 | 350 | 288/sq. mi. | 1/12 | 33/1000 | 4.4% | $258 | 70% |
| El Salvador | 5,221,000 | 4.1 | 671/sq. mi. | 1/12 | 62/1000 | 3.9% | $700 | 62%u/40%r |
| India | 850,067,000 | 246 | 658/sq. mi. | 1/62 | 91/1000 | 3.8% | $300 | 36% |
| Iraq | 18,782,000 | 34 | 104/sq. mi. | 1/18 | 69/1000 | 32.0% | $1,950 | 70% |
| Japan | 123,778,000 | 1800 | 844/sq. mi. | 1/4.1 | 5/1000 | 1.0% | $15,030 | 99% |
| Mexico | 88,335,000 | 126 | 115/sq. mi. | 1/8.7 | 42/1000 | .6% | $2,082 | 88% |
| Saudi Arabia | 16,758,000 | 70 | 15/sq. mi. | 1/3.5 | 74/1000 | 12.8% | | 50%(men) |
| Switzerland | 6,628,000 | 111 | 406/sq. mi. | 1/2.9 | 6.9/1000 | 2.2% | $26,309 | 99% |
| U.S.S.R. | 290,939,000 | 2.5 | 33/sq. mi. | 1/3.2 | 25.2/1000 | 17.0% | $3,000 | 99% |
| U.S.A. | 250,372,000 | 4.8 | 68/sq. mi. | 1/1.3 | 10/1000 | 5.7% | $16,444 | 99% |

**Figure 3.4**
Database on world statistics

2. If you knew nothing about any of these countries except for what is in the database, which one would you want to live in? Why?
3. How are infant mortality and literacy related to GNP?
4. Which are the most socially advanced countries? On what criteria do you base your answer?

The next database (Figure 3.5), which was developed by a science teacher, is on cells—their functions, locations, and so on. Many interesting queries can be written that require students to search and sort on different fields in order to come up with an answer:

1. Find all of the cell types of the tissue system connective tissue. Which cells are involved in bone formation? What is the interrelationship of these cells in bone formation?
2. Find all of the cell types with cilia. Where are the cilia located within the cells, and why are they important to those locations?
3. How are erythrocytes affected within sickle cells?

The next database (Figure 3.6) was developed by a math teacher to describe a variety of mathematical functions, including inverse, domain, and range. Seeing these functions contrasted in a database helps learners understand the underlying structure of algebra.

The following database (Figure 3.7) is not so much a collection of knowledge as it is a tool students can use for analyzing and comparing sentences from different works of literature. Sample sentences from different types of text (e.g., different authors, literary periods, or styles; different purposes for writing—narrative, exposition, argumentation) can be entered into the database. Each sentence is then analyzed for instances of each characteristic described by each field. Using search and sort functions, students can compare these sentences and the styles of writing they represent.

# Databases as Mindtools

When used as a Mindtool, a database management system helps students integrate and interrelate content ideas, which in turn makes the ideas more meaningful and more memorable (Figure 3.1). Building databases requires that learners organize information by identifying the relevant dimensions of the content. For example, health students studying vitamin therapy might want to set up a database in which each vitamin is a record and the characteristics of each vitamin (e.g., dietary sources, physiology,

| cell type | location | function | shape | related cell |
|---|---|---|---|---|
| Astocyte | CNS | Supply Nutrients | Radiating | Neurons, Capillaries |
| Basal | Stratum Basale | Produce New Cells | Cube, Columnar | Epithelial Cells |
| Basophils | Blood Plasma | Bind Imm.E | Lobed Nuclei, Gra | Neutrophil, Eosinophil |
| Cardiac Muscle | Heat | Pump Blood | Branched | Endomysium |
| Chondroblast | Cartilage | Produce Matrix | round | |
| Eosinophil | Blood Plasma | ?, Protazoans, Allergy | Two Lobes | Basophil, Neutrophil |
| Ependymal | Line CNS | Form Cerebralspinal Fluid | Cube | |
| Erythrocytes | Blood Plasma | Transport O2, Remove CC | Disc | Hemocytoblast, Proerythroblast |
| Fibroblast | Connective Tissue Proper | Fiber Production | Flat, Branched | |
| Goblet | Columnar Epithelial | Secretion | Columnar | |
| Keratinocytes | Stratum Basal | Strengthen other Cells | Round | Melanocytes |
| Melanocytes | Stratum Basale | U.V. Protection | Branched | Keratinocytes |
| Microglia | CNS | Protect | Ovoid | Neurons, Astrocytes? |
| Motor Neuron | CNS (Cell Body) | Impulse Away from CNS | Long, Thin | Sensory Neuron, Neuroglia |
| Neutrophil | Blood Plasma | Inflammation, Bacteria | Lobed Nuclei | Basophils, Eosinophil |
| Oligodendrocyte | CNS | Insulate | Long | Neurons |
| Osteoblast | Bone | Produce Organic Matrix | Spider | Osteoclasts |
| Osteoclast | Bone | Bone Restoration | Ruffled Border | Osteoblasts |
| Pseudostratified | Gland Ducts, Respiratory Tract | Secretion | Varies | Goblet |
| Satellite | PNS | Control | Cube | Schwann, Neurons |
| Schwann | PNS | Insulate | Cube | Neurons, Satellite |
| Sensory Neurons | PNS (Cell Body) | Impulse to CNS | Long, Thin | Motor Neuron, Neuroglia |
| Simple Columnar | Digestive Tract, Glands | Secretion, Absorption | Columnar | |
| Simple Cuboidal | Kidney Tubules, Gland Ducts | Secretion, Absorption | Cube | |
| Simple Squamous | Lungs, Kidney, Blood vessels | Diffusion of Materials | Flat | Basal |
| Skeletal Muscle | Bone, Skin | Movement, Heat, Posture | Long | Neurons |
| Smooth Muscle | Organ Walls | Movement | Disc | Endomysium |
| Stratified Columnar | Epithelial Junctions (Rare) | Protection, Secretion | Columnar | Simple Cuboidal, Goblet |

**Figure 3.5**
Part of a database on cells

| cell type | tissue systems | associate proteins | related disease | specialization | other | growth |
|---|---|---|---|---|---|---|
| Astocyte | Nervous | | | Half of Neural tissue | Neuroglia | No |
| Basal | Epithelial | | Cancer | Mitotic | | Yes |
| Basophils | Connective, Immune | Histamine, Heparin | | Basic, Possible Mast | | No? |
| Cardiac Muscle | Muscle | Actin, Myosin, Troponin | Athrosclerosis, Fibrosis | Intercalated discs | | No |
| Chondroblast | Connective | Collagen | | | Chondrocyte | Yes |
| Eosinophil | Connective, Immune | | | Acid, Phagocytos (Protein) | | No |
| Ependymal | Nervous | | | Cilia | Neuroglia | No |
| Erythrocytes | Connective | Hemoglobin | Sickle Cell Anemia | Transport | Reticulocyte | No |
| Fibroblast | Connective | Collagen, Elastin | Cancer? | Mitotic | Fibrocyte | yes |
| Goblet | Epithelial | | | Mucus | | No |
| Keratinocytes | Epithelial | Keratin | | | | No |
| Melanocytes | Epithelial | Melanin | Skin Cancer | Produce Melanin | | Yes |
| Microglia | Nervous | | | Macrophage | Neuroglia | No |
| Motor Neuron | Nervous | | | Multipolar, Neuromuscular, | Efferent | No |
| Neutrophil | Connective, Immune | Lysozyme | | Phagocytos, Neutral | | No |
| Oligodendrocyte | Nervous | | Multiple Sclerosis | Produce Myaline Sheath | Neuroglia | No |
| Osteoblast | Connective | Collagen | Osteoporosis, Rickets, P | Bone Salts | Osteocytes | Yes |
| Osteoclast | Connective | Lysosomal Enzyme, Actin | Osteoporosis, Paget's | Destroy Bone | | no |
| Pseudostratified | Epithelial | | | Cilia | | No |
| Satellite | Nervous | | | Chemical Env. | Neroglia | No |
| Schwann | Nervous | | Multiple Sclerosis | Form Myelin Sheath, Phago | Neuroglia | No |
| Sensory Neurons | Nervous | Neruotransmitters | | Unipolar, Action Potential | Afferent | No |
| Simple Columnar | Epithelial | | | Cilia | | No |
| Simple Cuboidal | Epithelial | | | Microvilli | | No |
| Simple Squamous | Epithelial | | | | | No |
| Skeletal Muscle | Muscle | Actin, Myosin, Acetylch | | Neuromuscular Junction, Ir | | No |
| Smooth Muscle | Muscle | Actin, Myosin, Calmoduli | | Gap Junction, Volentery | | No |
| Stratified Columnar | Epithelial | | | Cilia | | No |

| function | type | name | graph | inverse | domain | range | abs max | abs min |
|---|---|---|---|---|---|---|---|---|
| $y = x$ | polynomial | linear | line | $y = x$ | $(-\infty,\infty)$ | $(-\infty,\infty)$ | none | none |
| $y = x^2$ | polynomial | quadratic | parabola | | $(-\infty,\infty)$ | $[0,\infty)$ | none | $y = 0$ |
| $y = x^3$ | polynomial | cubic | cubic | $y = x^{1/3}$ | $(-\infty,\infty)$ | $(-\infty,\infty)$ | none | none |
| $y = x^4$ | polynomial | quartic | parabola | | $(-\infty,\infty)$ | $[0,\infty)$ | none | $y = 0$ |
| $y = x^5$ | polynomial | quintic | cubic | $y = x^{1/5}$ | $(-\infty,\infty)$ | $(-\infty,\infty)$ | none | none |
| $y = x^6$ | polynomial | 6th order | parabola | | $(-\infty,\infty)$ | $[0,\infty)$ | none | $y = 0$ |
| $y = x^7$ | polynomial | 7th order | cubic | $y = x^{1/7}$ | $(-\infty,\infty)$ | $(-\infty,\infty)$ | none | none |
| $y = x^n$ | polynomial | nth order | | | $(-\infty,\infty)$ | $(-\infty,\infty)$ | none | none |
| $y = 2^x$ | exponential | base 2 – exponential | exponential | $y = \log2(x)$ | $(-\infty,\infty)$ | $(0,\infty)$ | none | none |
| $y = 10^x$ | exponential | base 10 – exponential | exponential | $y = \log10(x)$ | $(-\infty,\infty)$ | $(0,\infty)$ | none | none |
| $y = e^x$ | exponential | base e – exponential | exponential | $y = \log e(x)$ | $(-\infty,\infty)$ | $(0,\infty)$ | none | none |
| $y = n^x$ | exponential | base n – exponential | exponential | $y = \log n(x)$ | $(-\infty,\infty)$ | $(0,\infty)$ | none | none |
| $y = \ln x$ | logarithmic | natural logarithm | logarithmic | $y = e^x$ | $(0,\infty)$ | $(-\infty,\infty)$ | none | none |
| $y = \log x$ | logarithmic | common logarithm | logarithmic | $y = 10^x$ | $(0,\infty)$ | $(-\infty,\infty)$ | none | none |
| $y = \log 7(x)$ | logarithmic | base 7 logarithm | logarithmic | $y = 7^x$ | $(0,\infty)$ | $(-\infty,\infty)$ | none | none |
| $y = 1/x$ | rational | | inverse varia | $y = 1/x$ | $(-\infty,0),(0,\infty)$ | $(-\infty,0),(0,\infty)$ | none | none |
| $y = 1/x^2$ | rational | | volcano | | $(-\infty,0),(0,\infty)$ | $(0,\infty)$ | none | none |
| $y = 1/x^3$ | rational | | inverse varia | $y = 1/x^{1/3}$ | $(-\infty,0),(0,\infty)$ | $(-\infty,0),(0,\infty)$ | none | none |
| $y = 1/x^4$ | rational | | volcano | | $(-\infty,0),(0,\infty)$ | $(0,\infty)$ | none | none |
| $y = 1/x^n$ | rational | | | | $(-\infty,0),(0,\infty)$ | | none | none |
| $y = \sin x$ | trigonometric | sine | sinusoidal | | $(-\infty,\infty)$ | $[-1,1]$ | $y = 1$ | $y = -1$ |
| $y = \cos x$ | trigonometric | cosine | sinusoidal | | $(-\infty,\infty)$ | $[-1,1]$ | $y = 1$ | $y = -1$ |
| $y = \tan x$ | trigonometric | tangent | cubic | | $x \neq n\pi/2), n = 1,3,5...$ | $(-\infty,\infty)$ | none | none |
| $y = \sec x$ | trigonometric | secant | sinusoidal | | $x \neq n\pi,n), n = 1,2,3...$ | $(-\infty,-1],[1,\infty)$ | none | none |
| $y = \csc x$ | trigonometric | cosecant | sinusoidal | | $x \neq n\pi/2), n = 1,3,5...$ | $(-\infty,-1],[1,\infty)$ | none | none |
| $y = \cot x$ | trigonometric | cotangent | reciprocal | | $x \neq n\pi, n = 1,2,3...$ | $(-\infty,\infty)$ | none | none |
| $y = |x|$ | absolute value | absolute value | bird | | $(-\infty,0)$ | $[0,\infty)$ | none | $y = 0$ |
| $y = 1/|x|$ | absolute value | absolute value | volcano | | $(-\infty,0)\ (0,\infty)$ | $(0,\infty)$ | none | none |

**Figure 3.6**
Database on mathematical functions

| function | increasing | decreasing | Vert asym | F1:1 | Horizontal Asymptote |
|---|---|---|---|---|---|
| y = x | $(-\infty,\infty)$ | $(\varnothing)$ | none | yes | none |
| y = x^2 | $[0,\infty)$ | $(-\infty,0)$ | none | no | none |
| y = x^3 | $(-\infty,\infty)$ | $(\varnothing)$ | none | yes | none |
| y = x^4 | $[0,\infty)$ | $(-\infty,0)$ | none | no | none |
| y = x^5 | $(-\infty,\infty)$ | $(\varnothing)$ | none | yes | none |
| y = x^6 | $[0,\infty)$ | $(-\infty,0)$ | none | no | none |
| y = x^7 | $(-\infty,\infty)$ | $(\varnothing)$ | none | yes | none |
| y = x^n | | | none | | none |
| y = 2^x | $(-\infty,\infty)$ | $(\varnothing)$ | none | yes | y = 0 |
| y = 10^x | $(-\infty,\infty)$ | $(\varnothing)$ | none | yes | y = 0 |
| y = e^x | $(-\infty,\infty)$ | $(\varnothing)$ | none | yes | y = 0 |
| y = n^x | $(-\infty,\infty)$ | $(\varnothing)$ | none | yes | y = 0 |
| y = ln x | $(-\infty,\infty)$ | $(\varnothing)$ | x = 0 | yes | none |
| y = log x | $(-\infty,\infty)$ | $(\varnothing)$ | x = 0 | yes | none |
| y = log7(x) | $(-\infty,\infty)$ | $(\varnothing)$ | x = 0 | yes | none |
| y = 1/x | $(\varnothing)$ | $(-\infty,0),(0,\infty)$ | x = 0 | yes | y = 0 |
| y = 1/x^2 | $(-\infty,0)$ | $(0,\infty)$ | x = 0 | no | y = 0 |
| y = 1/x^3 | $(\varnothing)$ | $(-\infty,0),(0,\infty)$ | x = 0 | yes | y = 0 |
| y = 1/x^4 | $(-\infty,0)$ | $(0,\infty)$ | x = 0 | no | y = 0 |
| y = 1/x^n | | | x = 0 | yes | y = 0 |
| y = sin x | $(-\pi/2,\pi/2)$ | $(\pi/2,3\pi/2)$ | none | no | none |
| y = cos x | $(-\pi,2\pi)$ | $(0,\pi)$ | none | no | none |
| y = tan x | $(-\infty,\infty)$ | $(\varnothing)$ | $x = n\pi/2$, n = | no | none |
| y = sec x | $(0,\pi/2)$ | $(\pi/2,\pi)$ | $x = n\pi$, n = | no | none |
| y = csc x | $(\pi/2,\pi)$ | $(0,\pi/2)$ | $x = n\pi/2$, n = | no | none |
| y = cot x | $(\varnothing)$ | $(-\infty,\infty)$ | $x = n\pi$, n = | no | none |
| y = |x| | $(0,\infty)$ | $(-\infty,0)$ | none | no | none |
| y = 1/|x| | $(-\infty,0)$ | $(0,\infty)$ | x = 0 | no | y = 0 |

| Sentence | One night a moth flew into the candle, was caught, burnt dry, and held. |
|---|---|

| Author | Annie Dillard | Dep Clause 1 | | Comma Rule | items in series |
|---|---|---|---|---|---|
| Title | Death of A Moth | Conjunction | | Comma Rule #2 | |
| Sentence Type | Simple | Clause Subj | | Punctuation Rule | |

| First 5 words | One night a moth flew |
|---|---|
| Main Clause | One night a moth flew into the candle, was caught, burnt dry, and held. |

| Subject | moth | Clause verb | | Compound Sent Connector | |
|---|---|---|---|---|---|
| Verb | flew, was caught, burnt dr | Dep Clause #2 | | Transition | One night--time |
| Phrase #1 | into the candle | Conj #2 | | Modifier #1 | one |
| Phrase #2 | | Clause Sub | | Modifier 2 | |
| Main Clause 2 | | Clause ver | | Modifier 3 | |
| Subject 2 | | Simile #1 | | Rhetorical Pattern | |
| Verb 2 | | Simile #2 | | Rhetorical Patt #2 | |
| Phrase 1 | | Onomatopoeia | | Number of words | 14 |
| Phrase 2 | | Alliteration | | Concrete words | 3 |
| | | Parallelism | was caught, burn | | |
| | | Apposition | | | |

**Figure 3.7**
Data structure of database for analyzing sentences

etc.) are the fields. The process of searching for information and creating the database—including deciding which fields are necessary, how large they should be, and how they should be ordered (creating the data structure)—can be a very meaningful instructional activity.

To build the data structure, students must first decide what the appropriate contextual relationships are. They must then search for the information in a systematic fashion in order to fill the database. The searching and sorting of the database required to answer queries can generate a variety of comparisons and contrasts based on which fields are selected for searching and sorting. Intellectually, these processes require the integration and organization of a content domain.

There are few examples of knowledge-oriented (Mindtool-type) databases described in the literature. Goldberg (1992) recommended using databases to classify types of seashells. According to Rooze (1988–89), the value of databases to the teaching of social studies is that creating databases places students in an active as opposed to a passive role. By preparing a database, students determine which information to collect and organize seemingly unrelated bits of information into meaningful categories. However, if students are to use the database effectively, the teacher must guide the development of categories and search procedures. Rooze recommended strategies for concept development and data interpretation in the development and use of databases.

Knight and Timmons (1986) also recommended the use of databases to meet the objectives of history instruction. Pon (1984) described the use of databases as an inquiry tool to aid higher-level thinking in a fourth-grade American Indian studies course. Watson and Strudler (1988–89) described a lesson based on Taba's Inductive Thinking Model that teaches higher-order thinking using databases. Building databases involves analyzing, synthesizing, and evaluating information, according to Watson and Strudler.

The Technical Education Research Center in Cambridge, Massachusetts, has created a simple-to-use database program called TableTop (Figure 3.8) to support database construction and analysis by school-age children (Hancock, Kaput, & Goldsmith, 1992). Their approach is to provide opportunities for children to analyze authentic data, so the database in Figure 3.8 was part of an elementary class's analysis of waste in school lunches.

| X ≫ meatballs | | | | | |
|---|---|---|---|---|---|
| lunch | like | best part | dislike | what eaten | what thrown away |
| bought | yes | meatballs | bread | meatball sub | bread |
| brought | yes | fruit cup | drink | sandwich | nothing |
| bought | yes | fruit cup | sub | fruit cup | nothing |
| bought | yes | meatball sub | peaches | meatball sub | peaches |
| bought | no | fruit cup | meatball sub | fruit cup | meatball sub |
| bought | yes | meatball sub | fruit cup | sub fruit cup milk juice | nothing |
| bought | yes | pear | sub | sub | nothing |
| bought | yes | meatballs | fruit and juice | meatball sub | fruit and juice |
| bought | no | milk | everything | milk meatball sub and pe. . | meatball sub and |
| bought | no | apple juice | meatball sub | fruit cup | meatball sub |
| bought | no | jello | pizza | pizza | milk |
| brought | yes | turkey sandwi . . | drink | turkey sandwich lettuce . . | nothing |

**Figure 3.8**
TableTop database

## Evaluation of Databases as Mindtools

**1.** *Computer-based.* Although databases were designed to replace filing cabinets of information, their power derives from the searching and sorting capabilities afforded by the computer. This is especially true with larger files of information. Computer databases are more powerful tools than paper ones because of their capacity to retrieve and organize information.

**2.** *Readily available, general applications.* After word processors, database management systems are the most widely used computer application. Databases provide catalog mailing lists and bank records, hospital records, and every other kind of record in every kind of business. In the home, they are useful for organizing addresses, hobbies, and many other collections of information.

**3.** *Affordable.* Database systems are bundled with many integrated software packages or office packages that provide spreadsheet and word-processing capabilities as well, making them relatively inexpensive. Many powerful, single-purpose database programs are available for less than $100. Also, there are many public-domain database systems available for every kind of computer from electronic bulletin boards and from organizations such as the Minnesota Educational Computing Consortium.

**4.** *Represent knowledge.* Databases support a rigid, associational form of knowledge representation. The content structure is defined by the fields, and examples are encoded in records. This form of organization is easy for beginners.

**5.** *Applicable in different subject domains.* Databases can be developed to describe the underlying structure of any content domain. They are especially effective in the social sciences.

**6.** *Engage critical thinking.* These skills are described in the next section.

**7.** *Facilitate transfer of learning.* Tabular database structures can be transferred to any kind of content domain. Their rigid structure is easier to understand, so it is easier to conceptualize in different content domains (see the section on Related Mindtools).

**8.** *Simple, powerful formalism.* Databases are probably the simplest Mindtool to understand. The formalism is concept-related and is especially useful for developing content hierarchies including concepts and their subordinate and superordinate concepts.

**9.** *(Reasonably) easy to learn.* Simple database systems can be learned quickly and easily, even by primary children.

## Critical, Creative, and Complex Thinking in Database Construction and Use

A large number of critical, creative, and complex thinking skills are required to use and construct knowledge-oriented databases. Tables 3.1, 3.2, and 3.3 identify the skills that are required querying a database, filling in an existing data structure by finding and inserting information, and designing and building a database structure. The skills in each table that are marked by an "×" are those that are employed by each process, based on an information-processing analysis of the tasks.

There are probably more critical thinking skills required to use and build databases than there are creative or complex skills (see Table 3.1). That is because database construction and use is an analytic process that makes extensive use of logical thinking. All three activities make heavy use of evaluating information, (especially) analyzing information, and connecting information. Querying a database requires that learners evaluate the question and determine a strategy to answer that query in terms of searching and sorting. For example, answering question 2 about the database in Figure 3.5 requires learners to search the field of cell types for cilia cells, identify the information in the location field, and compare information in the function

**Table 3.1**

Critical thinking skills in database construction and use

|  | Querying Database | Filling in Database | Designing Database Structure |
|---|:---:|:---:|:---:|
| **Evaluating** | | | |
| Assessing information | X | X | X |
| Determining criteria | | | X |
| Prioritizing | | X | X |
| Recognizing fallacies | X | | |
| Verifying | X | X | |
| **Analyzing** | | | |
| Recognizing patterns | X | | X |
| Classifying | | X | X |
| Identifying assumptions | X | | X |
| Identifying main ideas | X | X | X |
| Finding sequences | X | | |
| **Connecting** | | | |
| Comparing/contrasting | X | X | X |
| Logical thinking | X | | X |
| Inferring deductively | X | | X |
| Inferring inductively | | X | |
| Identifying causal relationships | X | | X |

field. That requires recognizing fallacies, verifying information, recognizing patterns, and identifying assumptions, main ideas, and sequences of information, as well as comparing and contrasting information, using logical, deductive thinking, and identifying causal relationships. Filling in a database such as that in Figure 3.4 requires using encyclopedias, atlases, and almanacs to assess, prioritize, and verify information, identify main ideas, and compare and contrast ideas. Developing a data structure engages nearly all critical thinking skills.

There are fewer creative thinking skills involved in constructing and using databases (see Table 3.2). Designing and using databases depends less on elaborating information than on analyzing information (a critical thinking skill). Some synthesizing is involved, but even fewer imagining skills are required, since one is essentially describing and classing what does exist. Most of the creative skills result from querying databases, which requires that learners predict, speculate, visualize, and intuit responses. Answering queries effectively requires that learners develop a "feel" for the database and its contents.

Finally, a number of complex thinking skills are required for querying and (especially) designing databases. Designing and building databases requires a number of planning operations that make heavy use of designing, problem-solving, and decision-making skills (see Table 3.3). For exam-

**Table 3.2**
Creative thinking skills in database construction and use

| | Querying Database | Filling in Database | Designing Database Structure |
|---|---|---|---|
| **Elaborating** | | | |
| Expanding | | X | |
| Modifying | | | X |
| Extending | | | X |
| Shifting categories | X | | |
| Concretizing | | X | |
| **Synthesizing** | | | |
| Analogical thinking | X | | |
| Summarizing | | X | |
| Hypothesizing | X | | |
| Planning | | | X |
| **Imagining** | | | |
| Fluency | | | |
| Predicting | X | | |
| Speculating | X | | |
| Visualizing | X | | X |
| Intuition | X | | |

**Table 3.3**
Complex thinking skills in database construction and use

| | Querying Database | Filling in Database | Designing Database Structure |
|---|---|---|---|
| **Designing** | | | |
| Imagining a goal | X | | X |
| Formulating a goal | X | | X |
| Inventing a product | | | X |
| Assessing a product | X | | X |
| Revising the product | | | X |
| **Problem Solving** | | | |
| Sensing the problem | X | | X |
| Researching the problem | | X | X |
| Formulating the problem | X | | |
| Finding alternatives | X | | X |
| Choosing the solution | | | X |
| Building acceptance | | | |
| **Decision Making** | | | |
| Identifying an issue | X | | X |
| Generating alternatives | | | X |
| Assessing the consequences | | | X |
| Making a choice | X | | X |
| Evaluating the choices | X | | X |

ple, deciding which attributes of British Romantic poems to include in order to describe them adequately required the designer of the database in Figure 3.3 to design the product (the database), but first to sense the problem, conduct research, and apply that research to the product.

The process of deciding when to develop a database in order to facilitate learning probably most engages problem-solving and decision-making skills, especially sensing and formulating the problem and comparing alternatives, making the choice, and evaluating that choice (to build a database) and selling team members on the process.

Database construction is a largely analytical task that calls on a variety of critical, creative (to a lesser extent), and complex thinking skills.

# Related Mindtools

Databases and spreadsheets (Chapter 4) look and function very much alike. Information can be passed back and forth between them, although spreadsheets offer much greater arithmetic sophistication. Since they can be used in conjunction with each other, information collected for one can be included in the other.

Conceptually, databases are similar to semantic networks (Chapter 5) in that both are used to define content domains in terms of their semantic relationships. Semantic networks are less structured and constrained than databases. The data structure (fields) selected for inclusion in a database constrains the kinds of information that can be included in it, whereas semantic networks can evolve in less structured ways. These reduced constraints may provide an advantage for knowledge construction, although it can also pose problems. I recommend learning to develop knowledge bases using databases first in order to take advantage of the more structured approach to knowledge construction.

In using computer-mediated telecommunications (Chapter 7) for information retrieval, much of the information learners seek is stored in large information databases. So, having experience in manipulating data structures will likely positively transfer to information-retrieval processes. This transfer is likely to help in searching for any information to include in any kind of knowledge base described in this book.

Finally, databases can provide a structure (albeit rigid) for developing multimedia and hypermedia knowledge bases (Chapter 8). Many critics claim that hypermedia is nothing more than multimedia databases (which is sometimes the case). The point is that database construction provides learners the opportunity to structure information in ways that can positively affect the use of most other Mindtools.

## Software Tools

DBMSs are commonly available for every type of computer in use today. Many database software packages are in the public domain, which makes them free or very inexpensive. For the Apple II series of computers, Quick File, PFS File, Data Factory, or AppleWorks will function well as Mindtool media. On DOS-based computers, PC File, PFS File, or a host of others can be used effectively to support Mindtools outcomes. The power of packages such as dBase, Lotus 1-2-3, Rbase, and Symphony are not required to implement Mindtools strategies.

For the Macintosh, the most commonly used databases are part of integrated software packages, such as Microsoft Works or ClarisWorks. These packages provide very adequate programs for constructing databases and spreadsheets (Chapter 4), as well as word processing and telecommunications (Chapter 7), so they represent especially good value. A number of more powerful, single-purpose DBMSs are available for the Macintosh, including FoxBase or FoxPro, FileMaker Pro, 4th Dimension, Dbase, Helix, NuBase, Reflex, and Panorama. These programs offer database templates, flexible reporting functions, scripting, and sophisticated graphics. Some provide file compatibility between Macintosh and DOS and Windows computers, allowing users on both systems to share files.

In evaluating hardware and software for supporting databases as Mindtools, one concern relates to the size of the database you intend to build. This is determined by the size and number of fields you intend to create times the number of records. You need to be certain that your database can be accommodated by the memory limits of your computer. A large database of information could exceed the random access memory (RAM) capacity of an older microcomputer. However, with today's microcomputers possessing megabytes of RAM, this should not usually pose a problem.

Selecting DBMSs can be a perplexing process, so keep a few simple criteria in mind. First and most important, you should not have to spend very much for a database system that performs the functions required by activities described in this chapter. Look at the list of features and decide which ones you really need. Generally, as the number of functions and capabilities provided by a database package increases, so do the complexity of the systems and the difficulty of use. Also consider usability. How easy is it to learn the system? If the software requires too much effort to learn, then the system will replace the Mindtool outcomes, or learners simply will not use it. One of the most serious problems with Mindtools or any computer application is the learning curve required to become an effective user. Select software that minimizes the time spent learning the software and maximizes the time spent analyzing content domains. Test out any new package to see how easy it is to use. If you are a novice database user, you may want to find the simplest one.

Some criteria apply to the hardware configuration you are using. How many computers do you have? How many will you assign to Mindtools applications? Can you afford a site license, or will you purchase individual packages? Are the computers networked? If so, does the package you want to use have a network version?

Finally, consider what other applications software you may want to use. Will you also want to perform word processing? Will you want to use other Mindtools, such as spreadsheets? If so, you may want to consider an integrated package such as AppleWorks for Apple IIs and Microsoft Works or ClarisWorks for Macintoshes.

# How to Construct and Use Content Databases in the Classroom

When should you use databases as Mindtools in the classroom? Databases are very useful for supplementing the learning of concept-rich content, such as that in geography, social studies, and the sciences. They are especially useful when you want students to compare and contrast different forms, styles, or approaches. For example, contrasting the uses of various chemical compounds, the demographics of different countries, or the stylistic elements used by authors in various literary periods are good candidates. Databases allow learners to examine the underlying structure of course content.

Using databases and performing the kinds of content analysis required to build them will probably require new skills for many learners. These skills should be developed carefully. The ultimate goal is for your students to be able to independently analyze a new content domain in order to determine the appropriate data structure, search for the information in texts, films, and other sources to fill in the database, and use the database to create and answer queries about the information it contains. In order to reach this goal, several stages of learning must occur. The following are some learning activities and strategies that will scaffold the learning of necessary database skills:

1. *Students query the completed databases.* In order to introduce students to the functions and organization of a database, you may want to prompt them by having them use an existing database to answer questions about the information contained in the database. Examples of the types of questions that can be asked are presented with earlier database examples (Figures 3.4 and 3.5). Do not begin with queries as complicated as these, however. Start with a familiar database, perhaps a database of personal information about the students in the class. Require them to search for information in the database (e.g., all students over 5 feet, 5 inches tall) or sort the database (e.g., arrange the class from youngest to oldest). They will need to be coached through these experiences, at least initially. These activities familiarize learners with database functions and structure. They also serve as advance organizers or overviews for lessons, and may also facilitate hypothesis generation.

2. *Students complete existing data structures.* Begin with a partially completed database and have students fill in gaps in the database by using their textbooks or going to the library to locate the necessary information. This provides them with some existing information for comparing new data to and from which to generalize. Later, require students to complete

full records; that is, provide them with a blank database in which only the fields (data structure) are defined. This activity stresses purposeful searching for information, rather than general memorization of all information. If you observe textbooks that students highlight during reading, it will be obvious that students do not know how to discriminate important from trivial information. This activity provides a model for searching and identifying the more important and relevant bits of information.

**3. *Students adapt existing data structures or design new data structures for other students to complete.*** Start with familiar content and require students to adapt existing databases, such as the classroom information database, or design new databases that they can collaboratively fill in. Here you are modeling the organizational skills required to develop data structures. Topics such as local sports teams, dating patterns, and television shows are popular.

**4. *Students create and complete data structures.*** Increase the complexity of the content by relating it to classroom studies. Starting with more concrete activities, such as geographical or demographic features in social studies, have students in groups determine what fields are required. This depends on what kinds of questions people have that need to be answered, that is, what kinds of information users may want from the database. This is perhaps the most difficult part of the process. Be certain to acquire a DBMS that allows you to add or delete fields after the initial design (some file management systems do not permit this). Compare the data structures in class and discuss the data structures in terms of how completely and accurately they reflect the content domain and how well they facilitate access to information in them. That is, do the fields allow for efficient searching? Do they represent the content faithfully? This is the most complete activity, requiring learners to identify variables and information needs, build data structures, access information and complete the database, and search the database.

**5. *Students write queries for other students.*** Have students write difficult queries that require other students to use multiple search criteria to answer the questions. Students are often challenged by the prospect of constructing queries that are difficult for their fellow students or for teachers. The value of this activity is that it requires learners to think about implications of the information contained in the database and the ability of the data structure to support various queries. It will very probably require a lot of coaching, as these are difficult skills to develop.

**6. *Students extrapolate from databases.*** Students can create new fields in existing databases to support other applications. For example, starting with a database of geographic information, adding political and economic fields of information to support geopolitical queries would be useful. Students may choose to restructure the databases or predict how others would respond to queries.

## Fostering Collaboration with Databases

Of all the Mindtools, the skills required to use Databases are likely the least novel to learners. Most students have learned to outline, and outlining has some transfer to database construction. The tabular form of database presentations will also make them easier to conceptualize.

Databases easily demonstrate that there are multiple perspectives on any problem or idea, especially if you ask different groups to develop databases on the same topic and then compare the products. The kinds of fields different groups use to define a domain can vary depending on what attributes of the domain the group finds most important.

Collaboratively constructed databases can result in the creation of large knowledge bases of information. Try building a database for an entire course over the period of an academic year. As new and related content is studied, see how you add it to the database.

1. *Form the teams.* Databases may be one of the few Mindtools that would benefit from homogeneous groupings, especially when you are getting started using Mindtools. These groups should be similar in terms of their background and abilities. This should help them generate attributes of a domain to use as the fields. As students gain skill and experience using databases, you may want to shift toward more heterogeneous groupings.

2. *Clarify the group goal.* Since databases are a good Mindtool to start with, you may want to provide the topics for the initial databases. Eventually you want groups to negotiate their own representations, although it may be easier to tutor learners who are working on the same content. Tutoring also facilitates comparison of the ideas students have and the approaches they take in completing the task.

3. *Negotiate tasks and subtasks to be completed.* Initially you may want the group to work together on the tasks. Databases are simpler for a group to develop, and having the group brainstorm optional fields and records for inclusion may be instructive. Later, when students begin building larger databases, it may be necessary to break down the required tasks and delegate them to various members of the group.

**4.** *Monitor individual and group performance.* Ensure that all members of each group are contributing. If the group leader assigns each student a part of the database, students are more accountable for their contributions.

**5.** *Reconcile differences in interpretations or approaches to the goal.* During the group work settings, learners must negotiate differences of opinion or interpretation in the content or the nature of the task. During work on the initial databases, it may be necessary for you to intervene in and coach the negotiations. Be sure that all members' ideas are considered.

## Advantages of Content Databases as Mindtools

A number of advantages accrue to learners from using databases as Mindtools. The process of creating and manipulating a database is inherently constructive, which means that learners are (mentally) actively engaged in learning rather than merely reading or responding to questions. They are actively building knowledge structures, because they are actively engaged in knowledge representation activities. In doing so, learners are required to define the nature of the relationships between concepts and then to construct records and fields that map those relationships. This is meaningful processing of information, as opposed to the rote recall too often required by instructional activities such as worksheets, which are designed to produce convergent thinking in learners.

Another advantage of these database learning strategies lies in the powerful searching and sorting capabilities of the DBMSs. It is here that the process of comparing concepts and relationships in the database is greatly facilitated by the speed and reporting capabilities of the DBMS. Learners can search their databases in any number of ways—to provide an overview, for example, of all of the kinds of cells, or to compare particular characteristics of different cells. They can also try to arrange the information in ways that may make more sense to them. For example, in seeking the answer to queries about what cell contributes to certain characteristics (Figure 3.5), searching two fields using common "and/or/not" logical connectors will yield the answer immediately. The ability to quickly compare and contrast relational information is tantamount to learning many different kinds of information.

A final advantage of DBMSs as Mindtools is the ease of data entry provided by most systems. Once the database has been structured, either by the student or the teacher, the program prompts learners to type in responses, which certainly takes no longer than writing notes longhand. Once the information has been entered, it can be rearranged and printed out in different ways to meet various information needs.

# Limitations of Content Databases as Mindtools

Critics may claim that these activities produce nothing more than a tabular summary of information, commonly available in textbooks. It is true that some textbooks do provide tabular summaries. However, using databases as Mindtools engages learners in constructing their own tables rather than trying to memorize those that already exist. Also, the table that each learner constructs will be more personally meaningful, since it will contain the learner's concepts and relationships between those concepts. This represents generative processing of information. There is a fundamental difference between this and memorizing tables.

Perhaps the most significant problem, as with most Mindtools, is the time and effort required to learn how to use DBMSs. However, the improvements in comprehension and retention should justify that effort. Once the skills are acquired, they are applied easily to new content domains as well as to other management problems.

Some teachers will be concerned that the interpretations of content produced by students may be too individualistic or idiosyncratic, and that the divergent database representations may confuse students more than enlighten them. Personal knowledge representations are individualistic. Students can compare representations that are too divergent or simply incorrect with other students' representations. The databases become a medium for socially negotiating a common understanding. For this reason, collaborative database projects will probably be more productive than individual projects.

## *Conclusion*

Database systems support the storage and retrieval of information in an organized manner. In order to develop and use databases, you must analyze and comprehend the information that you want to store and retrieve. This analysis requires identifying the underlying structural properties of the information. Although databases are more often used as organizational and retrieval tools in businesses, they can also function effectively as Mindtools. When students construct and query databases, they are building and exemplifying structural models of the content they are studying and are using those models to compare and contrast relationships among information contained in their models. That is the kind of meaningful processing of information that students should perform more regularly in schools. It necessarily engages higher-order thinking in learners, which results in better understanding.

## References

Goldberg, K. P. (1992, April). Database programs and the study of seashells. *The Computing Teacher*, pp. 32–34.

Hancock, C., Kaput, J. J., & Goldsmith, L. T. (1992). Authentic inquiry with data: Critical barriers to classroom implementation. *Educational Psychologist, 27*(3), 337–364.

Knight, P., & Timmons, G. (1986). Using databases in history teaching. *Journal of Computer-Assisted Learning, 2*(2), 93–101.

Pon, K. (1984). Databasing in the elementary (and secondary) classroom. *Computing Teacher, 12*(3), 28–30.

Rooze, G. E. (1988–89). Developing thinking using databases: What's really involved? *Michigan Social Studies Journal, 3*(1), 25–26.

Watson, J., & Strudler, N. (1988–89). Teaching higher order thinking skills with databases. *Computing Teacher, 16*(4), 47–50, 55.

# 4

## Spreadsheets:
### *Speculating with Numbers*

. . . . . . . . . . . . . . . . . . . . . . . . . . . . . . . . . . . . . . . . . . . . . . . . . . . . . . . .

## What Are Spreadsheets?

Spreadsheets are computerized, numerical record-keeping systems. They were originally designed to replace paper-based accounting systems. Essentially, a spreadsheet is a grid (or table or matrix) of empty cells, with columns identified by letters and rows identified by numbers (see Figure 4.2)—a ledger sheet spread in front of the user. Each cell may contain values, formulas, or functions, and the values may be numerical (numbers) or textual (words). The user moves around the matrix by scrolling, by identifying the cell number to go to, or by searching for the cell that contains a particular kind of information. A text label, a numerical value, a formula, or a function can be inserted into each cell.

Formulas consist of stated numerical relationships between the contents of different cells. For example, the formula B6+(C7/C6) would tell the program to go to cell B6, retrieve the value of the number in it, divide the contents of cell C7 by the contents of cell C6, and then add that value to the contents of cell B6. Formulas may refer to numerical values placed anywhere in the grid and may refer to any other cells by name.

Functions are mathematical or logical operations that may be performed on the values in a set of specified cells. Some are simple mathematical functions, such as SUM (B9 . . . B12), which sums the contents of cells B9, B10, B11, and B12, or AVG (B9 . . . B12), which would calculate the average of the values in those same cells. More sophisticated functions, such as ITERATE, perform operations a set number of times in a sequence. Functions are also logical, such as IF, MATCH, LOOKUP, or INDEX. These may be included in formulas, such as IF B9<E10,B9*E6

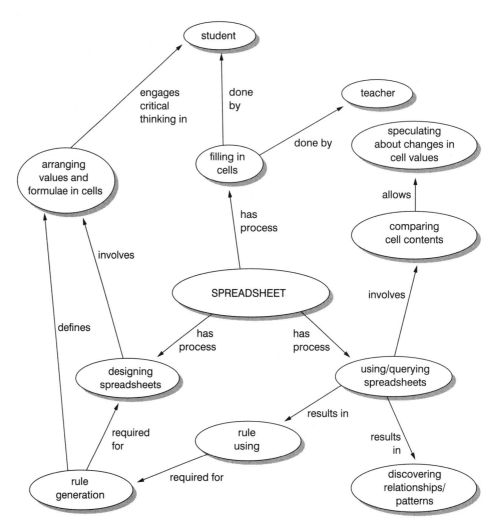

**Figure 4.1**
Spreadsheets as Mindtools

(if the value in cell B9 is less than that in E10, then multiply it by the value in E6). Other functions automatically match values in cells with other cells, look up values in a table of values, or create an index of values to be compared with other cells.

The primary differences among spreadsheets are the size of the grid and the number of functions available. Small spreadsheets, such as the first VisiCalc spreadsheets, provided a grid of approximately 250 by 400 cells, whereas large spreadsheets may provide grids that are thousands of

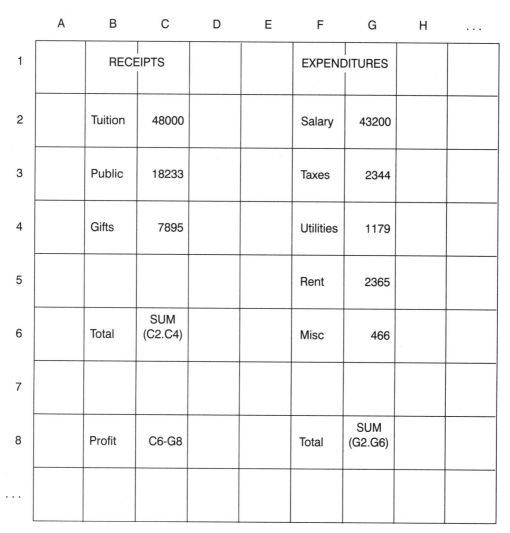

|   | A | B | C | D | E | F | G | H | ... |
|---|---|---|---|---|---|---|---|---|---|
| 1 |   | RECEIPTS |   |   |   | EXPENDITURES |   |   |   |
| 2 |   | Tuition | 48000 |   |   | Salary | 43200 |   |   |
| 3 |   | Public | 18233 |   |   | Taxes | 2344 |   |   |
| 4 |   | Gifts | 7895 |   |   | Utilities | 1179 |   |   |
| 5 |   |   |   |   |   | Rent | 2365 |   |   |
| 6 |   | Total | SUM (C2.C4) |   |   | Misc | 466 |   |   |
| 7 |   |   |   |   |   |   |   |   |   |
| 8 |   | Profit | C6-G8 |   |   | Total | SUM (G2.G6) |   |   |
| ... |   |   |   |   |   |   |   |   |   |

**Figure 4.2**
A simple profit/loss sheet

cells wide and deep. All spreadsheets provide the same basic functions, but more sophisticated ones provide more elaborate functions for interrelating content in the sheet.

Spreadsheets have three primary functions: storing, calculating, and presenting information. First, information, usually numerical, can be stored in a particular location (the cell), from which it can be readily accessed and retrieved. Second, and most important, spreadsheets support calculation functions, such that the numerical contents of any combination of cells can be mathematically related in just about any way the user wishes. (Most spreadsheets also provide other mathematical functions, such as logarithmic, trigonometric, etc.) Finally, spreadsheets present information in a variety of ways. All can display their contents in a two-dimensional grid, such as in Figure 4.2. Most also enable the user to label contents and to display the numerical information graphically in the form of charts or graphs. The user identifies a series of cells, and the program automatically provides graphs and charts of those quantities. By merely highlighting a group of cells (such as G2 to G6 in Figure 4.2) and clicking on a chart type, the program can produce a multicolored pie chart or a bar and line chart (Figure 4.3). Being able to visualize data instantaneously in several ways affords new ways of thinking about numbers.

Most spreadsheets provide advanced operations as well. These include replication, where the program will fill in formulas in cells by replicating a formula in another cell. During spreadsheet construction, the author is not required to copy a similar formula over and over again in different cells. The spreadsheet can change the formula relative to the position of the cell. Many spreadsheet programs also allow the user to write macros, which are miniprograms that identify a sequence of operations that the program should perform when a single, special key is struck. Macros are often used in spreadsheets for collecting information from the user. A macro can be included in a cell for getting the user to input a value (e.g., his or her age), which can then be related to other cells in the spreadsheet. Finally, some spreadsheets enable the user to open several "windows," each of which provides a different view of the spreadsheet. These

**Figure 4.3**
Graphic representation of expenditures in Figure 4.2

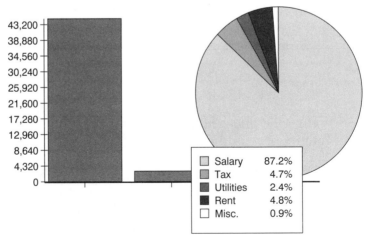

| | | |
|---|---|---|
| ☐ Salary | 87.2% |
| ☐ Tax | 4.7% |
| ☐ Utilities | 2.4% |
| ■ Rent | 4.8% |
| ☐ Misc. | 0.9% |

functions are normally reserved for the "power user" who has become skilled in spreadsheet use.

Spreadsheets were originally developed—and are most commonly used—to support business decision making. The electronic spreadsheet was designed by a couple of graduate accounting majors as a tool to support accounting operations. Their professors assigned them problems based on balance sheets and profit and loss statements (such as in Figure 4.2) that would ask them "what if" questions, such as, "What if interest rates increased by 1%?" Tired of having to recalculate all of the values that would be affected by the change, the students developed an electronic balance sheet where all of the values could be more easily manipulated. Changes would have to be made in only one location, and the spreadsheet would automatically recalculate all of the affected values. Use of this spreadsheet program, called VisiCalc, burgeoned immediately, triggering the phenomenal growth of microcomputers in business in the early 1980s.

Spreadsheets remain in common use today. Businesses use them not only for maintaining accounts but also for managing financial portfolios, determining service or interest rates, and modeling financial markets to support decision making. Spreadsheets are also commonly used for personal accounting and budgeting.

# Examples of Content Spreadsheets

Although spreadsheets have been used most consistently in schools as management tools for accounting, in some cases they have been used as Mindtools in nonbusiness courses. The literature is replete with examples of how spreadsheets have been used to engage and support problem solving. Spreadsheet applications include the following:

- tracking portfolio performance in a stock training simulation (Crisci, 1992)
- functioning as a calculator and demonstrating multiplicative relationships in elementary mathematics (Edwards & Bitter, 1989)
- analyzing lunchroom trash and projecting annual waste for an Earth Day project (Ramondetta, 1992)
- rootfinding in precalculus using synthetic division, bisection method, and Newton's Method (Pinter-Lucke, 1992)
- solving complex chemistry problems such as wet and dry analysis of flue gases, which may be expanded to include volumetric flow rate,

pressure, humidity, dew point, temperature, and combustion temperature, in a mass and energy balances course (Misovic & Biasca, 1990)
- modeling the stoichiometric relationships in chemical reactions and calculating how many bonds are broken, the energy required to break bonds, and the new masses and densities of the products and reagents in the reactions (Brosnan, 1990)
- calculating the force needed to lift assorted weights in various lever problems (Schlenker & Yoshida, 1991)
- helping to solve a number of science problems, including problems involving an incline plane and converting protein into energy (Goodfellow, 1990)
- helping children understand the meaning of large numbers (a million) by comparing quantities to everyday things (Parker & Widmer, 1991)
- calculating the dimensions of a scale model of the Milky Way in order to demonstrate its immensity (Whitmer, 1990)
- solving problems in physics laboratory experiments on time, displacement, and velocity and their interrelationships using a free-fall apparatus (Krieger & Stith, 1990)
- solving elementary mathematical story problems (Verderber, 1990)
- representing Keynesian versus classical macroeconomic models, such as savings-investment and inflation-unemployment (Adams & Kroch, 1989)
- supporting decision analysis by helping users find the best use of available information as well as evaluating any additional information that can be obtained (Sounderpandian, 1989)
- facilitating student grading of peer speech performances, providing a high level of motivation for the student (Dribin, 1985)
- implementing linear system-solving algorithms, that is, advanced mathematical formulas (Watkins & Taylor, 1989)
- estimating and comparing the relative velocities of various dinosaurs (Karlin, 1988)
- implementing Polya's problem-solving plan with arithmetic problems (Sgroi, 1992)
- analyzing field data on ecology of tree species (Sigismondi & Calise, 1990)
- solving rate equation chemical kinetics problems in a physical chemistry course (Blickensderfer, 1990)
- interrelating demographic variables in population geography courses using population templates (Rudnicki, 1990)
- calculating and graphing quantum mechanical functions such as atomic orbitals to simulate rotational and vibrational energy levels of atomic components in a physical chemistry class (Kari, 1990)

- creating and manipulating economic models (e.g., balance of payments, investment appraisal, elasticity, cost-benefit analysis) in an economics course (Cashien, 1990)

Many of these applications recommend activities and problems to structure their use. For example, in order to support higher level thinking skills such as collecting, describing, and interpreting data, Niess (1992) provided a spreadsheet with wind data for different towns. Wind directions (NE, SW, WSW) described rows of data with the percent of days for each month of the year representing the columns. She would then ask students to use the spreadsheets to answer queries, such as the following:

- Are the winds more predominant from one direction during certain months? Why do you think this is the case?
- In which months is the wind the calmest?
- Which wind direction is the most stable throughout the year?

The examples in this chapter demonstrate applications of spreadsheets as Mindtools. The first spreadsheet (Figure 4.4) supports a lab activity on blood analysis. The student is to collect the class data, arrange it by gender (this example is also arranged by descending white blood cell count), calculate averages by gender and by class, and compare his or her values with the averages for his or her gender and for the class. The data collected in this experiment were white blood count, red blood count, hematocrit, and hemoglobin.

Queries that would require students to add cells with formulas and functions might include the following:

- Are there gender differences in blood components such as red and white cells or hemoglobin?
- If white cell counts drop, what is the likely effect on red cells?
- If hemoglobin were administered to a patient, what is the likely effect on hematocrit readings?

The next spreadsheet (Figure 4.5) details solutions of the quadratic equation. It uses a variety of spreadsheet functions, especially the IF function to analyze the values in the spreadsheet during calculation. Having students trace the solution of these equations would help them to better understand the intermediate steps and how they combine in the solution.

**Figure 4.4**
Spreadsheet to support lab
experiment on blood

| | A | B | C | D | E |
|---|---|---|---|---|---|
| 1 | SEX | WBC | RBC(X10E6) | HCT (%) | HGB |
| 2 | FEMALE | 13,760 | 11 | 42.2 | 15.25 |
| 3 | FEMALE | 9,360 | 11.1 | 41.6 | 14.1 |
| 4 | FEMALE | 9,000 | 1.3 | 43.4 | 17 |
| 5 | FEMALE | 9,000 | 1.3 | 46.1 | 15 |
| 6 | FEMALE | 7,960 | 3.7 | 34.1 | 15 |
| 7 | FEMALE | 7,680 | 5.5 | 43.2 | 16 |
| 8 | FEMALE | 7,080 | 4.4 | 41.6 | 14 |
| 9 | FEMALE | 6,720 | 2.18 | 38.6 | 14.2 |
| 10 | FEMALE | 6,600 | 4.5 | 57.1 | 17.5 |
| 11 | FEMALE | 6,400 | 5.5 | 43.4 | 17 |
| 12 | FEMALE | 6,240 | 3.42 | 52 | 19 |
| 13 | FEMALE | 5,680 | 5.53 | 60 | 14.5 |
| 14 | FEMALE | 4,980 | 4.74 | 44.6 | 15 |
| 15 | FEMALE | 4,520 | 8.35 | 44.4 | 15.2 |
| 16 | MALE | 8,968 | 5.79 | 42.2 | 15.5 |
| 17 | MALE | 7,786 | 5.7 | 51.5 | 16.5 |
| 18 | MALE | 7,760 | 3.4 | 50 | 15.7 |
| 19 | MALE | 7,520 | 6.7 | 46.3 | 8.9 |
| 20 | MALE | 6,600 | 3.73 | 49.1 | 19 |
| 21 | MALE | 6,520 | 4.29 | 47 | 15 |
| 22 | MALE | 6,450 | 6.5 | 47.2 | 16.5 |
| 23 | MALE | 6,040 | 11 | 44 | 14.5 |
| 24 | MALE | 4,600 | 5.7 | 46.2 | 14 |
| 25 | MIN FEMALES | 4,520 | 1.3 | 34.1 | 14 |
| 26 | MAX FEMALES | 13,760 | 11.1 | 60 | 19 |
| 27 | RANGE FEMALES | 9,240 | 9.8 | 25.9 | 5 |
| 28 | AVE FEMALES | 7,499 | 5.18 | 45.2 | 15.6 |
| 29 | | | | | |
| 30 | MIN MALES | 4,600 | 3.4 | 42.2 | 8.9 |
| 31 | MAX MALES | 8,968 | 11 | 51.5 | 19 |
| 32 | RANGE MALES | 4,368 | 7.6 | 9.3 | 10.1 |
| 33 | AVE MALES | 6,916 | 5.9 | 47.1 | 15.1 |
| 34 | | | | | |
| 35 | MIN CLASS | 4,520 | 1.3 | 34.1 | 8.9 |
| 36 | MAX CLASS | 13,760 | 11.1 | 60 | 19 |
| 37 | RANGE CLASS | 9,240 | 9.8 | 25.9 | 10.1 |
| 38 | AVE CLASS | 7,271 | 5.4 | 45.9 | 15.4 |

| problem | equation | a | check a | b | check b | c | check c |
|---|---|---|---|---|---|---|---|
| 6 | 4n^2 - 3n + 5 = 0 | 4 | =If(C3=4,4,-99999) | -3 | =If(E3=-3,-3,-99999) | 5 | =If(G3=5,5,-99999) |
| 14 | 10w^2 + 3 - 7w = 1 | 10 | =If(C4=10,10,-99999) | -7 | =If(E4=-7,-7,-99999) | 2 | =If(G4=2,2,-99999) |
| 10 | 5 = 4x - 2x^2 | 2 | =If(C5=2,2,-99999) | -4 | =If(E5=-4,-4,-99999) | 5 | =If(G5=5,5,-99999) |
| 13 | 2y^2 = y - 2 - y^2 | 3 | =If(C6=3,3,-99999) | -1 | =If(E6=-1,-1,-99999) | 2 | =If(G6=2,2,-99999) |
| 3 | x^2 - 3x + 7 = 0 | 1 | =If(C7=1,1,-99999) | -3 | =If(E7=-3,-3,-99999) | 7 | =If(G7=7,7,-99999) |
| 2 | 9x^2 - 12x + 4 = 0 | 9 | =If(C8=9,9,-99999) | -12 | =If(E8=-12,-12,-99999) | 4 | =If(G8=4,4,-99999) |
| 7 | x^2 - 4x + 4 = 0 | 1 | =If(C9=1,1,-99999) | -4 | =If(E9=-4,-4,-99999) | 4 | =If(G9=4,4,-99999) |
| 15 | 8s + 9 = - 4s^2 + 5 | 4 | =If(C10=4,4,-99999) | 8 | =If(E10=8,8,-99999) | 4 | =If(G10=4,4,-99999) |
| 1 | 2x^2 + 5x - 3 = 0 | 2 | =If(C11=2,2,-99999) | 5 | =If(E11=5,5,-99999) | -3 | =If(G11=-3,-3,-99999) |
| 12 | -y^2 = -9y + 5 | -1 | =If(C12=-1,-1,-99999) | 9 | =If(E12=9,9,-99999) | -5 | =If(G12=-5,-5,-99999) |
| 4 | x^2 - 6x - 10 = 0 | 1 | =If(C13=1,1,-99999) | -6 | =If(E13=-6,-6,-99999) | -10 | =If(G13=-10,-10,-99999) |
| 11 | 3x^2 = 5 - 4x | 3 | =If(C14=3,3,-99999) | 4 | =If(E14=4,4,-99999) | -5 | =If(G14=-5,-5,-99999) |
| 8 | 9z^2 = 2z + 5 | 9 | =If(C15=9,9,-99999) | -2 | =If(E15=-2,-2,-99999) | -5 | =If(G15=-5,-5,-99999) |
| 5 | 3x^2 - 12x - 10 = 0 | 3 | =If(C16=3,3,-99999) | -12 | =If(E16=-12,-12,-99999) | -10 | =If(G16=-10,-10,-99999) |
| 9 | 16v^2 = 1 - 20v | 16 | =If(C17=16,16,-99999) | 20 | =If(E17=20,20,-99999) | -1 | =If(G17=-1,-1,-99999) |

Note: x^2 means (x)(x), which is x squared

**Figure 4.5**
Quadratic equation spreadsheet

| larger solution | smaller solution | discriminant | -b/a | sum of sq | c/a | product of |
|---|---|---|---|---|---|---|
| =(-E3+Sqrt((E3^2)-(4*C3*G3)))/(2*C3) | =(-E3-Sqrt((E3^2)-(4*C3*G3)))/(2*C3) | =(E3^2)-(4*C3*G3) | =-E3/C3 | =I3+J3 | =G3/C3 | =I3*J3 |
| =(-E4+Sqrt((E4^2)-(4*C4*G4)))/(2*C4) | =(-E4-Sqrt((E4^2)-(4*C4*G4)))/(2*C4) | =(E4^2)-(4*C4*G4) | =-E4/C4 | =I4+J4 | =G4/C4 | =I4*J4 |
| =(-E5+Sqrt((E5^2)-(4*C5*G5)))/(2*C5) | =(-E5-Sqrt((E5^2)-(4*C5*G5)))/(2*C5) | =(E5^2)-(4*C5*G5) | =-E5/C5 | =I5+J5 | =G5/C5 | =I5*J5 |
| =(-E6+Sqrt((E6^2)-(4*C6*G6)))/(2*C6) | =(-E6-Sqrt((E6^2)-(4*C6*G6)))/(2*C6) | =(E6^2)-(4*C6*G6) | =-E6/C6 | =I6+J6 | =G6/C6 | =I6*J6 |
| =(-E7+Sqrt((E7^2)-(4*C7*G7)))/(2*C7) | =(-E7-Sqrt((E7^2)-(4*C7*G7)))/(2*C7) | =(E7^2)-(4*C7*G7) | =-E7/C7 | =I7+J7 | =G7/C7 | =I7*J7 |
| =(-E8+Sqrt((E8^2)-(4*C8*G8)))/(2*C8) | =(-E8-Sqrt((E8^2)-(4*C8*G8)))/(2*C8) | =(E8^2)-(4*C8*G8) | =-E8/C8 | =I8+J8 | =G8/C8 | =I8*J8 |
| =(-E9+Sqrt((E9^2)-(4*C9*G9)))/(2*C9) | =(-E9-Sqrt((E9^2)-(4*C9*G9)))/(2*C9) | =(E9^2)-(4*C9*G9) | =-E9/C9 | =I9+J9 | =G9/C9 | =I9*J9 |
| =(-E10+Sqrt((E10^2)-(4*C10*G10)))/(2*C10) | =(-E10-Sqrt((E10^2)-(4*C10*G10)))/(2*C10) | =(E10^2)-(4*C10*G10) | =-E10/C10 | =I10+J10 | =G10/C10 | =I10*J10 |
| =(-E11+Sqrt((E11^2)-(4*C11*G11)))/(2*C11) | =(-E11-Sqrt((E11^2)-(4*C11*G11)))/(2*C11) | =(E11^2)-(4*C11*G11) | =-E11/C11 | =I11+J11 | =G11/C11 | =I11*J11 |
| =(-E12+Sqrt((E12^2)-(4*C12*G12)))/(2*C12) | =(-E12-Sqrt((E12^2)-(4*C12*G12)))/(2*C12) | =(E12^2)-(4*C12*G12) | =-E12/C12 | =I12+J12 | =G12/C12 | =I12*J12 |
| =(-E13+Sqrt((E13^2)-(4*C13*G13)))/(2*C13) | =(-E13-Sqrt((E13^2)-(4*C13*G13)))/(2*C13) | =(E13^2)-(4*C13*G13) | =-E13/C13 | =I13+J13 | =G13/C13 | =I13*J13 |
| =(-E14+Sqrt((E14^2)-(4*C14*G14)))/(2*C14) | =(-E14-Sqrt((E14^2)-(4*C14*G14)))/(2*C14) | =(E14^2)-(4*C14*G14) | =-E14/C14 | =I14+J14 | =G14/C14 | =I14*J14 |
| =(-E15+Sqrt((E15^2)-(4*C15*G15)))/(2*C15) | =(-E15-Sqrt((E15^2)-(4*C15*G15)))/(2*C15) | =(E15^2)-(4*C15*G15) | =-E15/C15 | =I15+J15 | =G15/C15 | =I15*J15 |
| =(-E16+Sqrt((E16^2)-(4*C16*G16)))/(2*C16) | =(-E16-Sqrt((E16^2)-(4*C16*G16)))/(2*C16) | =(E16^2)-(4*C16*G16) | =-E16/C16 | =I16+J16 | =G16/C16 | =I16*J16 |
| =(-E17+Sqrt((E17^2)-(4*C17*G17)))/(2*C17) | =(-E17-Sqrt((E17^2)-(4*C17*G17)))/(2*C17) | =(E17^2)-(4*C17*G17) | =-E17/C17 | =I17+J17 | =G17/C17 | =I17*J17 |

**Figure 4.5,** *continued*

# Spreadsheets as Mindtools

Spreadsheets are an example of a cognitive technology that amplifies and reorganizes mental functioning (see Chapter 1). They have restructured the work of budgeting, enabling the accountant to be a hypothesis tester (playing "what if" games) rather than merely a calculator (Pea, 1985). This was the original purpose of spreadsheets, as described in the first section of this chapter. In the same way that they have qualitatively changed the accounting process, spreadsheets can change any educational process with a quantitative base.

The spreadsheet engages a variety of mental processes, such as designing, using, and filling in values and formulas, that require learners to use existing rules, generate new rules describing relationships, and organize information (Figure 4.1). These processes engage critical thinking in students, which is the primary purpose of Mindtools.

The grid structure of spreadsheets facilitates the storage, calculation, and presentation of information. Merely transferring information into cells primarily involves knowledge- and comprehension-level learning, that is, identifying content that fits into a cell. Answering questions using the spreadsheets is primarily at the application level, that is, applying information from the spreadsheets to problem-solution scenarios.

However, the process of defining the organization structure for a spreadsheet involves analysis-level learning. The learner must analyze (break down) a knowledge domain into its components and then identify relationships (primarily mathematical) between the components of that content. The emphasis in a spreadsheet is on identifying relationships and describing those relationships in terms of higher order rules, so it is probable that if users learn to develop spreadsheets to describe content domains, they will be thinking more deeply.

So, spreadsheets are rule-using tools that require that users become rule makers (Vockell & Van Deusen, 1989). Calculating values in a spreadsheet requires users to identify relationships and patterns among the data they want to represent in the spreadsheet. Next, those relationships must be modeled mathematically using rules to describe the relationships in the model. Building spreadsheets requires abstract reasoning by the user. The Working Group for Technology of the National Curriculum Commission (1990), which helped frame the national curriculum in Great Britain, recognized the role of spreadsheets as tools that enable students to use information technology to explore patterns and relationships and to form and test sample hypotheses.

# Evaluation of Spreadsheets as Mindtools

1. *Computer-based.* Although they have the appearance of a ledger sheet, spreadsheets are computer-based computational tools that exploit the computational power of the computer.

2. *Readily available, general applications.* Spreadsheet applications are a part of most integrated software packages, so most computers in use in schools today probably have a spreadsheet program already installed.

3. *Affordable.* If the computer you use does not have an integrated office package, public-domain spreadsheet programs are available from a variety of sources, or powerful commercial spreadsheets are available for less than $100.

4. *Represent knowledge.* The knowledge represented in spreadsheets is quantitative and abstract. In addition to mathematical representations, spreadsheets easily convert quantities to graphical representations. However, facility with numerical relations is important. The ability to use variables is also important, since variable concepts are most effectively represented in spreadsheets.

5. *Applicable in different subject domains.* Although spreadsheets can be used to solve problems in any content domain, they are only appropriate for quantitative problem situations.

6. *Engage critical thinking.* These skills are described in the next section. Designing a spreadsheet and then speculating about outcomes ("what if" hypothesis testing) are the more engaging tasks.

7. *Facilitate transfer of learning.* Learning how to represent quantitative relationships between entities through building spreadsheets has significant transferability.

8. *Simple, powerful formalism.* The spreadsheet formalism is exclusively quantitative (numerical and graphic representations), so the relationships in the problem you want to investigate should be quantitative for a spreadsheet to be maximally effective.

9. *(Reasonably) easy to learn.* Spreadsheets are probably one of the more difficult Mindtools to master, not because of the inherent difficulty in the tool but because of the anxiety that most students exhibit about math. For mathematically able students, the use of spreadsheets should be easy to learn. For the mathematically challenged, spreadsheets can provide powerful lessons.

# Critical, Creative, and Complex Thinking
# in Spreadsheet Construction and Use

A large number of critical, creative, and complex thinking skills are required to use and construct knowledge-oriented spreadsheets. Tables 4.1, 4.2, and 4.3 identify the skills that are used when filling in, designing, and speculating (answering "what if" questions) with spreadsheets. The skills in each table that are marked by an "×" are those that are employed by each process, based on an information-processing analysis of the tasks.

As is the case with most other Mindtools, building and using spreadsheets probably requires more critical thinking skills than it does creative or complex thinking skills (see Table 4.1). That is because spreadsheet construction and use is an analytic process that makes heavy use of logical thinking. Spreadsheets are often used (as in Figure 4.4) to collect and analyze data from experiments. This kind of activity requires very little critical thinking. However, designing a spreadsheet to reflect the data-collection needs of an experiment requires a variety of evaluating, analyzing, and connecting skills, such as assessing information, determining criteria, verifying, classifying, and identifying assumptions. Speculating with spreadsheets about relationships or quantities makes heavy use of analyzing and connecting information, especially in identifying and explicating relationships between data points in the spreadsheet.

For example, having students speculate about the change in products from altering one of the factors in the quadratic equations represented in Figure 4.5 requires inferences, logical thinking, comparing/contrasting quantities, and looking for causal relationships.

There are also a number of creative thinking skills involved in constructing and speculating with spreadsheets (see Table 4.2). Designing spreadsheets depends more on elaborating, synthesizing, and imagining skills, such as modifying, expanding, planning, predicting, and visualizing. Building spreadsheets requires the designer to visualize the quantitative relationships between data, an activity that is supported by the graphing capabilities of most spreadsheet programs. Speculating with spreadsheets such as Figure 4.5 engages students in analogical thinking, hypothesizing, predicting, and, of course, speculation.

Finally, a number of complex thinking skills are required for designing and speculating with spreadsheets (see Table 4.3). Designing and building databases requires a number of planning operations that make heavy use of designing, problem-solving, and decision-making skills (see Table 3.3). With spreadsheets, on the other hand, heavier use of problem solving and

**Table 4.1**
Critical thinking skills in spreadsheet construction and use

| | Filling in Spreadsheet | Designing/ Building Spreadsheet | Speculating with Spreadsheet |
|---|:---:|:---:|:---:|
| **Evaluating** | | | |
| Assessing information | | X | |
| Determining criteria | | X | |
| Prioritizing | | | |
| Recognizing fallacies | | | X |
| Verifying | | X | |
| **Analyzing** | | | |
| Recognizing patterns | | | X |
| Classifying | X | X | |
| Identifying assumptions | | X | X |
| Identifying main ideas | | | |
| Finding sequences | | X | X |
| **Connecting** | | | |
| Comparing/contrasting | | | X |
| Logical thinking | | X | X |
| Inferring deductively | | X | X |
| Inferring inductively | | | |
| Identifying causal relationships | | X | X |

decision making takes place during speculating. This makes sense, because the purpose of using spreadsheets is to help users make decisions about what actions to take if a particular set of conditions evolves. Problem solving is an important outcome of using spreadsheets.

## Related Mindtools

Spreadsheets and databases (Chapter 3) look and function very much alike. They both display information in a matrix of rows and columns, and information can even be passed back and forth between them. Also, powerful spreadsheet programs have many database features, so these tools are often used in conjunction with each other.

Because of the mathematical skills and orientation required, spreadsheets are intellectually most like programming (Chapter 9), although spreadsheets require learning much less syntax than does computer programming. Spreadsheets can be used in lieu of computer programs, especially for mathematical calculations. I now tend to use spreadsheets for

**Table 4.2**
Creative thinking skills in spreadsheet construction and use

| | Filling in Spreadsheet | Designing/ Building Spreadsheet | Speculating with Spreadsheet |
|---|---|---|---|
| **Elaborating** | | | |
| Expanding | | X | |
| Modifying | X | X | |
| Extending | | | X |
| Shifting categories | X | | |
| Concretizing | X | X | |
| **Synthesizing** | | | |
| Analogical thinking | | | X |
| Summarizing | X | X | |
| Hypothesizing | | | X |
| Planning | | X | |
| **Imagining** | | | |
| Fluency | | | |
| Predicting | | X | X |
| Speculating | | | X |
| Visualizing | | X | |
| Intuition | | | X |

series of calculations where I used to write BASIC programs to manipulate data. It is much quicker and easier to create a spreadsheet than a computer program. Spreadsheets can also be used to develop prototypes of computer programs.

Spreadsheets also interact with statistical analysis programs, which, like word-processing and graphics programs, are not discussed in depth in this book but could be used as Mindtools. Many researchers collect data with computers and then load that data into a spreadsheet where the data are massaged and preprocessed before being loaded into a statistical analysis program. Spreadsheets are versatile programs for mathematically manipulating almost any kind of computerized information.

# Software Tools

Spreadsheet programs are commonly available for every type of computer in use today. Many spreadsheet software packages are in the public domain and thus very inexpensive. For the Apple II series of computers, AppleWorks or MultiPlan will work fine. The Minnesota Educational Computing Consortium also supplies an inexpensive, fully functional

**Table 4.3**
Complex thinking skills in spreadsheet construction and use

| | Filling in Spreadsheet | Designing/ Building Spreadsheet | Speculating with Spreadsheet |
|---|---|---|---|
| **Designing** | | | |
| Imagining a goal | | X | X |
| Formulating a goal | | X | X |
| Inventing a product | | X | |
| Assessing a product | | | |
| Revising the product | X | | |
| **Problem Solving** | | | |
| Sensing the problem | | | X |
| Researching the problem | | X | X |
| Formulating the problem | | X | X |
| Finding alternatives | | X | X |
| Choosing the solution | | X | |
| Building acceptance | | | |
| **Decision Making** | | | |
| Identifying an issue | | | X |
| Generating alternatives | | | X |
| Assessing the consequences | | | X |
| Making a choice | | X | |
| Evaluating the choices | | X | |

spreadsheet program. For the Macintosh, spreadsheets are part of most integrated packages, such as ClarisWorks or Microsoft Works. For users who seek more powerful spreadsheets, Microsoft's Excel has become an industry standard. A number of shareware spreadsheet programs are available through computer bulletin boards and computer users' groups. These are not as powerful, but they are typically inexpensive (users copy the program for free, and if they choose to keep it, they send in a nominal registration fee). Shareware programs are powerful enough to be used as Mindtools.

For DOS computers, Lotus 1-2-3, Symphony, Quattro Pro, SuperCalc, Excel (also running under Windows), and a host of other spreadsheet programs are available. By a large factor, Lotus is the most widely used spreadsheet program in the world. Less powerful programs, such as PC Quick, can be purchased very inexpensively, as can a number of shareware programs. Such programs would be adequate for most Mindtools uses. The power of programs such as Symphony and Excel is not required for most Mindtool applications.

Selecting a spreadsheet can be a perplexing process, so keep a few simple criteria in mind. The most important one is cost. It should not be necessary to spend very much for the kind of functionality described in this chapter. Look at the list of features and decide which ones you really need. Generally, as the number of functions and capabilities afforded by a package increases, so does the complexity of the system and the difficulty of use. Test out any new package to see how easy it is to use. If you are a novice spreadsheet user, you may want to select the simplest system, with the expectation that you will upgrade later if the program proves to be inadequate.

As with databases, you should consider what other applications software you want to use. Will you also want to perform word processing and use databases? If so, you may want to consider an integrated package such as AppleWorks for the Apple IIs or Microsoft Works or ClarisWorks for the Macintoshes.

Whichever software you purchase, it is always a good idea to try it out and spend some time using it. A potential problem with Mindtools or any computer application is the learning curve required to become an effective user. Try to select software that minimizes the time spent learning how to use the software and maximizes the time spent solving quantitative problems.

# How to Construct and Use Spreadsheets in the Classroom

Imagine that for Earth Day this year, your students want to calculate the impact of a new recycling policy on the county they live in. Identifying all of the disposable and recyclable products, the quantities discarded in each part of the county, and the costs (short term and long term) of burying or recycling those products would require extensive investigation. Then building a model to interrelate all of the products, costs, and savings on a spreadsheet would require extensive synthesis activities that would provide your students with feelings of satisfaction and accomplishment. Rather than having your elementary science students read about experiments in their science books, have them conduct the experiments and use spreadsheets to record and analyze the results. Or have your students construct a survey about the attitudes of students in different grades, administer the survey, and use spreadsheets to record and analyze the results. There are so many applications of spreadsheets in all grades.

Performing the kinds of content analysis required to set up and describe such problem situations for building spreadsheets will require many new skills. The ultimate goal is for your students to be able to independently analyze a new problem situation by identifying the problem variables and interrelationships among those variables and creating formulas and using functions to calculate and manipulate the quantities in those variables. The ability to create quantitative models of problem situations is a powerful, transferable skill. In order to reach this goal, several stages of learning must occur. This section recommends a series of stages and learning activities for preparing your students to achieve that goal.

1. *Provide spreadsheet template.* To introduce students to the structure and functions of spreadsheets, you may want to begin by having them complete some exercises using an existing spreadsheet. Begin with a spreadsheet template (a spreadsheet with formulas entered but no values) and require students to fill in gaps in the spreadsheet. For example, complete a simple science experiment and have students enter the data collected in particular cells. Or start with a familiar spreadsheet—perhaps a spreadsheet of personal information (height, weight, shoe size, age, parent data) about the students in the class—and require them to input their personal information in the spreadsheet and then calculate high, low, and averages of these values and other quantities, such as density (weight/height). Later, use a content spreadsheet that contains the formulas and have them look up information from almanacs, tables, or other reference materials to enter into the spreadsheet. Make sure that students trace all of the calculations that are completed by the spreadsheet. These activities familiarize learners with spreadsheet functions and structure.

2. *Students adapt existing spreadsheets or design new spreadsheets for other students to complete.* Start with familiar content and require students to adapt existing spreadsheets, such as adding nutritional information and relationships to the personal variables in the classroom information spreadsheet. Or design new spreadsheets that they can collaboratively fill in. Topics such as local sports teams, dating patterns, and television shows are popular.

3. *Students create and complete a problem-oriented spreadsheet.* Increase the complexity of the spreadsheet content by relating it to classroom studies. Starting with more concrete activities—such as geographical or demographic features in social studies or mathematical formulas in algebra—and working in small, collaborative groups, have students determine what values, formulas, and functions are required. This depends on what kinds of questions people have that need to be answered, that is, what kinds of relationships users may want to compare in the spreadsheet. This is perhaps the most difficult part of the process. Compare the spreadsheets in class and discuss the relationships in terms of how com-

pletely and accurately they reflect the content domain. This is the most complete activity, requiring learners to identify variables and information needs, develop formulas and functions, complete the spreadsheet, and use the spreadsheet to answer questions.

**4. *Students extrapolate from spreadsheets.*** Students can create new formulas in an existing spreadsheet to support other applications. For example, starting with a spreadsheet on geographic information, adding political and economic variables and relationships to support geopolitical relationship questions would be useful.

## Fostering Collaboration with Content Spreadsheets

The "what if" skills required to effectively use spreadsheets are likely to be new to learners, who have generally been told what the implications or importance of any content is. Spreadsheets are quantitative in nature, and this presents problems to students who fear mathematics, either because they are not competent or—more likely—because they believe they are not competent.

**1. *Form the teams.*** Since higher-ability math groups would easily outperform lower-ability groups, split the higher-ability students up between groups. This will allow these students to tutor and will provide more even performance across groups.

**2. *Clarify the group goal.*** This may be the most difficult part of the process, at least until students gain some familiarity with spreadsheets. Using a spreadsheet as a tool to solve a problem represents a major leap for most students. Spreadsheet use in schools is too often a rote activity, with students filling in formulas provided by the teacher. Identifying the problem and breaking the task into a set of steps is much like learning to program a computer (see Chapter 9). This part of the process will require you to coach the students extensively.

**3. *Negotiate tasks and subtasks to be completed.*** It is very easy for the higher-ability math students to take over and simply solve the problem for the rest of the group, so ensuring that each member contributes will be difficult. You may have the higher-ability students figure out the formulas for the first few cells and then have them coach the others to complete the remaining cells. You may need to scaffold this process by setting up specific work schedules and perhaps having students keep records of their activities in part of the spreadsheet that they are building.

**4. *Monitor individual and group performance.*** The higher-ability math students should become coaches for the other students. Teaching them to play that role rather than simply giving the others the answers will be difficult, so you will have to model those activities for them.

**5. *Reconcile differences in interpretations or approaches to the goal.*** Since many students would rather follow than lead, you may want to publicly compare the solutions of the various groups to demonstrate to your students that there are different approaches to solving the same problem.

## Advantages of Content Spreadsheets as Mindtools

A spreadsheet will always perform the calculations that are embedded into its cells, so if one value in the grid is changed, all of the values in the spreadsheet that are related to it are also automatically recalculated. This capability frees the user from reentering all of the values in a formula if one value changes, as is required by most calculators. Perhaps the major logistical advantage of spreadsheets is that they are easy to adapt and modify.

A spreadsheet is, in essence, a computer program for making multiple calculations. But since spreadsheets do not require the use of a complex programming language, they reduce the proliferation of syntax and logical errors that are common with these programming languages (Misovich & Biasca, 1990). If you like computer languages, many of the more powerful spreadsheet packages provide simple programming languages to enhance the capabilities of the spreadsheet, but you can access the power of programming without learning to program.

Spreadsheets support problem-solving activities. Given a problem situation with complex quantitative relationships, the experienced spreadsheet user can quickly create a spreadsheet to represent those relationships. Spreadsheets are perhaps best used for supporting "what if" analyses (e.g., What will be the effect on accounts payable and debt ratio if interest rates increase 1%?, or What will happen if the population of an emerging country increases at 7% rather than 5%?). This type of thinking is best supported by spreadsheets and is essential to decision analysis (Sounderpandian, 1989). Such questioning requires learners to consider the implications of various conditions or options, which entails higher-order reasoning.

Spreadsheets explicitly demonstrate values and relationships in any problem or content domain in numerical form. Identifying values and developing formulas to interrelate them enhances learners' understanding of the algorithms used to compare them and of the mathematical models used to describe content domains. Students understand calculations (both antecedents and consequents) because they are actively involved in identifying the interrelationships among the components of the calculation. Spreadsheet construction and use demonstrate all steps of problem solutions and show the progression of calculations as they are performed. The spreadsheet process models the mathematical logic that is implied by calculations. Making the underlying logic obvious to learners should improve their understanding of the interrelationships and procedures.

Finally, spreadsheets integrate graphics and calculations easily. Spreadsheets visualize quantitative relationships, both in the grid of cells and in graphs and charts that are generated by most spreadsheets. Research has shown that even children as young as 6 years are able to enter and graphically display information (Goodfellow, 1990).

# Limitations of Content Spreadsheets as Mindtools

Although the spreadsheet is a versatile tool, it is only effective in solving quantitative problems. Even though one can input text into spreadsheets, most programs are unable to process it in any meaningful way. Because spreadsheets are designed to manipulate quantitative information, they are most useful in mathematics and science, and in some social science applications (e.g., economics, psychology, and sociology). Spreadsheets are generally not very useful for humanities instruction, although there are a few types of analyses in this area that can be quantified and are therefore amenable to spreadsheet use (e.g., metric analysis of poems).

## *Conclusion*

Spreadsheets are versatile tools for identifying, manipulating, and visualizing quantitative relationships between entities. On the simplest level, they are programmable calculators that eliminate the need for time-consuming manipulation and calculation of numbers. They allow users to effectively organize a variety of calculations on a simple grid structure, using almost any kind of mathematical relationship. Spreadsheets are also effective problem-solving tools. While they are more often used as productivity tools, they can also function well as Mindtools. When students create spreadsheets, they are building quantitative models of the real world and using those models to speculate about changes in the phenomena contained in their models. Those are powerful skills to acquire.

## References

Adams, F. G., & Kroch, E. (1989). The computer in the teaching of economics. *Journal of Economic Education, 20*(3), 269–280.

Blickensderfer, R. (1990). Learning chemical kinetics with spreadsheets. *Journal of Computers in Mathematics and Science Teaching, 9*(4), 35–43.

Brosnan, T. (1990). Using spreadsheets in the teaching of chemistry: Two more ideas and some limitations. *School Science Review, 71*(256), 53–59.

Cashien, P. (1990). Spreadsheet investigations in economics teaching. *Economics, 26,* (Pt. 2, 110), 73–84.

Crisci, G. (1992, January). Play the market! *Instructor,* pp. 68–69.

Dribin, C. I. (1985, June). Spreadsheets and performance: A guide for student-graded presentations. *The Computing Teacher,* pp. 22–25.

Edwards, N. T., & Bitter, B. G. (1989, October). Changing variables using spreadsheet templates. *Arithmetic Teacher,* pp. 40–44.

Goodfellow, T. (1990). Spreadsheets: Powerful tools in science education. *School Science Review, 71*(257), 47–57.

Kari, R. (1990). Spreadsheets in advanced physical chemistry. *Journal of Computers in Mathematics and Science Teaching, 10*(1), 39–48.

Karlin, M. (1988, February). Beyond distance = rate * time. *The Computing Teacher,* pp. 20–23.

Krieger, M. E., & Stith, J. H. (1990, September). Spreadsheets in the physics laboratory. *The Physics Teacher,* pp. 378–384.

Misovich, M., & Biasca, K. (1990). The power of spreadsheets in a mass and energy balances course. *Chemical Engineering Education, 24,* 46–50.

National Curriculum Commission. (1990). *Technology in the national curriculum.* London: Author.

Niess, M. L. (1992, March). Winds of change. *The Computing Teacher,* pp. 32–35.

Parker, J., & Widmer, C. C. (1991, September). Teaching mathematics with technology. *Arithmetic Teacher,* pp. 38–41.

Pea, R. D. (1985). Beyond amplification: Using the computer to reorganize mental functioning. *Educational Psychologist, 20*(4), 167–182.

Pinter-Lucke, C. (1992). Rootfinding with a spreadsheet in pre-calculus. *Journal of Computers in Mathematics and Science Teaching, 11,* 85–93.

Ramondetta, J. (1992). Learning from lunchroom trash. *Learning Using Computers, 20*(8), 59.

Rudnicki, R. (1990). Using spreadsheets in population geography classes. *Journal of Geography, 89*(3), 118–122.

Schlenker, R. M., & Yoshida, S. J. (1991). A clever lever endeavor: You can't beat the spreadsheet. *The Science Teacher, 58*(2), 36–39.

Sgroi, R. J. (1992, March). Systematizing trial and error using spreadsheets. *Arithmetic Teacher,* pp. 8–12.

Sigismondi, L. A., & Calise, C. (1990). Integrating basic computer skills into science classes: Analysis of ecological data. *The American Biology Teacher, 52*(5), 296–301.

Sounderpandian, J. (1989). Decision analysis using spreadsheets. *Collegiate Micro-computer, 7*(2), 157–163.

Verderber, N. L. (1990). Spreadsheets and problem solving with AppleWorks in mathematics teaching. *Journal of Computers in Mathematics and Science Teaching, 9*(3), 45–51.

Vockell, E., & Van Deusen, R. M. (1989). *The computer and higher-order thinking skills.* Watsonville, CA: Mitchell Publishing.

Watkins, W., & Taylor, M. (1989). A spreadsheet in the mathematics classroom. *Collegiate Microcomputer, 7*(3), 233–239.

Whitmer, J. C. (1990). Modeling the Milky Way. *The Science Teacher, 57*(7), 19–21.

CHAPTER 5

# Semantic Networking Tools:
## *Mapping the Mind*

••••••••••••••••••••••••••••••••••••••••••••••••••••••••••••

## What Are Semantic Networks?

The past few years have seen the introduction of a new genre of Mindtool, the semantic networking tool. Programs such as SemNet (Fisher, 1990, 1992), Learning Tool (Kozma, 1987), and TextVision (Kommers, 1989) are powerful Mindtools that provide visual and verbal screen tools for developing concept maps, also known as semantic networks (nets). Semantic nets are spatial representations of ideas and their interrelationships. They enable learners to interrelate the ideas they are studying in multidimensional networks of concepts, to label the relationships between those concepts, and to describe the nature of the relationships among all of the ideas in the network.

Semantic networks are representations of human memory structures (Jonassen, Beissner, & Yacci, 1993). According to some psychological theories, those structures are organized semantically, that is, according to meaning that defines the relationships among the ideas in memory. These ideas, known as schemas, are arranged in networks of interconnected and interrelated ideas known as semantic networks. Semantic networking programs are computer-based visualizing tools for developing representations of these semantic networks in memory. These programs represent the mental semantic networks as concept maps.

The semantic networks in memory and the maps that represent them are composed of nodes (concepts or ideas) that are connected by links (statements of relationships). In computer-based semantic networks, nodes are represented as information blocks or cards (e.g., "structural knowledge" in Figure 5.1) and the links are labeled lines (e.g., "models"

**Figure 5.1**
Semantic networks as Mindtools

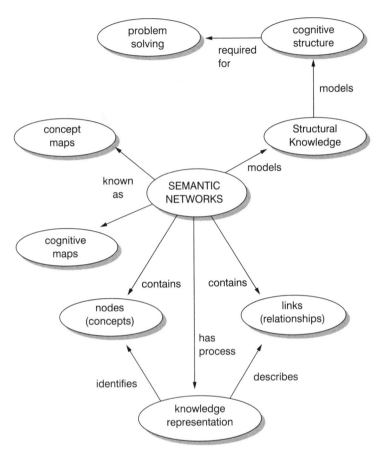

in Figure 5.1). Most semantic network programs also provide the capability of adding text and pictures to each node. The purpose of semantic networks is to represent the organization of someone's ideas or the underlying organization of ideas in a content domain. So, semantic networks function as Mindtools for engaging learners in critical thinking by engaging them in explicating the underlying ideas in the content being studied.

## Semantic Networks as Mindtools

Semantic networking aids learning by requiring learners to analyze the underlying structure of the ideas they are studying. The process of creating semantic networks engages learners in an analysis of their own knowledge structures, which helps them to integrate new knowledge with what they already know. The result is that the knowledge that is acquired can be used more effectively. Kozma (1987), one of the developers of Learning Tool, believes that semantic networking tools are cognitive tools that amplify, extend, and enhance human cognition. Constructing computer-based semantic nets engages learners in

* the reorganization of knowledge
* explicit description of concepts and their interrelationships
* deep processing of knowledge, which promotes better remembering and retrieval and the ability to apply knowledge in new situations
* relating new concepts to existing concepts and ideas, which improves understanding
* spatial learning through spatial representation of concepts in an area of study (Fisher et al., 1990)

Semantic networking tools are computer Mindtools for representing structural knowledge (Jonassen et al., 1993). Discussions of the psychology of knowing have often distinguished between declarative and procedural forms of knowledge. *Declarative* knowledge represents awareness of some object, event, or idea (knowing that). It enables learners to come to know, or define, ideas (verbal information or awareness of), and forms the basis for thinking about and using those ideas. However, merely knowing something does not mean that individuals can use that knowledge. *Procedural* knowledge is the knowledge of how to solve problems, form plans, and make decisions and arguments.

Declarative knowledge and procedural knowledge are interdependent. Some procedural knowledge is acquired by learning how to apply declarative knowledge, and some declarative knowledge is acquired in the context of learning how to do something. And most of us possess a considerable volume of declarative knowledge that we cannot apply and really have no use for (inert knowledge), while we know how to do some things that we cannot adequately articulate. Semantic networks represent an intermediate type of knowledge, *structural* knowledge, which aids the articulation of declarative and procedural knowledge. Structural knowledge is the knowledge of how the ideas within a domain are integrated and interrelated (Diekhoff, 1983). Awareness of those interrelationships and the ability to describe them are essential for higher-order thinking. It is not enough to know *that*. In order to know *how*, you must know *why*. Structural knowledge provides the conceptual bases for knowing why.

Structural knowledge is also known as cognitive structure, the pattern of relationships among concepts in memory (Preece, 1976), or, more specifically, the organization of the relationships among concepts in long-term memory (Shavelson, 1972). Semantic networking activities have been shown to be an accurate means for representing cognitive structure (Jonassen, 1987). That is, semantic networking, as described in this chapter, helps learners map their own cognitive structure.

Jonassen et al. (1993) describe a number of reasons for studying structural knowledge using semantic networks:

- Structure is inherent in all knowledge, so understanding the structural foundations of any content domain improves comprehension.
- Structural knowledge is essential to recall and comprehension because organization of knowledge has been shown by research to be facilitated by organization.
- When learners study, they necessarily acquire structural knowledge along with declarative knowledge.
- Memory structures reflect the world; people naturally learn the underlying organization of ideas while learning.
- Structural knowledge is essential to problem solving and procedural knowledge acquisition, so semantic networking will necessarily improve problem-solving ability.
- Experts' structural knowledge differs from novices'; understanding these differences is facilitated by semantic networking.

The usefulness of semantic nets and concepts maps in schools is shown by their relationship to other forms of higher-order thinking. For example, semantic nets have been significantly related to formal reasoning in chemistry (Schreiber & Abegg, 1991) and to reasoning ability in biology (Briscoe & LeMaster, 1991; Mikulecky, 1988). Learners with better structural knowledge are better problem solvers.

Semantic nets can also be used as evaluation tools for assessing learners' changes in thinking. If we agree that memory is organized as a semantic network, then learning can be thought of as a reorganization of semantic memory. Producing semantic networks reflects those changes in semantic memory, since the networks describe what a learner knows. So, the semantic nets learners generate before and after instruction should reflect growth in their knowledge structures. For this reason, concept maps were used in a geometry class to evaluate teaching outcomes and to monitor student progress in the course (Mansfield & Happs, 1991).

# Evaluation of Semantic Networks as Mindtools

**1.** *Computer-based.* Five different computer-based tools are described later in this chapter. These tools automate many of the processes for generating concept maps. They also enhance the maps with graphics, and they can automatically assess the net or changes to it. There are also many semantic networking methods that require only paper and pencil. These are described in Jonassen et al. (1993).

**2.** *Readily available, general applications.* Most of the limited number of semantic networking programs are available either from their authors or for purchase. Unlike other Mindtools, semantic networking programs are single purpose. They have no other, general productivity purpose. However, as described in the previous section, they can be used in a variety of ways.

**3.** *Affordable.* Some of the semantic networking programs are available from their authors at no charge. Others can be purchased, most for less than $100, if you are an educator.

**4.** *Represent knowledge.* Semantic networks represent structural knowledge more directly than any other Mindtool described in this book. Unlike other Mindtools, this was their original purpose.

**5.** *Applicable in different subject domains.* Semantic networking programs can be applied to any content domain. They are less applicable to very procedural domains, such as mathematics, but they are still useful for representing axioms, proofs, principles, concepts, and operators used in math. Learners enjoy the process and admit that they do think deeply about the content.

**6.** *Engage critical thinking.* These skills are described in the next section.

**7.** *Facilitate transfer of learning.* Research has shown that domain knowledge is as important or more important to higher-order thinking and problem solving than is previous experience in solving problems. Structural knowledge, as reflected in semantic nets, is very transferable.

**8.** *Simple, powerful formalism.* Visualizing relationships and semantic distance between ideas enhances comprehension and memory of the ideas. It is also enjoyable. I have experienced students coming to school while ill on days they were scheduled to work with these programs.

**9.** *(Reasonably) easy to learn.* Like all tools, semantic networking tools vary in complexity. However, learners can typically learn to use most semantic networking tools within an hour.

## Critical, Creative, and Complex Thinking in Semantic Network Construction and Use

The process of constructing semantic nets requires the learner to identify important concepts in a content domain. Deciding which are the important concepts is not easy for a novice. Experience with content (which develops procedural knowledge) is needed to become aware of which concepts are not only used most commonly but also which are most important to describing the domain.

Having identified the concepts in a domain that should go into the semantic net, the learner begins the more difficult and challenging part of the process: linking the concept nodes. We take relationships between concepts for granted. Having to describe precisely the relationship between two ideas is much more difficult and engaging than it initially appears. Why? The process of articulating those links requires learners to search through the range of possible relationships in order to define the relationship that exists in the context in which they are studying. What does that mean? Concepts can (and typically do) relate to each other in many different ways, depending on the context in which they are being used. For example, thinking about the concept "speed" in the context of physics class implies a different set of relationships than if you were studying the concept in the context of a drug education class. This variability is what contributes to the complexity of internal knowledge representations.

This linking process continues between all or most of the nodes in the net. While the linking is going on, new nodes or concepts are being added to the net in order to explain some of the existing concepts. Those concepts are linked, and additional concepts are added to explain them. This process of augmentation continues in a cycle until the builder feels that the domain is explained well enough. Interestingly, this process mirrors to some degree the natural pattern of knowledge acquisition. It is theoretically (although not practically) possible for learners to build nets consisting of all of the concepts they know in which those concepts are all linked together. What is also interesting and rewarding to students following the building of a large net is the realization of just how much they really know.

Tables 5.1, 5.2, and 5.3 identify the critical, creative, and complex thinking skills that are required for consulting an existing net (not building a new net, but simply studying an existing one), defining the nodes in a net, and linking those nodes. The skills in each table that are marked by an "×" are those that are employed by each process, based on an information-processing analysis of the tasks.

When learners consult an existing net in order to review content or try to understand the underlying organization of the content, they are not as deeply engaged as when they build nets. When studying an existing net, learners assess information in the net, identify the main ideas, and may compare and contrast those ideas (see Table 5.1). As with most Mindtools, more critical thinking skills are involved in building semantic nets than are creative or complex thinking skills. Net building is an analytic process of reflecting what one knows. Identifying and defining nodes involves identifying the main ideas and verifying them. The linking process engages the most critical thinking skills. Linking involves learners in evaluating the meaning of links (assessing and verifying meaning), analyzing the nature of the relationships, and then connecting the nodes where appropriate. This connecting process is the essence of semantic networking.

Using and building semantic nets engages fewer creative thinking skills (see Table 5.2). Consulting existing nets involves summarizing information and, perhaps, hypothesizing. Defining nodes requires summarizing, expanding, and concretizing the ideas represented by the nodes. This

**Table 5.1**
Critical thinking skills in using and constructing semantic nets

|  | Consulting Existing Semantic Nets | Defining Nodes | Linking/ Organizing Nodes |
|---|---|---|---|
| **Evaluating** | | | |
| Assessing information | X | | X |
| Determining criteria | | | X |
| Prioritizing | | | |
| Recognizing fallacies | | | X |
| Verifying | | X | X |
| **Analyzing** | | | |
| Recognizing patterns | | | X |
| Classifying | | | X |
| Identifying assumptions | | | X |
| Identifying main ideas | X | X | |
| Finding sequences | | | X |
| **Connecting** | | | |
| Comparing/contrasting | X | | X |
| Logical thinking | | | X |
| Inferring deductively | | | X |
| Inferring inductively | | | |
| Identifying causal relationships | | | X |

**Table 5.2**
Creative thinking skills in using
and constructing semantic nets

| | Consulting Existing Semantic Nets | Defining Nodes | Linking/ Organizing Nodes |
|---|---|---|---|
| **Elaborating** | | | |
| Expanding | | X | |
| Modifying | | | |
| Extending | | | X |
| Shifting categories | | X | X |
| Concretizing | | X | X |
| **Synthesizing** | | | |
| Analogical thinking | | | X |
| Summarizing | X | X | |
| Hypothesizing | X | | |
| Planning | | | X |
| **Imagining** | | | |
| Fluency | | X | X |
| Predicting | | | |
| Speculating | | | |
| Visualizing | | | X |
| Intuition | | | |

process requires the learner to elaborate on the concepts. This is accomplished by adding text or pictures to the node or determining what additional nodes are required to define the one being analyzed. Linking the nodes requires elaborating the nodes by connecting them to other nodes, finding analogical nodes, and planning the spatial relationships between nodes (visualizing).

Very little complex thinking is engaged by consulting nets (see Table 5.3). Identifying and defining nodes, however, engages more complex thinking skills than critical thinking skills, including skills associated with developing products, researching ideas, and identifying issues. Linking the nodes engages the most complex skills, primarily related to planning the net. Very limited problem solving or decision making is engaged by any aspect of net using or building.

Most of the cognitive activity in building semantic nets accrues from the linking process, in which students analyze the relationships between nodes and then evaluate the links they have created. This process involves a variety of evaluating, analyzing, and connecting skills. What makes this process difficult is the need to identify links that describe those relationships exactly and precisely. Most novices tend to use ambiguous terms, such as "is related to." These mean very little. That is why creative think-

**Table 5.3**
Complex thinking skills in using and constructing semantic nets

|  | Consulting Existing Semantic Nets | Defining Nodes | Linking/ Organizing Nodes |
|---|---|---|---|
| **Designing** |  |  |  |
| Imagining a goal |  | X | X |
| Formulating a goal |  |  |  |
| Inventing a product |  | X | X |
| Assessing a product | X |  |  |
| Revising the product |  | X | X |
| **Problem Solving** |  |  |  |
| Sensing the problem |  |  |  |
| Researching the problem |  | X | X |
| Formulating the problem |  |  |  |
| Finding alternatives |  |  | X |
| Choosing the solution |  |  |  |
| Building acceptance |  |  |  |
| **Decision Making** |  |  |  |
| Identifying an issue |  | X | X |
| Generating alternatives |  |  | X |
| Assessing the consequences |  |  |  |
| Making a choice |  |  |  |
| Evaluating the choices |  |  |  |

ing skills are involved in linking. Describing exactly how ideas are related to each other is difficult, and some suggestions for specific links are provided later in the chapter. Clearly, linking is the most critical, creative, and complex part of the net-building process.

## Related Mindtools

As just discussed, semantic nets are valuable planning and study tools that engage learners in critical thinking about the content they are studying. They are especially effective as study tools for preparing for examinations, especially long essay exams (experience has shown their particular value in comprehensive exams for graduate students). Many of the semantic networking tools have quizzing options built in.

Semantic networking is a powerful analyzing and organizing formalism that is often used for planning other constructions. A number of the expanded word-processing systems have semantic networking functionality built in to help writers plan their documents. Semantic networking is also used for eliciting knowledge from experts when building expert systems (see Chapter 6) (Cook & McDonald, 1987). Conceptually, semantic nets are very similar to databases. They both are used to analyze and define the structure of knowledge domains. However, semantic nets are most similar to hypertext and hypermedia knowledge bases (see Chapter 8), and they may be used as conceptual models for structuring hypertext and hypermedia systems (Jonassen, 1990, 1991). The nodes and links in the net become the nodes and links in the hypertext. In fact, Brock Allen at San Diego State University has developed a program called Wayfinder (distributed with the SemNet program) that automatically converts semantic nets into HyperCard stacks.

# Software Tools for Constructing Semantic Networks

A number of semantic networking programs are currently available for the Macintosh family of computers.

## SemNet

Probably the most powerful of the semantic networking programs is Sem-Net, which was developed by a research group at San Diego State University (Fisher, 1992; Fisher et al., 1990) and is available from the SemNet Research Group (1060 Johnson Avenue, San Diego, CA 92103). Using pull-down menus, SemNet enables the learner to create nodes and add text and pictures to them. Learners can also create links, the direction of which they determine using a clock face orientation. Two nodes connected by a link are called an instance. Nodes and links may be added by creating instances.

For each screen, the node that was selected by double-clicking on it is placed in the center of the screen, surrounded by all of its related concepts (Figure 5.2). The full web of interrelated concepts is available in a special menu, but SemNet developers argue that such a view is too confusing and that learners comprehend interrelationships better by having to navigate through the web. SemNet provides a number of powerful metrics for describing and evaluating the net, as well as guided tours and quizzes on concepts. All of this functionality makes SemNet more difficult to learn (though it is easily learnable by most students) but more powerful than most of the other tools.

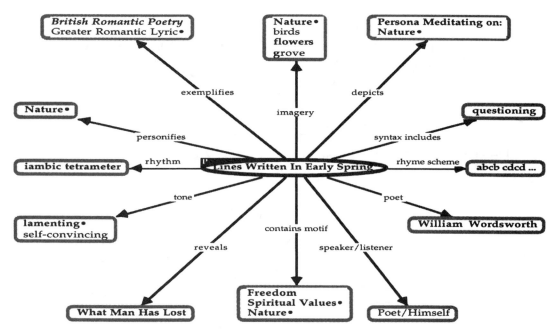

**Figure 5.2**
Screen from semantic net created with SemNet

## Learning Tool

One of the first semantic networking programs to be released, Learning Tool (Kozma, 1987, 1992) is available from the Intellimation software company. Like SemNet, it enables the learner to create and label nodes in the form of folders and to connect them with labeled links. Unlike Sem-Net, Learning Tool allows the display of a large number of interlinked concepts on the same screen (Figure 5.3). These nodes may have several intervening links displayed on the screen at once.

Learning Tool also permits the learner to create detailed submaps and text. For example, the concepts "self-efficacy theory" and "attribution the-ory" in Figure 5.3 have maps below the surface that describe those concepts in more detail. Double-clicking on the node brings up that submap. Finally, Learning Tool allows the learner to create the net in a graphic mode or in an outlining mode. It automatically creates the alternate representation and allows the learner to move freely between the two. The primary advantages of Learning Tool are its ease of learning and use, the amount of text that can be included, and the ease with which the net can be revised.

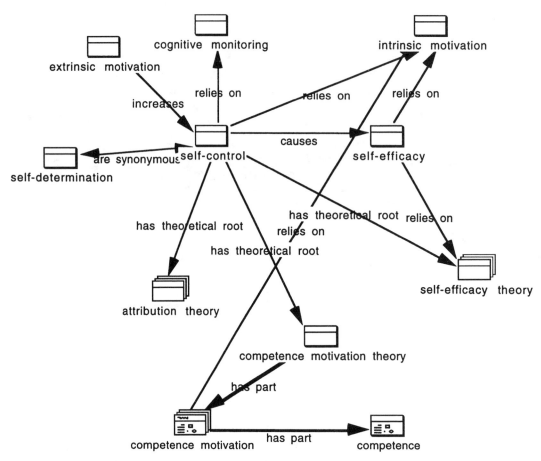

**Figure 5.3**
Beginning of a semantic net created with Learning Tool

## TextVision

TextVision is a mapping program developed by Piet Kommers and available from him at Twente University (Postbus 217, 7500 AE Enschede, Netherlands). Like the others, it lets learners create nodes and links. Its distinct advantage is its three-dimensional representation (Figure 5.4). Also, it permits the use of color as a cue to link direction. TextVision also makes calculations that identify the importance, or "centrality," of each node.

## CMap

CMap was developed by Hunter and Stahl in conjunction with John Novak at Cornell University and is available from ThinkTechnologies

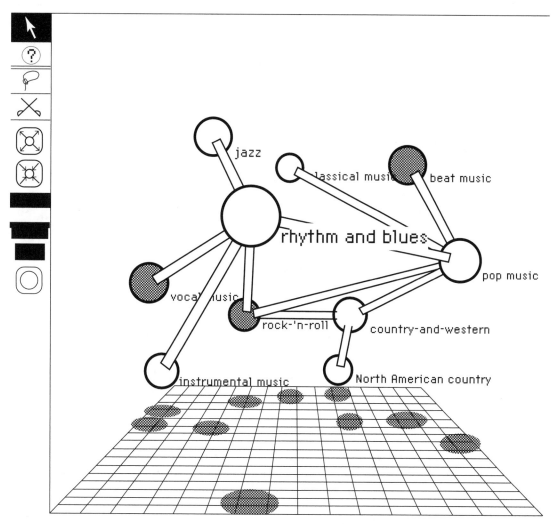

**Figure 5.4**
Semantic network created in TextVision

(Ithaca, NY). It is distributed as "freeware." CMap was developed to pro-vide a tool for creating concept maps as described by Novak and Gowin (1984), researchers who have been proponents of concept mapping for many years. It is a relatively simple tool that enables the learner to create concepts and links and to copy, move, and trace those links. Concept nodes may be moved anywhere on the screen (Figure 5.5). The links are elastic and follow the concepts. Its primary advantages are its ease of use and its cost, and it is an excellent mapping tool for beginners.

**Congress**

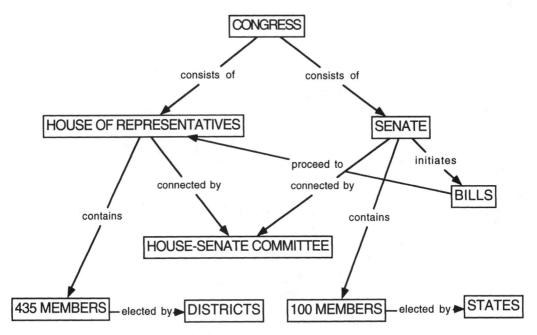

**Figure 5.5**
Simple map created with CMap

## Inspiration

Perhaps the most popular tool that can be used for semantic networking is Inspiration, a commercially available tool that supports different mapping techniques, including mind maps and organizational charts.

Thus far, the five programs being distributed to support the construction of semantic networks all run on Macintosh computers only. It is likely that similar software is being developed for the DOS family of computers running Windows.

# How to Construct and Use Semantic Networks in the Classroom

Semantic nets can be used in a variety of ways in the classroom. First, as a textbook study aid, students can identify the most important concepts in a

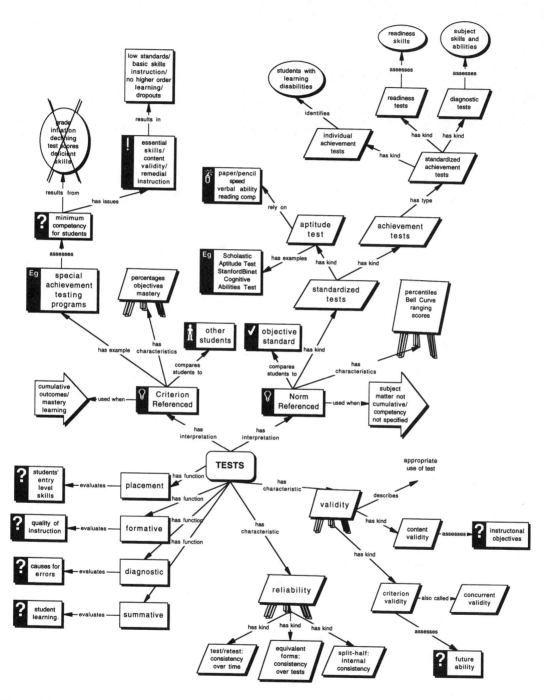

**Figure 5.6**
Mind map created with Inspiration

chapter and generate a semantic net as a review strategy. It serves the same purpose as outlining a chapter, but it engages learners more and requires deeper analysis of the content. Nets from different chapters can be merged or combined when studying for a large examination.

Another classroom application is as a planning tool. When groups of students are trying to get started on solving a large and complex problem, or when individual students have to write an essay, generating a semantic net can provide the organization and impetus for completing the project. Semantic nets are versatile tools that your students will learn to use quickly and want to apply in a variety of situations. The following sequence of activities will facilitate the integration of these tools in your classrooms.

1. *Set perspective for analyzing domain.* As reflections of knowledge structures, semantic networks are relative representations; that is, the ideas and relationships contained in a knowledge structure depend on the perspective from which they are being analyzed. For example, when studying concepts of Newtonian mechanics, such as speed, acceleration, mass, and force, unconstrained high school students are likely to immediately relate those concepts to their automobiles and feats they have performed in them. Although those may be acceptable and even relevant associations, it is also important to require them to "think like physicists" when analyzing the domain. If you were to analyze the same set of concepts but asked the learners to think like poets, a substantively different set of associations would be generated. Semantic networks (knowledge structures) are not static entities. They are dynamic and changeable, depending on the constructor's mood, frame of mind, recent events, and other factors. So help your learners establish the proper perspective or frame of mind for creating the net.

2. *Identify important concepts.* Understanding is made up of concepts. We communicate through our shared understanding of concepts, so identifying which are the important concepts in a content domain is crucial not only to understanding that content but also for collaborating on tasks. Important concepts are often highlighted for learners. They may appear in list form at the beginning or end of textbook chapters, or they may be highlighted in the text. You may analyze the textbook or supplementary materials and provide a list of concepts for the learners to define in the semantic net.

Students may also be responsible for highlighting important concepts in textbooks or supplementary readings. Rather than allowing them to highlight large sections of the textbook (producing pages of colorful text), you can suggest that they highlight only single words or short phrases that are essential to understanding the content and then use those for building semantic nets. You may want to focus a discussion on evaluating the relevance and importance of different concepts that might be included in the nets. Students could vote or argue for the inclusion of different concepts in the nets. This approach would result in all learners starting with the same list of concepts. However, it will become obvious through constructing semantic nets that the beginning list will likely be amended during the construction process as students discover the need for additional concepts to adequately describe and elaborate the concepts already in the net.

**3. Create, define, and elaborate nodes.** Create and label a node for each concept listed in step 2. Add pictures, descriptive text, and synonyms as appropriate. You may want to supply a net and require students to supply details about the concepts in it. Or the students may be responsible for developing the list as well as for defining the concepts in it. Each node may be embellished with graphics or a picture. Some of the semantic networking programs provide primitive graphics tools for drawing images. Most allow the learner to add descriptive text to each node, but the amount of text varies. These are areas where students could relate personal interpretations or beliefs about the concepts.

**4. Construct links and link concepts.** The most difficult part of semantic networking is the linking process. Describing precisely but completely the nature of the relationships among all the concepts is difficult. And, because concepts may be related to each other in several ways, it may be necessary to link the same two concepts with more than one relationship. Table 5.4 presents a fairly comprehensive list of link types that may be used to connect nodes.

What characterizes a good link? First, preciseness and succinctness. Try to avoid using links such as "is connected to," "is related to," or "involves." They do not tell anything meaningful about the relationship. Be sure not only to link new concepts that are added to the net, but also to interlink existing concepts as much as possible. Attempt to pair each concept with every other concept in the net and decide if there is a meaningful relationship between them. If there is, create a link between them. The more interconnected your net is, the more meaningful your understanding of the content domain will be.

**5. Evaluate the semantic net.** There are several criteria according to which learners and teachers may evaluate the semantic nets they have created. These occur in different categories.

**Table 5.4**
Possible links between nodes (adapted from Fisher 1988)

## Symmetric Links

| | |
|---|---|
| is opposite of | is same as |
| has sibling | is independent of |
| has synonym | is equal to |
| is near to | is opposed to |
| is similar to | |

## Asymmetric Links

*Inclusion Relations* (typically the most common)

| | |
|---|---|
| has part/is part of | contains/is contained in |
| composed of/is part in | includes/is included in |
| has example/is example of | has instance/is instance of |

*Characteristic Relations* (next most common)

| | |
|---|---|
| has characteristic/is characteristic of | has attribute/is attribute of |
| has property/is property of | has type/is type of |
| has kind/is kind of | defines/is defined by |
| describes/is described by | models/is modeled by |
| denotes/is denoted by | implies/is implied by |
| has advantage/is advantage of | has disadvantage/is disadvantage of |
| has function/is function of | has size/is size of |
| is above/is below | is higher than/is lower than |

*Action Relations*

| | |
|---|---|
| causes/is caused by | uses/is used by |
| solves/is solution for | exploits/is exploited by |
| decreases/is decreased by | increases/is increased by |
| destroys/is destroyed by | impedes/is impeded by |
| influences/is influenced by | determines/is determined by |
| enables/is enabled by | absorbs/is absorbed by |
| acts on/is acted on by | consumes/is consumed by |
| converted from/converted to | designs/is designed by |
| employs/is employed by | evolves into/is evolved from |
| generates/is generated by | modifies/is modified by |
| originates from/is origin of | provides/is provided by |
| requires/is required by | regulates/is regulated by |
| sends to/receives from | |

*Process Relations*

| | |
|---|---|
| has object/is object of | has output/is output of |
| has result/results from | has subprocess/is subprocess of |
| has process/is process in | organizes/is organized by |
| has input/is input to | proposes/is proposed by |
| depends on/has dependent | concludes/is concluded by |

*Temporal Relations*

| | |
|---|---|
| has step/is step in | has stage/is stage in |
| precedes/follows | |

**a.** *Evaluating the nodes (concepts):* To evaluate the adequacy of the nodes in a net, consider using some of these criteria:
- The number of nodes indicates the breadth of the net.
- The number of instances (two concepts linked by a relation) shows the extent of the net.
- The ratio of instances to concepts is an indicator of how well integrated the concepts in the domain are (also known as "embeddedness").
- The centrality of each node is indicated by its number of direct links (concepts linked directly to it) and indirect links (concepts linked to other concepts directly linked to it). Centrality is a measure of the importance of concepts in a domain. Look at the rank ordering of centrality for the most embedded (number of paths two nodes away). Often, the concepts that you believe are most important (typically those at the highest level of abstraction) are not very central to the net, at least according to this criterion.
- The depth (hierarchicalness) of the net is measured by the levels of nodes represented.

**b.** *Evaluating the links (relations):* To evaluate the adequacy of the links in a net, consider using some of these criteria:
- Links should be parsimonious. The law of parsimony pertains to the economy with which you express yourself. If six different links will describe all of the relationships in the net, then do not use more than six (i.e., don't use three different links that mean the same thing, e.g., "attribute of," "property of," and "characteristic of").
- On the other hand, don't use too few link types. Use enough links to discriminate meaningful differences. These two criteria require a balancing act of sorts.
- Use links consistently throughout the net. The meaning of any link should be the same each time it is used.
- Overreliance on one or two particular types of links shows a narrowness in thinking. Look at the proportions of link types that are used in the net. Calculate (roughly at least) the proportions of inclusion, characteristic, action, process, and temporal relations (see Table 5.4).
- Look at the number of "dead-end" nodes, that is, those that are only linked to one other concept. These are thought to be on the edge of the net. They prevent the browser of the net from traveling to any node other the one they came from.

- The ratio of the number of types of links to the number of nodes should be low. It is not appropriate to develop a different type of link for each concept (see earlier comments on parsimony).

The veracity of information included in the net is, of course, the most important criterion. Are learners making meaningful connections? Is the text in nodes correct? That is, is the information in the net correct?

## Models for Evaluating Semantic Nets

The richness, elaborateness, and complexity of a net are only measures of the meaningfulness of a net. Evaluating learners' nets requires standards against which to compare them. The following are models for evaluating nets.

1. *Compare learner's net with expert's (teacher's).* Much research focuses on the expert-novice distinction, comparing student knowledge representations with teacher or expert representations. Research has shown that during the process of learning, the learner's knowledge structure begins to resemble the knowledge structures of the instructor, and the degree of similarity is a good predictor of classroom examination performance (Diekhoff, 1983; Shavelson, 1974; Thro, 1978). Instruction, then, may be conceived of as the mapping of subject-matter knowledge (usually that possessed by the teacher or expert) onto the learner's knowledge structure. Semantic nets are a way of measuring that convergence. The closer a student's net resembles the teacher's, the more that student has (presumably) learned. This use of semantic nets represents a more traditional, objectivist notion of learning (i.e., the purpose of instruction is to get the learner to think like the teacher). The constructivist ideas on which this book is based would argue that this is not an appropriate use of semantic nets. However, learners do come to think like teachers, so semantic nets are a means for evaluating that change.

2. *Determine learner's knowledge growth.* The most significant problem with comparing a learner's knowledge with an expert's is that knowledge acquisition occurs in stages rather than in a single increment. Learners don't jump from novice to expert in a single bound. So, evaluating nets for their lack of convergence with an expert's may not be a fair comparison. Rather, evaluate a learner's net when he or she begins studying and at different points during the learning process. The net should be a visible sign of how much has been learned.

**3. *Accept learner's different perspectives.*** The multiple perspectives in knowledge representation often result from the variety of perspectives an individual can have on a particular content domain (like thinking about Newtonian concepts "like a scientist" versus "like a race car driver"). It is useful and informative to have learners create multiple nets on the same content. Each time they begin a net, ask them to assume a different perspective, or analyze a group of ideas in different classes so learners think about the same ideas from the perspective of social scientists, mathematicians, and writers.

**4. *Compare learner's nets to course goals.*** Semantic nets have been shown to be related to examination performance (Goldsmith, Johnson, & Acton, 1991). More research is needed to verify a consistent relationship between particular criteria for evaluating nets (listed above) and traditional measures of course performance, such as exams, research papers, and case studies.

# Fostering Collaboration with Semantic Networks

Semantic networking is likely to be novel to most learners. A number of teachers have had good results with paper-and-pencil concept mapping. For students who have practiced concept mapping, semantic networking with computer tools should be easy. For other students, the task is engaging because of the visualization involved, so they will catch on quickly. Semantic networking can be done individually with effective results. However, collaboration is likely to produce even better nets.

The best semantic nets are very large. In fact, the best use of semantic networking is to spend the entire academic year contributing to a map of the ideas studied throughout an entire course. Very large nets help learners to see the complexity of knowledge and how it is all interrelated. Nets with thousands of nodes will require collaboration. The entire class can work on a net, as can a group of six or more students. From a constructivist perspective, an important goal of semantic networking is for learners to recognize that there are multiple perspectives on any content. Creating visual maps of ideas helps students compare how they think with how others think.

**1. *Form the teams.*** Grouping should probably be either heterogeneous or by interest in the topic of the net. Interest groups are likely to be more motivated to build larger nets, while heterogeneous groups will provide the multiple perspectives that are desirable.

2. *Clarify the group goal.* The parameters of the content domain being represented in the net need to be negotiated. Although semantic memory is virtually endless because of the integrated nature of ideas in memory, computer-based semantic nets need to have some boundaries. The groups may wish to focus on particular perspectives on the content (e.g., political and economic perspectives on historical events).

3. *Negotiate tasks and subtasks to be completed.* Once the group agrees on the domain and frame of reference, students should carefully plan how concepts and links are to be generated. Certain students might provide all the concepts and others the links, or some students might concentrate on certain types of links. This process will require careful negotiation. To foster parsimonious link types, students should establish a process for including link types. Similarly, they should establish a process for monitoring achievement of the criteria described above.

4. *Monitor individual and group performance.* You may wish to have students tag their concepts or links in a net to ensure that all members are contributing. If brainstorming is used to generate ideas for the net, this kind of attribution is difficult, so students will have to monitor themselves more carefully. Leadership skills need to be developed and practiced carefully to avoid conflicts.

5. *Reconcile differences in interpretations or approaches to the goal.* During the group settings, learners may want to negotiate differences of opinion or interpretation in the content. Or they may choose to exploit the ability of semantic nets to demonstrate multiple points of view. The same concepts can have different links representing various perspectives.

## Advantages of Semantic Networks as Mindtools

- Semantic networking tools are easy to use. Most learners can gain proficiency within 1 to 2 hours.
- Semantic networking tools provide for spatial representations of content, which helps memory.
- Semantic networking tools enhance comprehension of ideas being studied by helping learners construct structural knowledge. In addition to improving comprehension, structural knowledge improves retention of content being studied.
- Semantic networks demonstrate the interconnectedness of ideas from different subjects and different courses.

- Semantic networking should improve problem-solving performance in learners.

# Limitations of Semantic Networks as Mindtools

- Semantic networks have a limited ability to represent causal relationships. One can define a causal link, but it doesn't provide the implications and inferences that accompany causal relations.
- Semantic networks can be too readily thought to reify the structures of the mind, implying that our semantic stores of information can be cognitively mapped and literally searched, just as a computer searches its memory stores. Semantic nets are not truly maps of the mind, but rather representations of what we think is in the mind.
- The knowledge that semantic nets represent is dynamic. It changes depending on the context and on the experiences and backgrounds of those producing the nets. Structural knowledge also changes over time. To truly and accurately represent knowledge, semantic networking tools would need to enable minute-by-minute, context-by-context changes in the concepts, relationships, and structures that are represented in them.
- The propositional networks in the mind, in whatever form they really exist, are far more complex than anything that can be represented in a concept map. The ideas that we know are interrelated and multiply encoded in rich, very redundant networks of ideas. These networks are multidimensional, yet $n$-dimensionality is a concept that is extremely difficult to grasp, and even harder to represent in two-dimensional space.

# *Conclusion*

Semantic networking programs provide a set of graphic conceptualization tools for creating concept maps. These concept maps represent the structure of ideas in memory or in a content domain. Semantic networking engages learners in an analysis of content domains that helps them organize their knowledge for better comprehension and retention. Semantic networking is also effective for planning other kinds of productions and knowledge bases. Semantic networks are among the most versatile of the Mindtools described in this book.

## References

Briscoe, C., & LeMaster, S. U. (1991). Meaningful learning in college biology through concept mapping. *American Biology Teacher, 53*(4), 214–219.

Cook, N. M., & McDonald, J. E. (1987). The application of psychological scaling techniques to knowledge elicitation for knowledge-based systems. *International Journal of Man-Machine Studies, 26,* 533–550.

Diekhoff, G. M. (1983). Relationship judgments in the evaluation of structural understanding. *Journal of Educational Psychology, 75,* 227–233.

Fisher, K. M. (1988, April). *Relations used in student-generated knowledge representations.* Paper presented at the annual meeting of the American Educational Research Association, San Francisco, CA.

Fisher, K. M. (1990). Semantic networking: New kid on the block. *Journal of Research in Science Teaching, 27*(10), 1001–1018.

Fisher, K. M. (1992). SemNet: A tool for personal knowledge construction. In P. Kommers, D. Jonassen, & T. Mayes (Eds.), *Cognitive tools for learning.* Berlin: Springer-Verlag.

Fisher, K. M., Faletti, J., Patterson, H., Thornton, R., Lipson, J., & Spring, C. (1990). Computer-assisted concept mapping. *Journal of College Science Teaching, 19*(6), 347–352.

Goldsmith, T. E., Johnson, P. J., & Acton, W. H. (1991). Assessing structural knowledge. *Journal of Educational Psychology, 83,* 88–96.

Jonassen, D. H. (1987). Assessing cognitive structure: Verifying a method using pattern notes. *Journal of Research and Development in Education, 20*(3), 1–14.

Jonassen, D. H. (1990). Semantic network elicitation: Tools for structuring of hypertext. In R. McAleese & C. Green (Eds.), *Hypertext: The state of the art.* London: Intellect.

Jonassen, D. H. (1991). Representing the expert's knowledge in hypertext. *Impact Assessment Bulletin, 9*(1), 93–105.

Jonassen, D. H., Beissner, K., & Yacci, M. A. (1993). *Structural knowledge: Techniques for representing, conveying, and acquiring structural knowledge.* Hillsdale, NJ: Lawrence Erlbaum Associates.

Kommers, P. A. M. (1989). *TextVision.* Enschede, Netherlands: University of Twente, Faculty of Education.

Kozma, R. B. (1987). The implications of cognitive psychology for computer-based learning tools. *Educational Technology, 24*(11), 20–24.

Kozma, R. B. (1992). Constructing knowledge with Learning Tool. In P. Kommers, D. Jonassen, & T. Mayes (Eds)., *Cognitive tools for learning.* Berlin: Springer-Verlag.

Mansfield, H., & Happs, J. (1991). Concept maps. *Australian Mathematics Teacher, 47*(3), 30–33.

Mikulecky, L. (1988). *Development of interactive computer programs to help students transfer basic skills to college-level science and behavioral sciences courses.* Bloomington, IN: Indiana University.

Novak, J. D., & Gowin, D. B. (1984). *Learning how to learn.* New York: Cambridge University Press.

Preece, P. F. W. (1976). Mapping cognitive structure: A comparison of methods. *Journal of Educational Psychology, 68,* 1–8.

Schreiber, D. A., & Abegg, G. L. (1991, April). *Scoring student-generated concept maps in introductory college chemistry.* Paper presented at the annual meeting of National Association for Research in Science Teaching, Lake Geneva, WI.

Shavelson, R. J. (1972). Some aspects of the correspondence between content structure and cognitive structure in physics instruction. *Journal of Educational Psychology, 63,* 225–234.

Shavelson, R. J. (1974). Methods for examining representations of subject matter structure in students' memory. *Journal of Research in Science Teaching, 11,* 231–249.

Thro, M. P. (1978). Relationships between associative and content structure of physics concepts. *Journal of Educational Psychology, 70,* 971–978.

# Expert Systems:
## *Decisions, Decisions, Decisions*

## What Are Expert Systems?

Expert systems are computer-based tools designed to function as intelligent aids (i.e., experts) to facilitate decision making in all sorts of tasks. Early expert systems, such as MYCIN, were developed to help physicians diagnose bacterial infections with which they were unfamiliar. Prominent expert systems have also been developed to help geologists decide where to drill for oil, firefighters decide how to extinguish different kinds of fires, computer sales technicians configure computer systems, and employees decide among a large number of company benefits alternatives. Problems whose solutions include recommendations based on a variety of decisions are good candidates for expert systems. It is fairly easy to understand the concept of expert systems at the verbal information level of knowledge, that is, to be able to recite definitions, but it is more difficult to develop procedural knowledge of expert systems. Only through building expert system knowledge bases will you come to understand their power.

Expert systems have evolved from research in the field of artificial intelligence. *Artificial intelligence* (AI) is a specialty in computer and cognitive science that focuses on the development of both hardware innovations and programming techniques that enable machines to perform tasks that are regarded as intelligent when done by people. *Artificial* means simulated, and *intelligence* is the capacity to learn, reason, and understand, so AI researchers and expert system builders attempt to develop programs that simulate the human capability to reason and to learn. *Simulated* means only imitating a real object or event. For example, flight simulators

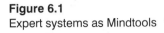

**Figure 6.1**
Expert systems as Mindtools

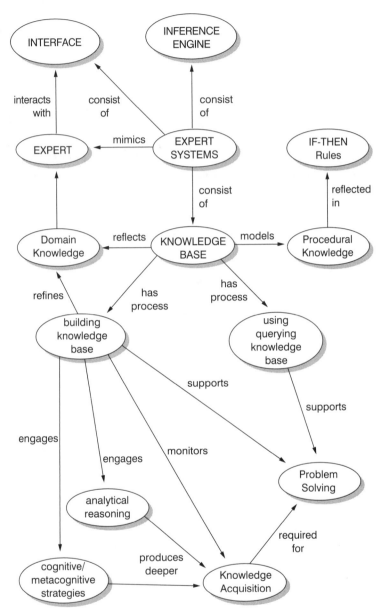

look real and feel real to flight trainers; however, a flight simulator is an *artificial* airplane that never actually flies and could not replace an airplane's primary function—to fly.

AI programs, including expert systems, may perform functions that resemble human thinking, such as decision making. In reality, though, AI programs are just *programs* that imitate what we believe to be human mental activity in a certain situation. Human intelligence is generalizable and transferable to new situations, but most forms of computer intelligence are not, and that includes expert systems. For example, a computer that is programmed to play chess cannot transfer that capability to playing Monopoly.

An expert system, then, is a computer program that attempts to simulate the way human experts solve problems—an artificial decision maker. For example, when you consult an expert (e.g., doctor, lawyer, teacher) about a problem, the expert asks for current information about your condition, searches his or her knowledge base (memory) for existing knowledge to relate elements of the current situation to, processes the information (thinks), arrives at a decision, and presents a solution. Like a human expert, an expert system (computer program) is approached by an individual (novice) with a problem. The system queries the individual about the current status of the problem, searches its knowledge base (which contains previously stored expert knowledge) for pertinent facts and rules, processes the information, arrives at a decision, and reports the solution to the user.

## Components of Expert Systems

Figure 6.2 diagrams the integration of the components of an expert system. I will describe each component briefly.

### User

Like a human expert, an expert system cannot put its knowledge and skills to use unless a need arises. The computer must await input from a user with a need or problem. For example, imagine that a novice loan officer in a bank must decide whether an individual should be granted a personal, unsecured loan. There are many factors to consider when making the decision (e.g., applicant's income and past credit record, amount of loan, reason for the loan, size of monthly payment, etc.)—so many factors that it may take months or years of training to prepare the loan officer to consider everything involved. An alternative is to build an expert system that asks the loan officer to input all data necessary for making an informed decision. The expert system, which is composed of facts and rules that an experienced or expert loan officer uses in making a decision, relates the information provided by the loan applicant to the rules and presents a decision that provides valuable advice to the loan officer. In

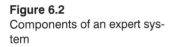

**Figure 6.2**
Components of an expert system

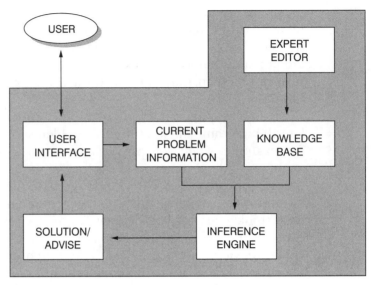

this way, the expert system increases productivity because it saves both analysis time and training time.

## Current Problem Information

Because an expert system is based on programming techniques derived from AI, it is designed to deal with changing conditions in the problem situation it was designed to help. In order to handle these changing conditions, data about the current situation are collected from the user and entered into computer memory to help guide the expert system to a solution. For example, an expert system designed to help an undergraduate select courses for the current semester might ask the student the following questions:

```
What is your major?
What courses have you completed?
Do you have a job that prevents you from taking
classes at certain times?
When do you expect to graduate?
Do you plan to take summer school courses?
```

The questions asked by the expert system through the user interface (described on page 123) gather information that may change with each individual situation. The answers to these questions are integrated within an existing knowledge base of information (facts and rules) that remains relatively stable (although it may be changed by the expert through the expert editor, described on page 124).

## User Interface

The user interface is built by the expert system designer (also known as a knowledge engineer) to facilitate the program's communication with the user. This communication process gathers current problem data from the user, explains the expert's reasoning, and presents the solution or advice for the problem being solved. The user interface gathers information from the user through questions and answers that define the conditions that will be evaluated by the rules in the knowledge base (see below). The interface also provides explanations about the questions being asked and the decisions being made. Typically, the interface allows users to ask why they were asked for information or why the program made a particular decision, and the expert system will retrieve that information from the knowledge base and display it for the user.

Finally, the inference engine (see page 124) evaluates all of the available information and presents its solution to the user through the interface. As in other computer programs, the interface is a critical feature. The program must carry on a dialogue with the user, so the nature of the dialogue, as well as the format of the presentation, must be developed and tested carefully to ensure easy input of the information sought.

## Knowledge Base

Information placed in the knowledge base (analogous to long-term memory) is relatively stable. It is composed of facts about objects and rules about the relationships among those objects that represent knowledge structures used by a human expert to reach a decision. Facts simply state given conditions (e.g., Calculus I is offered at 8 a.m., 10 a.m., and 2 p.m. on Monday, Wednesday, and Friday), and rules consist of conditions and decisions. That is, rules state that IF a set of conditions exists, THEN some decision is reached. Conditions may be combined in a number of ways into sets. Sets of IF conditions may be combined using conjunctions (condition 1 AND condition 2 must exist), disjunctions (condition 1 OR condition 2 must exist), and negations (condition 1 but NOT condition 2 must exist) in order for a decision to be reached. A decision may be an action or it may state another condition, which is then combined with other conditions to reach another decision. In the previous situation, the knowledge base would have stored lists of required courses for every major, as exemplified by the following rules:

```
IF student's major is mechanical engineering, THEN
Differential Equations is required.
IF student's major is mechanical engineering OR stu-
dent's major is electrical engineering, THEN Calculus
2 is required.
IF Differential Equations is NOT taken AND Calculus 2
is complete AND Differential Equations is offered at a
time student is available, THEN advise student to sign
up for Differential Equations.
```

Variables may be used to carry current problem information or to carry a preliminary decision value on through the process. The knowledge base also may contain explanations for why questions are being asked and why certain rules are activated, that is, why certain decisions are reached.

## Expert Editor

Most expert system programs provide an editor that enables the expert or the knowledge engineer to enter information into the knowledge base. Editors consist of text editors and parsers. The text editor allows the engineer to input facts and rules into the knowledge base in a prespecified format. The parser will check the syntax of the information that is input, as well as the validity or logic of the information that is entered. For example, the parser will usually decide if the rules are consistent and mutually exclusive or whether any redundancy exists.

## Inference Engine

The inference engine is the part of an expert system that incorporates AI techniques. This component is not usually accessible to an expert system designer; instead, it is built into the system that the designer uses. It is constructed of AI programming techniques that act on the knowledge base and current problem data to generate solutions. In an expert system, the inference engine does its work when the user poses a specific problem and enters current problem information. The inference engine contains the logical programming to examine the information provided by the user, as well as the facts and rules specified within the knowledge base. It evaluates the current problem situation and then seeks out rules that will provide advice about that situation.

Inference engines are usually of two types: *backward-chaining* and *forward-chaining*. The backward-chaining engine (goal-driven model) starts with a solution or decision and then searches the knowledge base for rules containing the conditions necessary to fulfill that solution. If sufficient conditions are not found, it asks the user to supply information or searches the knowledge base for subgoals that contribute to the solution. The forward-chaining engine (data-driven model) starts by trying to match existing data with a condition or conditions stated in the rules and examines the knowledge base to see if a solution is viable with only that information. It successively acquires information in an effort to be able to make a decision.

### Solution/Advice

The final feature of an expert system is its presentation of a solution generated by the inference engine based on the permanent knowledge base and current problem information. The student advisor example considers all of the data entered by the student, relates those data to the rules in the knowledge base, and presents a solution, such as the following:

```
Recommend Calculus I, Section 2, 10–11, MWF
```

# Examples of Content Expert Systems

The following examples represent very divergent goals in very divergent curricula. The first knowledge base (Figure 6.3), which was developed by a student using a simple shell called PC Expert (Starfield, Smith, & Bleloch, 1990), attempts to reflect the reasoning that Truman may have used in deciding whether or not to drop an atomic bomb on Hiroshima. Although the content is gruesome and many factors were not considered, it describes a deeper reflection on historical events than the typical memorization of names, dates, and places. In this kind of rule base, the decisions are stated first. This requires that the designers identify the goals before clarifying any of the decision factors.

Next the designer identifies the decision factors in the form of questions that will be asked of the user. This is the essence of the design process. Writing questions that are simple enough for any novice user to be able to answer is difficult. With this expert system shell, the designer next writes the rules, using IF-THEN (Boolean) logic to relate the decisions to the decision factors or questions. This rule base consists of 20 rules that comprise the heart of the knowledge base. For example, the

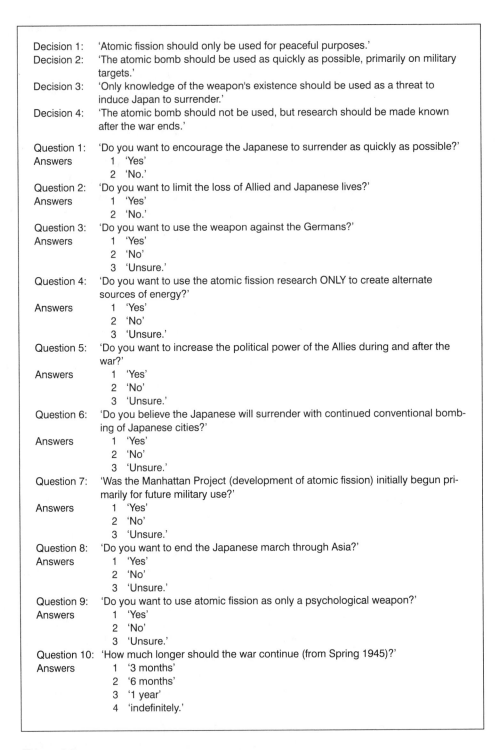

| | | |
|---|---|---|
| Decision 1: | 'Atomic fission should only be used for peaceful purposes.' | |
| Decision 2: | 'The atomic bomb should be used as quickly as possible, primarily on military targets.' | |
| Decision 3: | 'Only knowledge of the weapon's existence should be used as a threat to induce Japan to surrender.' | |
| Decision 4: | 'The atomic bomb should not be used, but research should be made known after the war ends.' | |
| | | |
| Question 1: | 'Do you want to encourage the Japanese to surrender as quickly as possible?' | |
| Answers | 1 'Yes' | |
| | 2 'No.' | |
| Question 2: | 'Do you want to limit the loss of Allied and Japanese lives?' | |
| Answers | 1 'Yes' | |
| | 2 'No.' | |
| Question 3: | 'Do you want to use the weapon against the Germans?' | |
| Answers | 1 'Yes' | |
| | 2 'No' | |
| | 3 'Unsure.' | |
| Question 4: | 'Do you want to use the atomic fission research ONLY to create alternate sources of energy?' | |
| Answers | 1 'Yes' | |
| | 2 'No' | |
| | 3 'Unsure.' | |
| Question 5: | 'Do you want to increase the political power of the Allies during and after the war?' | |
| Answers | 1 'Yes' | |
| | 2 'No' | |
| | 3 'Unsure.' | |
| Question 6: | 'Do you believe the Japanese will surrender with continued conventional bombing of Japanese cities?' | |
| Answers | 1 'Yes' | |
| | 2 'No' | |
| | 3 'Unsure.' | |
| Question 7: | 'Was the Manhattan Project (development of atomic fission) initially begun primarily for future military use?' | |
| Answers | 1 'Yes' | |
| | 2 'No' | |
| | 3 'Unsure.' | |
| Question 8: | 'Do you want to end the Japanese march through Asia?' | |
| Answers | 1 'Yes' | |
| | 2 'No' | |
| | 3 'Unsure.' | |
| Question 9: | 'Do you want to use atomic fission as only a psychological weapon?' | |
| Answers | 1 'Yes' | |
| | 2 'No' | |
| | 3 'Unsure.' | |
| Question 10: | 'How much longer should the war continue (from Spring 1945)?' | |
| Answers | 1 '3 months' | |
| | 2 '6 months' | |
| | 3 '1 year' | |
| | 4 'indefinitely.' | |

**Figure 6.3**
Knowledge base example

Rule 1:
IF Question1=Answer1 & Question2=Answer1 & Question5=Answer1 THEN Decision2.
Rule 2:
IF Question3=Answer2 THEN Decision4.
Rule 3:
IF Question4=Answer1 THEN Decision3.
Rule 4:
IF Question4=Answer2 THEN Decision2.
Rule 5:
IF Question5=Answer1 & Question6=Answer2 THEN Decision2.
Rule 6:
IF Question6=Answer1 THEN Decision4.
Rule 7:
IF Question6=Answer2 & Question1=Answer1 & Question8=Answer1 THEN Decision2.
Rule 8:
IF Question6=Answer3 THEN Decision3.
Rule 9:
IF Question7=Answer1 & Question1=Answer1 THEN Decision2.
Rule 10:
IF Question7=Answer2 THEN Decision1.
Rule 11:
IF Question7=Answer3 THEN Decision4.
Rule 12:
IF Question8=Answer1 & Question6=Answer2 & Question1=Answer1 THEN Decision2.
Rule 13:
IF Question8=Answer2 THEN Decision3.
Rule 14:
IF Question9=Answer1 THEN Decision3.
Rule 15:
IF Question9=Answer2 & Question8=Answer1 & Question7=Answer1 &
Question1=Answer1 THEN Decision2.
Rule 16:
IF Question4=Answer1 & Question5=Answer1 & Question7=Answer3 THEN Decision4.
Rule 17:
IF Question10=Answer1 & Question2=Answer1 & Question6=Answer3 THEN Decision2.
Rule 18:
IF Question10=Answer2 & Question3=Answer1 & Question5=Answer1 THEN Decision2.
Rule 19:
IF Question10=Answer3 & Question6=Answer1 & Question8=Answer3 THEN Decision4.
Rule 20:
IF Question10=Answer4 & Question4=Answer1 & Question6=Answer3 THEN Decision4.

first rule states that IF the answer to question 1 is yes AND the answer to question 2 is also yes AND the answer to question 5 is also yes, THEN the atomic bomb should be used as quickly as possible, primarily on military targets. The remainder of the rules specify alternative conditions that may have existed at that time.

The next set of rules is part of a knowledge base developed by students in a home economics class for advising classmates or the public on how to order from a fast-food menu (Figure 6.4). It was developed using a shell called McSmarts, which uses a different syntax from the previous rule base. In each rule, the advice is presented first, followed by the conditions that will lead to that advice.

The final set of rules is excerpted from a knowledge base on classifying geometric figures (Figure 6.5). Students who determine these rules for themselves will be better able to apply them than students who are required to memorize and later apply the rules. This rule base includes links to graphics files, so when a decision is made the shell program automatically loads a picture of the figure.

These rule bases are simple examples of how students can think about the content they are studying in different ways. When students become expert system designers, they have to become the authorities (a role reversal that they enjoy), and this engages deeper thinking about the subject.

# Expert Systems as Mindtools

Expert systems have many applications in education. Their primary uses in business have been to control manufacturing processes and assist managers in decision making. A good deal of research has focused on developing expert system advisors to help teachers identify and classify students with learning disabilities. Expert system advisors have also been developed to guide novices through the instructional development process (Tennyson & Christensen, 1991) and to assist students in selecting the correct statistical test (Karake, 1990; Saleem & Azad, 1992). No research comparing the learning effects of using an advisor compared with building a rule base has been reported.

Expert systems can serve as computer-based cognitive amplification tools (see Figure 6.1). Trollip, Lippert, Starfield, and Smith (1992) believe that the development of expert systems results in deeper understanding because they provide an intellectual environment that demands the refinement of domain knowledge, supports problem solving, and monitors the acquisition of knowledge.

2 Eat: Chunky chicken salad, diet soft drink, and low-fat yogurt cone

IF YES: Question 1 Do you want a balanced, nutritious meal? (Meal will represent all of the basic four food groups)

IF YES: Question 2  Do you desire a low-fat meal? (<30% calories come from fat)

IF YES: Question 3 Do you desire a low-cholesterol meal? (>84 mg)

IF YES: Question 4 Do you desire a low-carbohydrate (sugar and starch) meal? (<30% calories come from carbohydrates)

IF NO: Question 5 Do you desire a low-salt meal? (<650 mg)

6 Eat: Chunky chicken salad and 2% milk

IF YES: Question 1 Do you want a balanced, nutritious meal? (Meal will represent all of the basic four food groups.)

IF YES: Question 2 Do you desire a low-fat meal? (<30% calories come from fat)

IF NO: Question 3 Do you desire a low-cholesterol meal? (>84 mg)

IF YES: Question 4 Do you desire a low-carbohydrate (sugar and starch) meal? (<30% calories come from carbohydrates)

IF NO: Question 5 Do you desire a low-salt meal? (<650 mg)

9 Eat: Garden salad and a diet drink

IF YES: Question 1 Do you want a balanced, nutritious meal? (Meal will represent all of the basic four food groups.)

IF NO: Question 2 Do you desire a low-fat meal? (<30% calories come from fat)

IF YES: Question 3 Do you desire a low-cholesterol meal? (>84 mg)

IF YES: Question 4 Do you desire a low-carbohydrate (sugar and starch) meal? (<30% calories come from carbohydrates)

IF YES: Question 5 Do you desire a low-salt meal? (<650 mg)

12 Eat: Hamburger, sm. fries, and dairy drink OR 6ct. McNuggets, sm. fries, and van. shake OR Filet-o-fish, sm. fries, and van. shake

IF YES: Question 1 Do you want a balanced, nutritious meal? (Meal will represent all of the basic four food groups.)

IF NO: Question 2 Do you desire a low-fat meal? (<30% calories come from fat)

IF YES: Question 3 Do you desire a low-cholesterol meal? (>84 mg)

IF NO: Question 4 Do you desire a low-carbohydrate (sugar and starch) meal? (<30% calories come from carbohydrates)

IF NO: Question 5 Do you desire a low-salt meal? (<650 mg)

14 Eat: McDLT and diet soft drink OR 6ct. McNuggets, side salad, and 2% milk OR Chunky chicken salad and 2% milk

IF YES: Question 1 Do you want a balanced, nutritious meal? (Meal will represent all of the basic four food groups.)

IF NO: Question 2 Do you desire a low-fat meal? (<30% calories come from fat)

IF NO: Question 3 Do you desire a low-cholesterol meal? (>84 mg)

IF YES: Question 4 Do you desire a low-carbohydrate (sugar and starch) meal? (<30% calories come from carbohydrates)

IF NO: Question 5 Do you desire a low-salt meal? (<650 mg)

17 Eat: Any food menu item of your choice

IF NO: Question 1 Do you want a balanced, nutritious meal? (Meal will represent all of the basic four food groups.)

**Figure 6.4**
Part of a knowledge base of fast-food recommendations

9  The figure is a simple quadrilateral.          PRIMARY LINK: quadrilateral
IF YES: Does the polygon have more than 3 sides?
IF NO: Does the polygon have more than 4 sides?
IF NO: Does the polygon have 2 pairs of parallel opposite sides?
IF NO: Does the polygon have 1 pair of parallel opposite sides?
IF NO: Does the polygon have 2 different pairs of congruent adjacent sides?

10  The figure is an isosceles trapezoid.          PRIMARY LINK: isosceles trapezoid
IF YES: Does the polygon have more than 3 sides?
IF NO: Does the polygon have more than 4 sides?
IF NO: Does the polygon have 2 pairs of parallel opposite sides?
IF YES: Does the polygon have 1 pair of parallel opposite sides?
IF YES: Does the polygon have congruent nonparallel sides?

11  The figure is a simple trapezoid.          PRIMARY LINK: trapezoid
IF YES: Does the polygon have more than 3 sides?
IF NO: Does the polygon have more than 4 sides?
IF NO: Does the polygon have 2 pairs of parallel opposite sides?
IF YES: Does the polygon have 1 pair of parallel opposite sides?
IF NO: Does the polygon have congruent nonparallel sides?

12  The figure is a square.          PRIMARY LINK: square
IF YES: Does the polygon have more than 3 sides?
IF NO: Does the polygon have more than 4 sides?
IF YES: Does the polygon have 2 pairs of parallel opposite sides?
IF YES: Does the polygon have a right (90-degree) angle?
IF YES: Does the polygon have a pair of congruent adjacent sides?

14  The figure is a rhombus.          PRIMARY LINK: rhombus
IF YES: Does the polygon have more than 3 sides?
IF NO: Does the polygon have more than 4 sides?
IF YES: Does the polygon have 2 pairs of parallel opposite sides?
IF NO: Does the polygon have a right (90-degree) angle?
IF YES: Does the polygon have a pair of congruent adjacent sides?

16  The figure is a regular pentagon.          PRIMARY LINK: regular pentagon
IF YES: Does the polygon have more than 3 sides?
IF YES: Does the polygon have more than 4 sides?
IF NO: Does the polygon have more than 5 sides?
IF YES: Does the polygon have all sides congruent?

**Figure 6.5**
Part of a knowledge base for classifying geometric figures

Building expert systems requires the developer to explicitly model the knowledge of the expert. This requires identifying declarative knowledge (facts and concepts), structural knowledge (knowledge of interrelationships among ideas), and procedural knowledge (how to apply declarative knowledge) that an expert (or at least a knowledgeable person) possesses. The expert system is one of the few formalisms for depicting procedural knowledge. Psychologists usually represent procedural knowledge as a series of IF-THEN rules (Gagné, 1985). Such a representation mode is obviously well suited to expert systems. As learners identify the IF-THEN structure of a domain, they tend to understand the nature of decision-making tasks better, so this deeper understanding should make subsequent practice opportunities more meaningful. This is not to suggest that the mere development of an expert system necessarily leads learners to acquire the compiled procedural knowledge of a domain. For example, a student project may correctly identify many of the IF-THEN rules involved in flying an airplane, but actually acquiring the procedural expertise would require extended practice opportunities in realistic performance settings.

Trollip et al. (1992) believe that learning environments, whether computer based or not, should provide a mechanism for helping learners monitor their own knowledge growth. This involves metacognitive awareness of their knowledge, which is a necessary component of problem solving (Flavell & Wellman, 1977). Clearly, building expert systems requires learners to synthesize knowledge by making explicit their own reasoning, thereby improving retention, transfer, and problem-solving ability. While all of this sounds complex and beyond the grasp of most school-age students, experience has indicated otherwise. Using a simple shell, most students are able to begin building simple rule bases within an hour.

The use of expert systems as Mindtools is relatively new. Lippert (1987) found that the analysis of subject matter that is required to develop expert systems is so deep and so incisive that learners develop a greater comprehension of the subject matter. Building expert system rule bases engages learners in analytical reasoning, elaboration strategies such as synthesis, and metacognitive strategies. Among the early advocates of expert systems as Mindtools, Lippert (1988) argued that having students construct small knowledge bases is a valuable method for teaching problem solving and knowledge structuring for students from sixth grade to adults. Learning is more meaningful because learners evaluate not only their own thinking processes but also the product of those processes, the resulting knowledge base. Developing the knowledge base requires learners to isolate facts, variables, and rules about the relationships in a domain. Additional research has verified these effects:

- Lai (1989) found that when nursing students developed medical expert systems, they developed enhanced reasoning skills and acquired a deeper understanding of the subject domain.

- Six first-year physics students who used an expert system to create questions, decisions, rules, and explanations pertaining to classical projectile motion developed more refined, domain-specific knowledge due to greater degrees of elaboration during encoding and greater quantity of material processed in an explicit, coherent context, and therefore in greater semantic depth (Lippert & Finley, 1988).

- Students who used an expert system to select the most appropriate statistical analysis procedure were more accurate in their selections and also retained the information better than students who used traditional computer-assisted instruction (Marcoulides, 1988).

- Lippert (1988) described physics students' development of rule bases to solve problems about forces. Students identified factors such as kind of force acting on an object (gravitational, centripetal, etc.), motion of the object (free fall, circular, sliding, etc.), velocity of the object, and so on. The decisions that students reached include the laws that affect the motion, the formulas that should be applied, and so on. Students reported meaningful learning from evaluating their own thought processes, more enthusiasm for learning, and the learning of content that they were not expected to master.

- Knox-Quinn (1992) reported that MBA students who developed knowledge bases on tax laws in an accounting course were consistently engaged in higher-order thinking, such as classifying information, breaking down content, organizing information, and integrating and elaborating information. All of the students who developed rule bases showed substantial gains in the quantity and quality of declarative and procedural knowledge and improved their problem-solving strategies. Students who built expert systems reasoned more similarly to experts.

When analyzing outcomes from building and using expert systems, a distinction needs to be drawn between using an existing expert system rule base to support decision making and creating a knowledge base (as advocated in this chapter). Consulting a knowledge base does not engage users as deeply as building a knowledge base that reflects their own thinking. Querying a knowledge base to help solve a problem primarily involves comprehension of the problem and its factors and application of some predetermined rules for solving it. Building an expert system knowledge base necessarily involves deeper thinking. Expert system builders must analyze a knowledge domain and synthesize rules and rule sequences to make that knowledge domain useful. Analysis skills include identifying outcomes, factors, and values for those factors. Restructuring that information into IF-THEN rules requires builders to synthesize that knowledge into a new form. Anyone who has attempted to build even a simple rule base realizes how engaging this process is.

## Evaluation of Expert Systems as Mindtools

1. *Computer-based.* Although expert system logic can be simulated using decision tables, the complexity and flexibility of reasoning requires a computer-based system. Many computer-based expert system shells and languages are available, with a wide variety of functionality.

2. *Readily available, general applications.* Although they have mostly been used in the applied sciences, expert systems can be applied to any problem or domain with causal elements.

3. *Affordable.* Expert system shells vary tremendously in cost. However, all of the functionality that you need for using expert systems as Mindtools can be found in an inexpensive shell. The shell that I prefer to use (PC Expert) is in the public domain. Many others that are somewhat more powerful can be purchased for less than $100.

4. *Represent knowledge.* As indicated before, expert systems are most applicable for representing causal knowledge. They also represent factual knowledge. Their purpose, however, is to represent the knowledge of an expert.

5. *Applicable in different subject domains.* Every domain has causal reasoning involved, especially where the content is used to solve problems.

6. *Engage critical thinking.* These skills are described in the next section.

7. *Facilitate transfer of learning.* Problem solving is the essence of transfer. Any formalism (like expert systems) that facilitates problem solving should also facilitate transfer of learning.

8. *Simple, powerful formalism.* Although many people are afraid of expert systems because of their association with AI, the underlying ideas (causal reasoning) are not that complex. Research on solving everyday problems has shown that even very young learners are able to use complex chains of causal reasoning.

**9.** *(Reasonably) easy to learn.* PC Expert (available for DOS machines from Anthony Starfield at the University of Minnesota) normally requires less than an hour to learn. The more complex the shell, the longer it would require to learn.

## Critical, Creative, and Complex Thinking in Expert System Construction and Use

Tables 6.1, 6.2, and 6.3 identify the critical, creative, and complex thinking skills that are required to consult an expert system rule base and to design and construct a rule base. The skills in each table that are marked by an "×" are those that are employed by each process, based on an information-processing analysis of the tasks.

As with databases, there are probably more critical thinking skills required to use and build knowledge bases than there are creative thinking skills (see Table 6.1). However, building knowledge bases requires more complex thinking skills than nearly any other Mindtool. Clearly there are more thinking skills required to build a rule base than simply to consult one. This is because knowledge base construction is an analytic

**Table 6.1**
Critical thinking skills in expert system construction and use

| | Querying Knowledge Base | Designing Knowledge Base |
|---|---|---|
| **Evaluating** | | |
| Assessing information | X | X |
| Determining criteria | | X |
| Prioritizing | | |
| Recognizing fallacies | | X |
| Verifying | | X |
| **Analyzing** | | |
| Recognizing patterns | | X |
| Classifying | X | X |
| Identifying assumptions | | X |
| Identifying main ideas | | |
| Finding sequences | | X |
| **Connecting** | | |
| Comparing/contrasting | X | |
| Logical thinking | X | X |
| Inferring deductively | | X |
| Inferring inductively | | X |
| Identifying causal relationships | | X |

**Table 6.2**
Creative thinking skills in expert
system construction and use

| | Querying Knowledge Base | Designing Knowledge Base |
|---|---|---|
| **Elaborating** | | |
| Expanding | | |
| Modifying | | |
| Extending | | |
| Shifting categories | X | |
| Concretizing | X | X |
| **Synthesizing** | | |
| Analogical thinking | | |
| Summarizing | X | |
| Hypothesizing | | X |
| Planning | | X |
| **Imagining** | | |
| Fluency | | |
| Predicting | | X |
| Speculating | | X |
| Visualizing | | |
| Intuition | | |

process that makes heavy use of logical thinking, a major component of critical thinking. Building the rule base on the atom bomb (see Figure 6.3), for example, required assessing the information available, determining criteria for using it, verifying the information, and, most especially, making inferences. Building rule bases probably requires learners to make more inferences than any other Mindtool. The rule base on polygons (see Figure 6.5), for example, required a lot of classifying skills.

Under creative thinking skills, building rule bases engages a lot of hypothesizing, planning, predicting, and speculating about causal relations (see Table 6.2). In the rule base on fast food (see Figure 6.4), students had to hypothesize about combinations of foods and their nutritional provisions before confirming that information.

Finally, a number of complex thinking skills are required for querying and (especially) designing knowledge bases. Designing and building knowledge bases requires the use of almost every kind of designing, problem-solving, and decision-making skill (see Table 6.3). Keeping the potential user in mind (imagining and formulating the goal) and then balancing the goals of the rule base against the factors and the rules requires researching and formulating the problem, finding alternatives, and

**Table 6.3**
Complex thinking skills in expert system construction and use

| | Querying Knowledge Base | Designing Knowledge Base |
|---|---|---|
| **Designing** | | |
| Imagining a goal | X | X |
| Formulating a goal | X | X |
| Inventing a product | | X |
| Assessing a product | X | X |
| Revising the product | | X |
| **Problem Solving** | | |
| Sensing the problem | X | X |
| Researching the problem | | X |
| Formulating the problem | | X |
| Finding alternatives | X | X |
| Choosing the solution | | X |
| Building acceptance | | |
| **Decision Making** | | |
| Identifying an issue | X | X |
| Generating alternatives | | X |
| Assessing the consequences | | X |
| Making a choice | X | X |
| Evaluating the choices | X | X |

choosing a solution. Decision making is at the heart of expert systems, so identifying issues and alternatives, assessing them, and making choices are essential to constructing rule bases. Building a knowledge base is a complex process consisting of cycles of hypothesizing and testing.

## Related Mindtools

As indicated in Chapter 5, building semantic networks is sometimes used as a process for identifying the ideas that will go into an expert system knowledge base. This is a process known in the AI literature as knowledge elicitation. Identifying the issues and their relationships is important to expert system construction.

Another related Mindtool is the database management system. As will be described in the next section, some expert system shells are able to induce rules from a database, so an easy approach to building knowledge bases is to create a database of instances and let the program generate the rules. This approach limits the kind of logic that can be used, but it is valuable for demonstrating the interrelated nature of Mindtools.

# Software Tools

Expert system rule bases are often built using a procedural language, such as BASIC, Pascal, or C; an AI-oriented language, such as Lisp or Prolog; or an expert system shell program. Building expert system knowledge bases in a language requires that the expert system builder understand the language and its syntax, such as the following Lisp code for combining lists:

```
(DE APPEND (L1 L2)
  (COND ((NULL L1) L2)
    ((ATOM L1) (CONS L1 L2))
      (TRUE (CONS (CAR L1) (APPEND (CDR L1) L2)))))
```

Computer languages are complex to learn; however, they may be used when no shell is available or when the computer's memory is too restricted (Goodall, 1985). Computer languages are often compiled, so knowledge bases constructed in them typically run faster than expert system shells can run them. This is not a problem with most small rule bases that are built as Mindtools, but large rule bases with hundreds or thousands of rules run more efficiently when composed in a computer language.

When using expert systems as Mindtools, most people use expert system shell programs, which typically consist of a knowledge input editor, an inference engine, and an output generator—all of the components necessary for building and running an expert system rule base. Be careful, though. Shells differ dramatically in capability. For example, some shells permit the builder to use only binary, yes-no options to questions. This would prevent the builder from asking a question such as "How full is the tank? Empty, Half Full, Full." This question would have to be rephrased as a series of binary questions, such as "Is the tank empty?" "Is the tank half full?" and "Is the tank full?" (yes or no to each). Such a limitation can be very restrictive.

A variety of expert system shells is available. For the DOS family of computers, IBM Personal Consultant, Personal Consultant Easy, M1, Personal Consultant Plus, VP Expert, First Class, and Knowledge Pro are available. A number of shells are also available for the Macintosh, including Super Expert, Instant Expert, Expert Ease, MacSmarts, Primex and others. Most of these shells permit the use of IF-THEN rules, so they are easier to use. They vary in capability and price, ranging from a few dollars to hundreds or even thousands of dollars. PC Expert is probably the easiest to learn and most flexible. VP Expert is also very flexible, powerful, and inexpensive.

## Additional Shell Features

A shell may provide many other features besides the basic components of an expert system (see Figure 6.2).

### Induction

Many expert system shells are able to induce rules automatically from examples. In order to do this, the user creates a database (some shells provide for database construction; others read a variety of files created by database programs) of examples, with each of the factors designated by a field and each example consisting of a record (see Figure 6.6). The shell reads these examples and creates rules automatically, such as

```
IF purpose = commuting
AND economy > 30 mph
AND price < 6000
THEN purchase = Geo
AND body = 2-dr. sedan.
```

### Chaining

Some shells enable the inference engine to use a backward-chaining or forward-chaining sequence of rule firing when searching the knowledge

| Factors | | | Decisions | |
|---|---|---|---|---|
| Purpose | Economy | Price | Purchase | Body |
| commuting | >30 mph | <6,000 | Geo | 2-dr. sedan |
| family | 20-30 mph | 10,000-12,000 | Taurus | wagon |
| status | <20 mph | >30,000 | Lexus | sedan |
| commuting | 20-30 mph | >25,000 | BMW | convertible |
| | | | | |
| | | | | |

**Figure 6.6**
Database of examples used for inducing rules

base. These sequences will produce a different sequence of queries for the users, emphasizing different factors within the knowledge base.

## Confidence Factors

Confidence factors state a level of certainty in the rule decisions or in the input. The knowledge engineer designing the rule base can identify the degree of certainty in the THEN portion of the rule. For example, in the rule stated earlier, the conclusion is to buy a Geo. The builder could state the conclusion, "THEN purchase = Geo CNF = .40," indicating that the conclusion has a 40% chance of being correct. Many shells also allow the user to enter levels of confidence when answering queries from the inference engine. For example, if the program asked "What is the primary purpose for this car?," users could enter "commuting CNF = 70." This means either that the users are 70% certain of their answer or that they intend to use the car for commuting 70% of the time.

## Explanatory Support

Many shells enable linking decisions or questions to hypertext or graphics. That is, when a rule is fired, rather than merely presenting the solution in text, the program may call up a hypertext sequence (see Chapter 8) or graphics files and display them on the screen. This capability makes the explanations more detailed and useful. Some shells also display graphics along with the text. For example, if the rule base were supporting identification of bacteria from microscopic displays, the program could display graphics and ask the user which most closely resembled what they were seeing in the microscope.

# How to Construct and Use Expert Systems in the Classroom

Expert system rule bases are reflective tools that can be used in a variety of classroom situations. Imagine that you have just completed a science lab. As a way of reviewing what was learned, have the students construct a rule base that reflects the decisions they had to make in order to complete the lab. In social studies, have students create a rule base that will predict who will win an election, or whether a health care reform bill will pass through Congress, and why. For any content that you ask your students to remember and think about, expert systems require you to consider how you could have them use that information to predict outcomes, explain results, or infer reasoning. This probably will represent a new way of thinking that will have to be modeled for students.

**1. *Identify the purpose for building the expert system and the problem domain.*** This will determine the overall approach students take in seeking information to fill in the knowledge base. If your goal is to understand students' current mental models, then they will do very little outside research to create the knowledge base (Knox-Quinn, 1988). However, if your goal is student mastery and problem solving of new content, then research may be very integral to the process. This decision will depend, to a large degree, on students' current level of knowledge about the subject domain.

Regardless of learners' age or amount of prior subject knowledge, it will be necessary to help them develop the skills needed for constructing expert systems. Getting them to understand the IF-THEN logic of rules and the syntax of even simple expert system shells is not easy, so it is desirable to start with familiar content. Have students develop rule bases on which fast-food restaurant to eat in, what kind of person to ask out on a date, or which popular music groups are best. They will be surprised by how much they know, how much they don't know, and how difficult it is to articulate what they do know.

**2. *Specify problem solutions or decisions.*** Once students have determined the problem domain, they work to identify the solutions, decisions, or outcomes the expert system is expected to provide. In the atom bomb example (see Figure 6.3), there are only four decisions (threaten to drop the bomb, drop the bomb, don't drop the bomb, and a general statement of advice about using fission for peaceful purposes). Decisions are not necessarily mutually exclusive; that is, you may want to provide more than one recommendation to the same individual.

There are several reasons for beginning with the solutions or decisions. Most problems suitable for implementation in an expert system have many alternative solutions, so the first part of the goal-identification stage involves generating all possible solutions *within the defined problem area.* "All possible solutions" refers to all those you can think of. It is important that you not make judgments about the feasibility or value of each solution (brainstorming can help here). It is critical that you identify as many alternative solutions as possible so that none are overlooked.

Having identified all possible solutions, you may want to limit the options, since in most cases it is neither practical nor necessary to deal with each one. You can identify the most probable solutions or develop classes of solutions that have common attributes. For example, you could decide to reject any goal with less than a 25% likelihood of happening. You have to decide how important any particular solution is and whether it is worth including in the knowledge base.

**3. Isolate problem attributes, factors, or variables.** The *problem attributes* provide the set of factors an expert considers when making a decision. They are decision points used during the problem-solving process to determine the most appropriate solution. The expert gathers and analyzes information and then decides what other information is needed in order to solve the problem. Each decision point adopts a value that is called an *attribute value*. In other words, each problem attribute used in an expert system must have at least two alternatives or options to help direct the process to a solution. For example, in the automobile advisor described before (see Figure 6.6), the goal is to select the most appropriate car for purchase. The problem attributes in this case are the factors the buyer should consider when deciding which car to buy: purpose, economy, price, and so on. Problem attributes, then, are those arguments used by an expert when arriving at a decision. In most problem situations there are tangible and intangible elements that influence the direction of the decision-making process. Tangible elements are items that are discrete or calculated quantities such as price and miles per gallon. Intangible elements are such factors as purpose, style, and image.

There are three major steps to identifying the primary problem attributes used in an expert system: (1) identify the problem factors or attributes used when making the decision (the questions that will be asked by the expert system); (2) separate the critical problem attributes from the trivial attributes; and (3) assign the significant values for each attribute (i.e., the answers to the questions).

**4. Generate rules and examples.** Rules represent the knowledge or expertise in an expert system. They are used to arrive at a decision. For example, "IF the consumer makes $1,200 per month and has a job and has a good credit rating and is over 24, THEN a loan of $10,000 is permitted." Rules are a series of IF-THEN statements that describe the means of reaching a specific decision in narrative form. They set forth the conditional relationships among the problem attribute values.

Rules consist of two essential elements: the premise (antecedent) and the conclusion (consequent). The premise begins with the word *if* and states the conditions that are compared with the situation or the desires of the user. Conditions are combined logically using the logical operators *and* and *or*. If conditions are connected by *and*, both conditions must be met in order for the rule to be true. If the conditions are connected by *or*, one or both conditions must be true in order for the rule to be true. Conclusions are signaled by the word *then*.

Rules in expert systems vary in complexity and certainty (confidence levels). Rule complexity refers to the number of premises that must be satisfied before reaching a decision for solving the problem. The number of antecedents may vary, as well as the number of consequents. For example, a rule that must meet only one condition is simple, such as

```
IF the subject in a picture is more than 40 yards away
THEN use a 400-millimeter lens.
```

The only condition in that rule is the subject's distance from the camera. A rule that meets more than one condition or a rule that contains alternative solutions is complex, such as

```
IF the purpose of the car is commuting
AND IF number of commuters is less than 4
AND IF distance to work is greater than 25 miles
OR IF more than one return trip per day is made
THEN buy a 2-door sedan
ELSE take the bus.
```

The conditions or attributes in this rule include the purpose of use, number of commuters using the car, distance to work, and number of trips per day. Given a particular combination of these conditions, the alternative solutions include either buying a two-door sedan or taking the bus. You will probably want to use complex rules with a number of conditions and alternatives. A few simple rules do not warrant the development time involved in creating an expert system, nor will they be able to provide advice on any significant problem.

**5.** *Refine logic and efficiency of decision making.* In order to make construction of the rule base easier, you may want to generate interim decisions and use those as factors rather than writing very complex rules with eight or more factors. For example, in the car selection example you may want to make an interim decision about the size of car (compact, midsize, luxury) and use section factors to first determine the size of the car needed:

```
IF the purpose of the car is commuting
AND IF number of commuters is less than 3
```

```
AND IF distance to work is greater than 25 miles
AND IF the roads are good
THEN size needed is compact.
```

This conclusion can then be combined with other factors to make the final decision:

```
IF size needed is compact
AND IF price must be below $6,000
AND IF status need is low.
THEN buy a Yugo.
```

Interim decisions help the flow of knowledge base development by preventing long, complex rules. You can also collaborate with others by breaking the final decision up into a set of subdecisions and assigning the subdecisions to different groups.

**6.** *Test the system.* Although the purpose of a Mindtool knowledge base is not absolute fidelity of the knowledge base to real-world occurrences, it is useful to ensure that the system works. Have different people query the system and note any improper conclusions or sets of conditions that do not produce a conclusion. As the number of factors increases, the number of possible combinations of rules increases geometrically. Writing a rule for every possible combination of circumstances may not be feasible or even desirable. However, if users' queries lead to dead ends, you should probably generate a rule for those combinations.

# Fostering Collaboration with Expert Systems

Group development of knowledge bases is extremely valuable, not only because it reduces workload, but also because problem solving has frequently been shown to improve as a result of collaborative efforts. Lippert (1988) reports that intragroup interactions contribute to greater cognitive growth because development must accommodate different interpretations and because the public airing and defense of a system provides for a cross-fertilization of ideas. She also reports that a great deal of incidental learning occurs when students attempt to extract information from "experts." Also, seeing the consequences of their decisions is very reinforcing for the groups.

The final reason for collaboration is to address the different perspectives that are the nature of expertise. Physicians, for example, frequently disagree on diagnoses and the proper treatment of various medical problems. So, too, do all experts. Individuals' perspectives on any problem or issue will diverge somewhat. Recognizing those differences and resolving them in the development of knowledge bases is an extremely valuable exercise.

**1. *Form the teams.*** As described in Chapter 1, the most probable predictor of ability to produce expert systems is analytical reasoning. Although analytical reasoning is correlated with achievement, there are many low achievers who are also very analytical. If you are not able to assess this ability, random groups may work the best. Otherwise, be sure that each group has some analytics in it.

**2. *Clarify the group goal.*** This is the key to the expert system construction process. The goal of the expert system may be to classify an unknown object, to provide advice about what type of formula to use in math, or to decide whether to increase or decrease investments in economics. Until all members of the group agree and understand, determining the factors to consider or generating rules will not be possible.

**3. *Negotiate tasks and subtasks to be completed.*** Brainstorming the factors to consider and then having individuals or subgroups investigate them may be appropriate. Decide who will test the rule base once it has been completed. This may consist first of group members but should also involve students outside the group, teachers, or parents.

**4. *Monitor individual and group performance.*** Be sure that each member is involved in rule writing. If individuals write the questions and rules for their own factors, then the whole group needs to integrate them into the whole system. This process will require leadership skills in order to avoid conflicts. A leader is likely to emerge from the group. Foster that emergence.

**5. *Reconcile differences in interpretations or approaches to the goal.*** During the group settings, learners must negotiate differences of opinion or interpretation in the content or in the nature of the task. Differences are more likely with expert systems than with any other Mindtool, except for multimedia/hypermedia construction.

## Advantages of Expert Systems as Mindtools

- More than other Mindtools, expert systems focus thinking on causal reasoning and problem-solving activities.

- Expert systems engage learners in metacognitive reasoning. Reflecting on and representing the thinking involved in problem solving provides valuable insights to learners.
- Expert systems emphasize inferential and implicational reasoning. Few activities in schools stress going beyond existing information to infer why something happened or to consider the implications of what might happen if a set of conditions exists. Building expert systems engages learners in this form of deeper-level processing.
- Expert systems highlight the natural complexity that exists in most problem-solving situations. Becoming aware of how complex problems can really be is also enlightening.

# Limitations of Expert Systems as Mindtools

- The process of building coherent knowledge bases requires novel thinking for many learners, so the work is difficult.
- Formal operational reasoning is probably required. Even though Lippert (1988) reports that expert systems may be used as Mindtools for children as young as sixth grade, experience has shown others that it is much more difficult for students who have not yet achieved formal operational reasoning. Wideman and Owston (1991) found that expert system development most benefited learners with higher abstract reasoning ability and that students with lower abstract reasoning ability were not affected as much or as capable.

## *Conclusion*

Expert system knowledge bases represent causal, procedural knowledge about content domains. They are especially effective in representing problem-solving tasks that require decision making. Expert systems represent inferential thinking about the implications of findings. Building expert system rule bases engages learners in reflective thinking about the dynamic, causal relationships among concepts in any knowledge domain. The thinking required to build expert systems may be the most difficult of any Mindtool because of the formal, logical reasoning. They are perhaps the most intellectually engaging and challenging of all of the Mindtools.

### References

Flavell, J. H., & Wellman, H. M. (1977). Metamemory. In R. V. Kail & J. W. Hagen (Eds.), *Perspectives on the development of memory and cognition.* Hillsdale, NJ: Lawrence Erlbaum Associates.

Gagné, E. (1985). *The cognitive psychology of school learning.* Boston: Little, Brown.

Goodall, A. (1985). *The guide to expert systems.* Oxford: Learned Information.

Karake, Z. A. (1990). Enhancing the learning process with expert systems. *Computers and Education, 14*(6), 495–503.

Knox-Quinn, C. (1988). A simple application and a powerful idea: Using expert systems shells in the classroom. *Computing Teacher, 16*(3), 12–15.

Knox-Quinn, C. (1992, April). *Student construction of expert systems in the classroom.* Paper presented at the annual meeting of the American Educational Research Association, San Francisco, CA.

Lai, K. W. (1989, March). *Acquiring expertise and cognitive skills in the process of constructing an expert system: A preliminary study.* Paper presented at the annual meeting of the American Educational Research Association, San Francisco, CA. (ERIC Document Reproduction Service No. ED 312986)

Lippert, R. (1987). Teaching problem solving in mathematics and science with expert systems. *School Science and Mathematics, 87,* 407–413.

Lippert, R. C. (1988). An expert system shell to teach problem solving. *Tech Trends, 33*(2), 22–26.

Lippert, R., & Finley, F. (1988, April). *Students' refinement of knowledge during the development of knowledge bases for expert systems.* Paper presented at the annual meeting of the National Association for Research in Science Teaching, Lake of the Ozarks, MO. (ERIC Document Reproduction Service No. ED 293872)

Marcoulides, G. A. (1988). An intelligent computer-based learning program. *Collegiate Microcomputer, 6*(2), 123–126.

Saleem, N., & Azad, A. N. (1992). Expert systems as a statistics tutor on call. *Journal of Computers in Mathematics and Science Teaching, 11,* 179–191.

Starfield, A. M., Smith, K. A., & Bleloch, A. L. (1990). *How to model it: Problem solving for the computer age.* New York: McGraw-Hill.

Tennyson, R. D., & Christensen, D. L. (1991). Automating instructional systems development. *Proceedings of selected research presentations at the annual convention of the Association for Educational Communications and Technology.* (ERIC Document Reproduction Service No. ED 335018)

Trollip, S., Lippert, R., Starfield, A., & Smith, K. A. (1992). Building knowledge bases: An environment for making cognitive connections. In P. Kommers, D. H. Jonassen, & T. Mayes (Eds.), *Cognitive tools for learning.* Heidelberg, Germany: Springer-Verlag.

Wideman, H. H., & Owston, R. D. (1991, April). *Promoting cognitive development through knowledge base construction.* Paper presented at the annual meeting of the American Educational Research Association, New Orleans, LA.

# 7

# Computer-Mediated Communication:
## *Connecting Communities of Learners*

∙∙∙∙∙∙∙∙∙∙∙∙∙∙∙∙∙∙∙∙∙∙∙∙∙∙∙∙∙∙∙∙∙∙∙∙∙∙∙∙∙∙∙∙∙∙∙∙∙∙∙∙∙∙∙∙∙∙∙∙∙∙

## What Is Computer-Mediated Communication?

There is a tacit assumption of most educational institutions, from kindergarten through graduate school, that the best way for learning to take place is for a fixed number of students to spend a fixed amount of time per year in face-to-face communication with a teacher. While interpersonal communication with teachers is an important part of a person's education, computer-mediated communication (CMC) begins with a different set of assumptions about learning and instruction—including the assumption that learning need not necessarily be conducted face to face.

CMC facilitates (and mediates) communication between individuals or groups of people. It relies on computer technologies to enable individuals who may or may not be proximate to each other to share computer files and programs and to work and learn together. This is accomplished through computer networks, which are sets of computers connected to other computers through telephone wires, coaxial cable (like that which delivers cable television programming), fiber-optic cable, microwave antennas, and even satellites, which allow data (ones and zeros encoding messages, databases, graphics, and even video) to be passed back and forth, across a room or around the world. "Internet" is a generic term for the tens of thousands of local, regional, national, and international computer networks that are all interconnected. It is the metanetwork that interconnects millions of computers around the world.

CMC is often associated with distance learning initiatives, which connect learners in remote or distant locations to each other, usually through electronic mail (e-mail). However, many of the services provided through

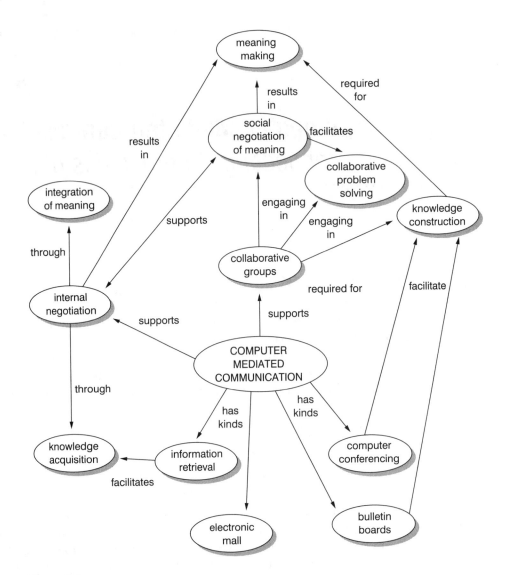

**Figure 7.1**
Computer-mediated communication as a Mindtool

CMC can prove just as useful to learners and teachers in the same class-room or building. To an increasing degree, as computers are integrated more into learning and as time becomes a more precious commodity, teachers and learners will pass ideas and information back and forth via computers.

One of the most important distinctions in CMC is between synchronous and asynchronous communication. *Synchronous* communication (also known as real-time communication) occurs most often face to face with two or more people communicating with each other at the same time (and typically, though not necessarily, in the same place, thanks to telephones, video conferences, etc.). Synchronous CMC occurs when two or more people are connected to each other via their computers and communicating at the same time. *Asynchronous* communication (not at the same time; also known as delayed communication) occurs when only one person can communicate at a time. Telephone answering machines and faxes are asynchronous. One person leaves a message, and the other returns the call, often having to leave an asynchronous message for the original sender.

Synchronous and asynchronous communication also refers to the technical connections in electronic communication. Synchronous connections are open to each other, while asynchronous connections are not open both ways at the same time. The latter are simpler and cheaper to maintain. Most CMC is asynchronous, where users leave notes, papers, pictures, or any other type of communication for each other that can be encoded into digital form, transmitted, and later decoded. CMC does support synchronous communication as well, but it is more expensive because it requires more active, available communication links.

CMC supports synchronous and asynchronous communication in different combinations: one person working alone accessing information, one person communicating with another, one person communicating with many people, and many people communicating with many other people. As shown in Figure 7.2, one-alone communication is supported by information retrieval processes and produces notebooks and files for the individual. One-to-one correspondence is supported by e-mail and results in messages and lectures and conversations (asynchronous) or real-time conversations (synchronous). One-to-many communication is supported by e-mail and bulletin boards and produces lectures and postings, while many-to-many communication is supported by both bulletin boards and computer conferencing, resulting in postings, online journals, and conferences and colloquia.

In the next section, I will describe the types of activities and systems CMC affords, followed by a description of the products of CMC. Products are the artifacts or archives that are created by engaging in CMC processes. Finally, I will briefly describe the means by which CMC is accomplished. This part becomes a bit technical, but, as you will see, the technological overhead is worth the effort. Refer to Figure 7.2 as often as needed to understand the relationships between processes and products.

**Figure 7.2**
Types of CMC processes and products

## Types of Computer-Mediated Communication

### Information Access and Retrieval (One Alone)

Retrieving information is a common activity in schools, especially for supporting research papers. Online information retrieval greatly expands the number of available resources. Information is stored everywhere on the Internet, and these archives are rapidly proliferating, and CMC has made it possible to access thousands of archives around the world. Individuals with a computer and a modem in their home, classroom, library, or office can access many of these databases or information pools around the world to find information on nearly any subject. These remote databases consist of library catalogs, organizational databases, text files, games, and graphics that various organizations maintain on bulletin boards or in databases. Information pools on everything from the president's daily schedule to the contents and descriptions of the Wellington, New Zealand, zoo are a few mouse clicks or keystrokes away.

Another frequently accessed database is the library catalog. You can log on to your library's computer and search the holdings of your library or groups of libraries (see Figure 7.3), or you can search remote databases such as the Educational Research Information Clearinghouse (ERIC), almanacs, encyclopedias, and literally thousands of other knowledge bases.

Information access is supported through file transfer sessions using helpers (known as clients, described later) such as Archie and Gopher or through remote logons (TELNET). File transfer protocol (FTP) sessions enable you to connect to a remote computer on the network and search for and retrieve any unprotected files. In these sessions, you can look up information or download files, that is, copy them through the network from the remote computer to your computer. When you TELNET to another computer, you can log on remotely and work as if you were directly connected. So, I can sit at my home computer in Pennsylvania and work on a computer in the Netherlands, just as if I were there. FTP sessions will enable you to access remote computers and log on as an anonymous user. When you do this, your access to the computer's files and applications is usually restricted.

## E-Mail (One-to-One)

The most common CMC process is to send and receive e-mail. E-mail consists of messages that are sent through networks of computers from your host computer (school system, university, or commercial service, such as Prodigy or CompuServe) to another computer, anywhere in the world. You use a mail program on your computer to compose a message, and the computer sends it through the network to an address on any other computer connected to the Internet. That is, you ask that your message be deposited in someone's mailbox, which is really dedicated file space on

```
1. Libraries  2. Articles  3. Information  4. Other Systems  5. News
                        LIBRARY CATALOGS
  6. Auraria Library                17. Regis University
  7. Colorado School of Mines       18. Luther College Network (IA)
  8. Univ Colo at Boulder           19. Northwest College (WY)
  9. Univ Colo Health Sciences Center  20. State Department of Education
 10. Univ Colo Law Library          21. Bemis Public Library(Littleton)
 11. Denver Public Library          22. Government Publications
 12. Denver University              23. Univ Colo Film/Video - Stadium
 13. Denver University Law Library  24. CCLINK — Community Colleges
 14. University of Northern Colorado 25. Med InfoNet-Medical Libraries
 15. University of Wyoming          26. High Plains Regional Libraries
 16. Colorado State University      27. Teikyo Loretto Hts

          CURRENT ARTICLE INDEXES AND ACCESS
      ARTICLE INDEXES                CURRENT RECEIPTS
 50. UnCover — Article Access        53. New Journal Issues
     (Article Access & Delivery)
 52. ERIC (Access Restricted as of 11/1/92)
 57. British Library Document        UNION LISTS
 80. Magazine Index & ASAP (full text available)
 81. Business Index & ASAP
          NATIONAL SERIALS CATALOGING DATABASE (full text available)
 55. CONSER                         56. Online Libraries
 87. Expanded Academic Index
 86. National Newspaper Index

              INFORMATION DATABASES
              60. Choice Book Reviews
              61. Encyclopedia
              63. Metro Denver Facts
              64. School Model Programs
              65. Internet Resource Guide
              66. Department of Energy
              67. Journal Graphics
                  (Television/Radio Transcripts)
              82. Company ProFile
              88. Federal Domestic Assistance Catalog
              89. Librarian's Yellow Pages
                  OTHER LIBRARY SYSTEMS
 69. Atlanta Public Library (GA)    109. Capitol Region Lib.Council (CT)
 70. Boulder Public Library (CO)    110. C/W MARS (MA)
 71. MARMOT Library System (CO)     111. Denver Public Schools (CO)
 72. Pikes Peak Library System (CO) 112. Foothill/DeAnza Coll. (CA)
 73. University of Hawaii System    113. Houston Area Library
 74. Montgomery Cnty Dept. of            Automation Network (TX)
     Public Libraries (MD)          114. Inland Northwest Library
 75. Northeastern University (MA)        Automation Network (WA)
 76. Sno-Isle Regional Library (WA) 115. Maryland Interlibrary
 77. University of Maryland Systems      Consortium
 78. MELVYL (Univ of California System) 116. Morgan State Univ (MD)
 79. Arizona Libraries (Arizona State 117. Solano, Napa & Partners (CA)
     Univ. & Northern Arizona Univ.) 118. Lane Medical Library (CA)
119. Monroe County Public Lib (NY)  120. Broward County Public Lib (FL)
121. Los Angeles Public Library
```

**Figure 7.3**

Library databases offered by the Colorado Alliance of Research Libraries system their host computer. Addresses can be complicated, but typically they observe the following pattern:

*user@host_computer.institution.domain.network or country code*

Sending a message to *user335@psuvm.psu.edu* would direct a message to the person identified as user335 through a network to the IBM mainframe (known as psuvm) at Penn State University (psu), which is in the educational domain (edu). A message to *president@white_house.gov* would presumably direct your message to the president on the White House computer, which is in the government domain.

Messages can include any form of text characters and be about any subject. Most e-mail programs also allow you to send formatted documents and files to the recipient's address. You can also send graphics or applications programs after they have been converted to a binary file (encoded into ones and zeros).

E-mail can support a number of learning techniques, such as learning contracts, mentorship and apprenticeship, and correspondence study (Paulsen, 1994). Learning contracts are formal agreements between teacher and learner that set out learning goals, methods, and timelines. Each of these is facilitated by the direct correspondence between teacher and learner that e-mail affords. Likewise, teachers may continue to mentor or apprentice learners through e-mail. These tele-apprenticeships resemble face-to-face apprenticeships (Levin, Haesun, & Reil, 1990). Finally, correspondence study is greatly enhanced by e-mail. Rather than playing telephone tag for weeks with a tutor, students in many courses at England's Open University receive fairly rapid and direct feedback from their tutors via e-mail. E-mail generally ensures that messages are received, and those messages are typically more directly related to students' questions than those tutors would receive in a classroom.

## Bulletin Boards (One-to-Many)

Bulletin board services (BBSs) are special-purpose computer programs that enable individuals to post messages to a bulletin board (just as you might pin a notice to a physical board) or to read messages and copy them to your computer. BBSs are usually established to disseminate information about a finite topic or set of topics, although there are a growing number of NetNews services (BBSs that provide access to newspapers and magazines). Large BBSs are also available to support special-interest discussion groups oriented to a wide range of topics, from computers to sexual deviancies. Many of these also contain computer application programs, such as games, that can be copied (downloaded) to your computer.

There are six main functions of BBSs: e-mail, conferencing, chat (online conversations), questionnaires or polling, file access, and random access of databases (Hudspeth, 1990). While e-mail is the oldest and most frequently used, many BBSs are used more for conferencing and file access.

BBSs may be supported by large organizations, such as universities (on large mainframe computers), or by individuals on their personal computers. Mainframe services offer a greater variety of topics and services. If you would like to host a bulletin board, however, it is relatively easy to set one up simply by connecting a dedicated microcomputer to a dedicated telephone line (usually) and loading bulletin board software on it. This software manages access to the computer and receipt and distribution of files. These types of bulletin boards have grown rapidly to support teaching in remote parts of the country and world, where teachers can ask their computer to call up the bulletin board computer in order to get or send such things as innovative teaching ideas or lesson plans.

## Computer Conferencing (Many-to-Many)

As new technologies and issues confront education daily, individuals want to discuss them with each other. With travel costs soaring, however, physically assembling to discuss them is becoming increasingly difficult, so professionals often connect to computer conferences in order to discuss ideas. Computer conferences are asynchronous discussions, debates, and collaborative efforts among a group of people who share an interest in the topic. These virtual conferences connect people who may be continents away from each other as if they had come together for the discussion. This form of knowledge sharing is gratifying and informative. Technically, there is little, if any, difference between bulletin boards and computer conferences. The differences are in the intent and form of the communication.

Computer conferencing also supports efforts to create virtual classrooms. Virtual classrooms are communications and learning spaces located within a computer system (Hiltz, 1986). The Electronic Information Exchange System was created at the New Jersey Institute of Technology as a classroom without walls, in order to supplement existing courses and deliver entire courses and simulations through CMC.

Computer conferencing asks why it is necessary for students to share the same physical space with a teacher in order to listen to the teacher, ask questions, get assignments, and otherwise communicate with the teacher. Most of those forms of communication can easily and effectively be mediated by the computer, enabling students at a distance to join classes they would otherwise be prevented from attending. Urban universities, for example, could effectively create virtual classrooms through computer conferencing, thereby reducing traffic, pollution, and parking costs.

Computer conferencing also supports long-distance collaboration among learners. Whether on different continents or at the school across town, learners can correspond and collaboratively construct newspapers, newsletters, or other documents, solve problems, conduct experiments, debate, or simply share ideas and perspectives. As will be discussed later, when learners have a wider audience for their writing or other scholarly activities, they tend to invest more effort in the process and learn more.

Computer conferencing has given rise to numerous online interest groups—people with a common interest who convene in electronic conferences about that interest. Over 2,000 such groups send hundreds of thousands of messages to each other daily (Howse, 1992). Many of these groups support teachers and education, such as the electronic Academic Village at the University of Virginia, which links public school teachers, teacher education students, and university faculty with teachers across the United States and in foreign countries (Bull, Harris, & Drucker, 1992).

In addition to discussion groups, computer conferencing also supports debates, simulations, role playing, and collaborative construction of knowledge bases (Paulsen, 1994). Debates are natural applications of computer conferences, with teams of learners assigned issues and positions to argue. The research skills engaged to develop arguments that will adequately present the group's position are considerable. Many business simulations are mediated by computer conferences in which individuals are assigned roles and interact with each other. Effective simulations require a well-structured set of activities and very careful monitoring of the contributions, but the experience can be very powerful.

Role plays are like simulations in that learners may assume a variety of roles and attempt to reason like the individuals they represent. For example, the University of Michigan involved schools all over the world in an Arab-Israeli conflict simulation in which students were assigned roles as either the combatants, the United States, or the former Soviet Union (Goodman, 1992). Other students represented the religious interests of the Muslims, Christians, and so on. These types of interactions are more engaging than hearing only the teacher's perspective, and they enhance multicultural awareness among the participants. Students can also conduct experiments or observe the environment and collaboratively contribute to a common knowledge base. Examples of this are described later in this chapter.

Computer conferencing is technologically accomplished in three ways: bulletin boards, e-mail, and special conferencing software. BBSs can be used to support postings about ideas in special-interest folders, but they often lack some of the functions that are desirable in a conference. Computer conferencing is most commonly conducted via e-mail, which supports conferencing through LISTSERVs. Individuals can subscribe to a LISTSERV much as they might subscribe to a newspaper. Any message that is sent to the LISTSERV mailbox is automatically forwarded to every other subscriber to the service.

LISTSERV conferences are usually focused on a single topic or issue. They are effective because they do not require more sophisticated software and do not use much storage space on the host computer. Once like-minded individuals have located one another through the general conference, they can correspond individually or in small groups by sending personal messages to each other.

Computer conferencing is also supported by special conferencing software, such as VAXnotes, Caucus, or CoSys. This software requires users to log on to a remote computer in order to post and receive messages. These systems provide more functions to support the conferencing process.

## Products of Computer-Mediated Communication

The processes of information retrieval, e-mail, bulletin boards, and computer conferencing produce a variety of artifacts.

### Files

Information retrieval from remote databases and e-mail services involves transmitting files of data. The files that are transmitted are most often text files, consisting of words and numbers. Text files are converted to ASCII (American Standard Code for Information Interchange, a code used to represent alphabetic and numeric characters on any computer without formatting) characters before they are transmitted. Graphics files (pictures), sound files, and even video files (motion graphics) can also be digitized and transmitted as ASCII characters through the networks. Formatted files (word-processing files with special codes embedded in them as text-formatting characters), executable files, and graphics, sound, and video files travel as binary (zeros and ones) or hexadecimal files (codes converted to base 16). Every form of asynchronous communication creates a file of some kind.

## Messages

The most personal and perhaps most meaningful CMC application is e-mail. This service allows you to write a message or send a text, graphics, or video file to one person or a group of people. It is the most direct CMC service, because the sender addresses his or her message to the intended audience. Only those individuals whose mailboxes are listed in the header of the message will receive the message. If the header cites a LISTSERV, then all of the subscribers to that LISTSERV will receive the message.

## Bulletin Boards and Online Journals

Electronic bulletin boards function like physical bulletin boards, for posting announcements and information that is accessible to anyone who looks at them. While both physical and electronic bulletin boards are publicly accessible, electronic ones tend to be more specialized. Postings on bulletin boards can be messages, articles, replies, reviews, pictures, games, applications, or any other type of computer file.

The cost and time delays of publishing and distributing print journals—especially academic ones with a limited number of subscribers—are forcing many to consider electronic publishing. Posting articles on a BBS and restricting access to them through subscriptions allows articles to be published much more quickly (often within hours as opposed to months or even years). Electronic journals also support more collaborative authorship between distant authors. Authors may send versions of the article back and forth, cowriting and coediting the article up until its publication.

## News Networks

More than 2,000 news networks—NetNews or Usenet services—provide news and announcements in a bulletin board fashion on many social, recreational, computer, or alternative topics. Over 500 Usenet groups provide information and discussion space on computer issues, such as data compression techniques, computer languages in common use, computer platforms and operating systems available, and software sources. Usenets also list jobs, items for sale, and services such as tax preparation and investment guidance. More than 300 groups provide information on topics as diverse as baseball, poetry, model railroading, and *Star Trek* memorabilia. Cultural information on more than 100 countries can also be accessed. Many nationally prominent newspapers offer their news online, and there are numerous "talk" groups focusing on current issues such as abortion and gun control. It is likely that any topic you have an interest in is serviced by one or more Usenet groups. These services enable you to post a question to be answered, give your opinion about a topic, or make friends with like-minded individuals. Unlike bulletin boards, news networks are updated continuously.

## Lectures

Transcripts of speeches or lectures may be posted to bulletin boards, news networks, or computer conferences so they will be available for additional reflection and/or analysis. The full text of nearly every speech delivered by the president is immediately available through the Internet. If you missed a class lecture or a presentation by a prominent speaker, you may be able to obtain the lecture immediately on a network. Such a lecture may be more comprehensible to visually oriented learners than the live lecture, since it can be reviewed and scrutinized more easily and does not require note taking.

## Discussion Groups/Colloquia

Computer discussion groups provide a public forum or communication space in which anyone who is a subscriber or member of the conference can contribute ideas to the group. Groups may start with specific contributions in the form of a lecture or an article and then be opened up for discussion, interpretation, and argumentation by the members of the group or class. Discussion in most conferencing systems may be held at the whole-group level or be broken up into more specific or user-focused discussions of subtopics. Individuals may comment on the original ideas or on comments by other participants, thus creating an electronic discussion of ideas.

These groups are open to individuals who may be great distances apart, and ideas can be added at any time of day or night, both by the teacher and by the students. In fact, the teacher who monitors an electronic classroom discussion has much better access to how each of the students is thinking about the topics than in a face-to-face class. As Romiszowski and de Haas (1989) point out, these interactions are more democratic because all students have the same tools for communicating their ideas. These authors also mention that there is increased potential for deeper or more thoughtful classroom interaction because individuals can reflect on and think over ideas—or even look up information—before responding (typically not possible in real classrooms). Perhaps most important is that learners end up with a complete record of the discussion, reducing the anxiety that one will miss something important in note taking, which often disrupts the communication process.

# Means of Computer-Mediated Communication: Telecommunications

CMC relies on sophisticated technologies for connecting computers together. Computers all respond to the same binary, digital language; however, different programs and operating systems on different computers must agree on a protocol (see discussion later in the chapter) and a syntax for sending and receiving messages and files so that any computer can read those files or pass them along to another computer. Using CMC involves a combination of transmission technologies, as illustrated in Figure 7.4.

## Networks

Networks are groups of computers that are connected to each other for the purpose of passing data back and forth. There are different levels of networks. Local area networks (LANs) are used to connect computers within an organization or a local area. They are frequently used to connect all of the computers in a school or lab so they can share programs from a server, which has a large disk drive for storing programs. LANs may be connected by fiber-optic or coaxial cable or special high-capacity telephone lines to wide area networks (WANs) or metropolitan area networks (MANs), which connect all of the computers in a community or region.

A personal computer can be connected to a host computer either directly (hardwired) through a network or through the telephone line via a modem (see Figure 7.4). A modem (stands for modulator-demodulator) is a device that converts binary code into sound for transmission over telephone lines. A direct connection is usually through a coaxial, fiber-optic, or twisted-pair cable. Such a cable may form a LAN that is connected to all of the computers in your school building or to a central host computer connected to the Internet.

A host computer is identified by a specific locator name to which other computers may address files. The host computer is connected to other host computers (which are also dedicated as servers) directly through fiber-optic or coaxial cable, special high-capacity phone lines, microwave transmitters, or satellites; or indirectly through normal telephone lines.

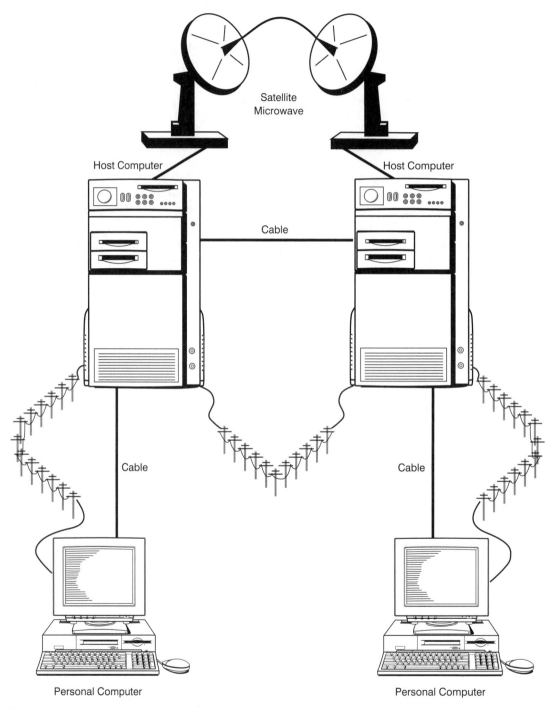

Satellite
Microwave

Host Computer · · · · · · · · · · · · · · · · · · · · · Host Computer

Cable

Cable · · · · · · · · · · · · · · · · · · · · · · · · · · · Cable

Personal Computer · · · · · · · · · · · · · · · · · · · · Personal Computer

**Figure 7.4**
Computer-mediated communication technologies

These host computers are interconnected in larger, regional WANs. Networks such as PREPnet, BITNet, NSFnet, and ARPANet in the United States and national networks in many foreign countries each consist of hundreds or thousands of interconnected host computers. These networks are interconnected throughout the world in one giant meganetwork, the Internet. When you send an e-mail message to another computer, routing patterns are worked out by each network, which passes your message file from your host computer to other switching computers, which receive and pass along your message to other computers. As your message leaves the network to which your computer is connected, it goes through a gateway to another network, which passes it along to another network, and so on until your message arrives at the destination computer, much like your local phone company is connected to a variety of long-distance telephone networks that connect to other local systems. "Gateway" is a technical term used to describe computers that translate messages into different protocols. BITNet- and Internet-connected computers operate on different languages and command sets. Once a message is received by a host computer, it is held in the users' mailboxes until they log on to the computer and retrieve it or delete it from the computer's memory. This process is typically completed in a matter of seconds, depending on the required switching, how busy the networks are, and so on.

## Protocols

Computers, like humans, need to speak the same language in order to understand each other. At the most basic level, all computers understand zeros and ones, just as humans use alphabets to depict sounds and words. However, the particular arrangements of those zeros and ones affects the meaning of the message, just as the arrangement of letters in different languages affects the meaning. Networks have established conventions, or protocols, for addressing and interpreting files. Protocols define how computers will act when talking to each other. They allow communication between computers made by different manufacturers and using different software. The referent standard protocol for file transfer on the Internet is TCP/IP (transmission control protocol/Internet protocol). There are versions of TCP/IP for virtually every kind of computer available. So, your personal computer transmits a message to the host computer, which converts it to TCP/IP before passing it along through the network to its destination computer, which reads and interprets the TCP/IP-encoded message. Although there are many other protocols used, TCP/IP is the most common.

## Clients

Clients are special-purpose software programs that provide the CMC capabilities. Client programs reside on individual personal computers. They create a connection between your personal computer and a server, accept input from users, reformat it into a standard such as TCP/IP, send the input to a server, accept output from a server in the same format, and reformat the information for display on your personal computer. Client programs are available for every kind of personal computer and workstation. Information retrieval clients, such as Gopher, developed at the University of Minnesota, have done more to increase the use of CMC than any other innovation. Gopher (named after the Minnesota mascot and the "go-fer" function it serves) client programs enable you to search a vast network of computers throughout the world for useful and interesting information by simply navigating layers of menus.

## Servers

Servers refer to special-purpose software loaded onto central host computers (which may or may not be dedicated to functioning solely as a server) that support the types of CMC described earlier. Servers provide the services, archives, and files that clients allow you to access and retrieve. Some servers provide bulletin boards, while others, such as Confer and CoSys, serve computer conferencing. Still other servers support the transfer of e-mail. Servers send and receive data to and from client programs on individual personal computers or other servers. Putting it all together, clients are connected to servers, which pass information to other servers, which are connected to other clients.

# Examples of Computer-Mediated Communication

The applications of CMC are too numerous to recount. Wells (1992) briefly describes nearly 100 educational applications of CMC, including the following:

- Athabasca University offers a master's degree in Distance Education via CMC.
- Earth Lab is a LAN in New York that supports collaborative work among sixth graders.
- FrEdMail connects teachers and students in large- and small-group discussions in the United States, Argentina, and Australia.

- Kids Network, funded by the National Science Foundation and National Geographic, connects 4,000 children at 200 sites to support data collection on acid rain.
- Students throughout Europe gather and share data on weather and pollution through the Pluto Project.

The following descriptions of selected applications provide a more detailed description of the potentials of CMC.

## Learning Circles

Developers of the Global Learning Circles Project, in which classrooms in the United States are connected to classrooms around the world via the AT&T Learning Network, believe that when students write for a larger, networked audience of peers, they are more motivated to perform than when they write only for their teacher's red pen. Cohen and Reil (1989) found that papers written to communicate with peers were more fluent, better organized, and clearer than those written merely for a grade. Collaboratively authoring newspapers and booklets by collecting articles from partner schools around the world also results in better use of grammar and syntax (Reil, 1990).

The Learning Circles Project facilitates collaboration among small groups of classrooms (therefore learning *circles*, rather than large, amorphous groups of readers). Collaboration, of course, requires closer communication and is easier with a known audience than an imaginary audience. The project staff has worked with elementary, middle, and high school students by outlining group tasks and time lines, with each school managing one project around its curriculum for the group, which as a whole produces a publication. This is a good example of a global application of reciprocal teaching (Palinscar & Brown, 1984). Classes in each learning circle agree on a project, and the students become authors, reporters, poets, and researchers, responding to requests from the other classes in the circle regularly via e-mail. Joint publications are planned and carried out, and students reflect on the experiences they have had. Reil (1993) described a number of learning circles, such as the following:

- Elementary students in Saudi Arabia sponsored a project on solutions to the Gulf crisis. Together with their partners in different countries, they discussed world dependence on oil, kingdoms, democracies, and conflicts between political and religious beliefs.
- Intermediate students in West Virginia have sponsored a project in which inmates are answering the questions of students in the Learning

Circle about a range of social problems from their personal life experiences. The inmates' reflections on their life decisions have had a very strong effect on students, who live in a range of social settings and conditions.

- Students in British Columbia sponsored the "Environmental Investigator" as their section of their collective newspaper, The Global Grapevine. They asked the eight schools in their Learning Circle for essays or poetry centered on local environmental issues.

- High school students designed studies of the homeless, illiteracy, or substance abuse, or explored differences in family patterns or causes of suicide across cultures.

- Students in Belgium sponsored a research project on waste caused by excessive packaging of goods. Students collected and compared the packaging of many different types of products and assessed the best and worst examples in different countries.

Learning Circles are designed to expose students to different points of view, enhance multicultural awareness on a global scale, and develop cooperative skills for dealing with people in different cultures (Reil, 1993). These are powerful learning outcomes by anyone's standards.

## In-Service Teacher Education

In Catalonia, Spain, the Department of Education has set up a network, XTEC, to provide databases of educational resources for teachers and a computer conferencing service that enables students to get to know students and teachers in other schools and to consult expert teachers and students in other schools (Simón, 1992). Courses on educational innovations such as spreadsheets and online retrieval (Mindtools are popular in Spain, too) are offered through conferences to teachers all over the region. Tutorial instruction is supplied by the conference, with teachers submitting their assignments to the tutor via a file transfer system. Teachers then engage in "tele-debates" on suggested teaching methods via the conferencing system. Both students and teachers think the technology is exciting and effective because of the individualization afforded by the system—especially the e-mail correspondence with distant tutors.

In the United States, the Beginning Teacher Computer Network was begun at Harvard in 1987 to provide support and mentoring for graduates in their first year of teaching (Merseth, Beals, & Cutler, 1992). The network enables rookie teachers to ask questions, make comments, and request materials. Conversations on the net have included questions on teaching methods, such as collecting homework and fostering classroom discussion; values topics, such as how to counsel a sexually active teenager; content suggestions; case studies; and content discussions. The new teachers are spread all over the country but find it helpful to maintain an umbilical link to their teacher-preparation program during that crucial period.

## Collaborative Writing

One of the most common uses of CMC is to support collaborative writing, with several individuals contributing to a common project (this is one of the goals of Learning Circles). The Daedalus system at Texas Tech University enables first-year composition students to respond and critique each other's writing and encourages "community brainstorming." With students critiquing class work, instructors may assume different roles as coaches and guides. The Daedalus system supports text sharing by managing multiple copies of works, handling critiques, and providing real-time conferencing among students for sharing ideas (brainstorming).

## Situated Language Learning

Perhaps the most frustrating job in education is teaching foreign-language courses, such as German and French, to junior and senior high school students in the United States. The subject is academic and decontextualized, as the students have little opportunity or encouragement to speak the language outside the classroom. The cultural isolation of students in the United States makes it difficult to make real-world use of a foreign language, an opportunity regularly available to learners in Europe, Africa, and Asia. However, the Internet can support electronic pen pals, social forums and comparisons, discussions of issues, or just plain gossip between learners in classes all over the world. Rather than studying language textbooks that contain outdated articles or literature that is "foreign" to students in different ways, students can engage in dialogues with learners in their native tongues. A French class in the United States, for example, can compare fashion, customs, or favorite rock stars in French with a class in Lyon.

# Computer-Mediated Communication as a Mindtool

Communicating with others via CMC has been shown to be a reflective and constructive activity. Harasim (1990) found that learners perceive themselves as reflecting more on their thoughts while computer conferencing than when engaged in face-to-face or telephone conversations. Carefully considering and constructing responses to issues involves more analytical thinking. The "need to verbalize all aspects of interaction within the text-based environment can enhance such metacognitive skills as self-reflection and revision in learning" (Harasim, 1990, p. 49). These are important thinking skills.

As described in Chapter 1, meaningful learning results from reflective thinking, which results in knowledge construction. These are constructivist activities, which engage learners in meaning making. No Mindtool described in this book better facilitates these constructivist processes than CMC, because it supports reflection on what one knows and, through communication of that with others, may lead to conceptual change.

Most of the computer-mediated activities I have described facilitate forms of constructive thinking. For example, e-mail often supports collaborative writing, personal negotiation, and collaborative problem solving. Computer conferencing supports the social negotiation of ideas about the content that is being studied, as well as the collaborative construction of new knowledge. As groups of individuals provide different perspectives and interpretations, debate, argue, and compromise on the meaning of ideas, they are deeply engaged in knowledge construction. Knowledge construction also involves acquiring ideas. The information retrieval capability of CMC supports potentially vast amounts of knowledge acquisition as individuals search the thousands of databases of information available to them. All of these processes are important to meaning-making among learners.

Yet, not all learners are inclined to take advantage of these resources. In fact, when usage is voluntary, participation is usually low. More mature students, particularly graduate students, are most inclined to participate in CMC options (Wells, 1992). Also, students more accustomed to independent study and distance learning are more likely to benefit. CMC is not an immediately comfortable learning strategy for most students, who have been directed and spoon-fed for most of their educational careers. On the other hand, dedicated and capable extraverted learners may prefer live interactions to computer-mediated interactions, believing that CMC removes many interpersonal communication cues.

## Evaluation of Computer-Mediated Communication as a Mindtool

   **1. *Computer-based.*** The Internet is the largest computer-based communication network in the world, connecting millions of computers.

While it is not yet as widespread as telephone networks, it accesses a lot more information. All of the capabilities described in this chapter rely on computer networks.

**2.** *Readily available, general applications.* The range of services, including e-mail, conferencing, bulletin boards, and information access, are available to almost any educator through his or her school district, university, or other educational agency. In addition, access to all of the services described in this chapter is available commercially.

**3.** *Affordable.* Most of the software required to access the Internet is either in the public domain or will be bundled with any communications equipment you purchase. The only costs that you may incur are for the computer modem and the account. High-speed modems are commercially available for less than $100. Commercial communications services will charge a monthly fee for connecting and accessing the services described in this chapter. If you can get an account on a university or agency computer, this cost is typically borne by the institution.

**4.** *Represent knowledge.* CMC is a communication tool that does not represent knowledge directly as do other Mindtools. Rather, CMC is a vehicle for allowing individuals to transmit the products and representations of other Mindtools and (more importantly) to collaboratively negotiate knowledge representations with other individuals. In this way, CMC provides access to multiple interpretations of ideas, which leads directly to an advanced level of knowledge acquisition and representation.

**5.** *Applicable to different subject domains.* The Internet provides access to information on nearly every subject.

**6.** *Engage critical thinking.* These skills are described in the next section.

**7.** *Facilitate transfer of learning.* Knowledge acquisition and negotiation of meaning are among the most fundamental and important learning processes in education. They can be applied in any content domain and related to any kind of problem. It is critical that learners become self-directed and acquire and use these skills always.

**8.** *Simple, powerful formalism.* Communication is the most common and important meaning-making medium available. Facilitating meaningful communication enhances that process.

**9.** *(Reasonably) easy to learn.* The new generation of client servers has eliminated the need to learn a process before engaging in many CMC activities. The process of correspondence is more natural and available to learners. The programs that facilitate that correspondence are so friendly and easy to use that learners will enter the exploration mode very quickly.

# Critical, Creative, and Complex Thinking in Computer-Mediated Communication

Tables 7.1, 7.2, and 7.3 evaluate the critical, creative, and complex thinking skills engaged by the three major computer-mediated activities: information retrieval, e-mail, and computer conferencing. The skills in each table that are marked by an "×" are those that are employed by each process, based on an information-processing analysis of the tasks.

Information retrieval involves interacting with computer networks to identify and retrieve relevant information from notebooks, news networks, or other information sources. It is like using a giant reference library, so it primarily involves using research skills and evaluating information. E-mail refers primarily to manipulating text to support one-to-one correspondence. Computer conferencing refers to using LISTSERVs, bulletin boards, or special conferencing software to interact with others in a conversation about specific topics.

The bulk of critical, creative, and complex thinking skills results from computer conferencing, probably because it engages the most complex

**Table 7.1**
Critical thinking skills in CMC activities

| | Information Retrieval | Electronic Mail | Computer Conferencing |
|---|:---:|:---:|:---:|
| **Evaluating** | | | |
| Assessing information | X | X | X |
| Determining criteria | X | | X |
| Prioritizing | X | | X |
| Recognizing fallacies | | | X |
| Verifying | X | X | X |
| **Analyzing** | | | |
| Recognizing patterns | X | | X |
| Classifying | X | | X |
| Identifying assumptions | | X | X |
| Identifying main ideas | X | | X |
| Finding sequences | | | X |
| **Connecting** | | | |
| Comparing/contrasting | X | | X |
| Logical thinking | | X | X |
| Inferring deductively | | | X |
| Inferring inductively | | | X |
| Identifying causal relationships | | | X |

forms of communication. As indicated in Table 7.1, however, information retrieval also engages a fair number of critical thinking skills. Locating and evaluating the relevance and usability of information that is found on the Internet engages mostly evaluating and analyzing skills, though almost no connecting skills. Being able to select relevant information is a very important skill in all forms of problem solving and higher-order thinking.

Depending on the nature of the correspondence, e-mail may or may not engage many critical thinking skills. Assessing what the sender provided and identifying its assumptions are the primary activities. Computer conferencing, on the other hand, engages every evaluating and analyzing skill. Analyzing and evaluating the issues being discussed and connecting those ideas with others in the conference are necessary for meaningful participation.

Creative thinking is most commonly used in computer conferencing and, to a lesser degree, with e-mail correspondence (see Table 7.2). Computer conferencing engages learners in elaborating on ideas and then synthesizing various positions. E-mail uses fewer elaborating and synthesizing activities, presumably because of the specificity and intentionality of the correspondence. If one is corresponding with a known audience, the effort in developing and explaining issues is not as great.

| **Table 7.2** Creative thinking skills in CMC activities | **Information Retrieval** | **Electronic Mail** | **Computer Conferencing** |
|---|---|---|---|
| **Elaborating** | | | |
| Expanding | | | X |
| Modifying | | | X |
| Extending | | X | X |
| Shifting categories | X | | X |
| Concretizing | | X | |
| **Synthesizing** | | | |
| Analogical thinking | | | X |
| Summarizing | | X | X |
| Hypothesizing | | | |
| Planning | X | | X |
| **Imagining** | | | |
| Fluency | | X | X |
| Predicting | | | X |
| Speculating | | | X |
| Visualizing | | | |
| Intuition | X | | X |

Complex thinking skills are most required for information retrieval and computer conferencing (see Table 7.3). Information retrieval involves designing queries and some problem solving and decision making in determining search goals, routes, or sources of information. Computer conferencing also involves a fair amount of problem solving and decision making, as those are the primary goals of many conferences that seek collaboratively developed answers to difficult issues. Again, conferencing is more complex because of the multiple interactions and the differences of opinions and perspectives that are typically represented in most conferences.

## Related Mindtools

CMC is perhaps the most independent or unrelated of the Mindtools, probably because its direct purpose is not to represent knowledge. CMC is able to act as a vehicle for delivering and sharing the products of any other Mindtool. It is also able to act as a medium for collaboratively constructing any of the other Mindtools, but the ends of CMC are not directly facilitated by any other Mindtool.

**Table 7.3**
Complex thinking skills in CMC activities

|  | Information Retrieval | Electronic Mail | Computer Conferencing |
|---|---|---|---|
| **Designing** | | | |
| Imagining a goal | X | | X |
| Formulating a goal | X | | X |
| Inventing a product | | X | X |
| Assessing a product | X | | X |
| Revising the product | | X | X |
| **Problem Solving** | | | |
| Sensing the problem | X | | X |
| Researching the problem | X | | X |
| Formulating the problem | X | | X |
| Finding alternatives | | | X |
| Choosing the solution | | | X |
| Building acceptance | | | X |
| **Decision Making** | | | |
| Identifying an issue | | X | X |
| Generating alternatives | | | X |
| Assessing the consequences | | X | |
| Making a choice | X | X | X |
| Evaluating the choices | X | | X |

# Software Tools

A large variety of communications software is currently in use, and many other types of programs are being investigated to aid the CMC process.

## Communications Software

Essential software for many CMC projects includes communications packages that are installed on a computer. This software sets up a conversation between your computer, the modem, and the remote computer. The modem converts your files into a series of tones that are sent from your computer, through the modem, and on through telephone lines to a modem connected to the remote computer, which converts them back into digital information.

Communications software is typically bundled with the modem. Modem programs provide important functions, such as alternative FTPs and the capability to emulate different types of terminals that are commonly connected to the remote computers. They also support the uploading (sending) and downloading (capturing) of data files and, most importantly, dialing the phone and connecting to the remote computer (this is a complex process—called "handshaking"—between your computer and the host computer). Setting up your modem and communications software by identifying speed, parity, and protocols can be very confusing, though after it is configured to run properly, communications software is normally easy to use. A detailed description of these processes is beyond the scope of this book and fairly specific to the hardware that you purchase, so read the documentation carefully and ask a lot of questions.

### Client Programs

Client programs are special-purpose application programs that support different CMC processes, unlike communications software, which enables a variety of telecommunications activities. You need a client program to use the telecommunications described in this chapter. They are usually available from the computer center to which you apply for an account in order to connect to the Internet. There are e-mail software programs for nearly every type of personal computer. Programs such as Eudora combine a simple interface with all of the mail functions that anyone would need, making e-mail a simple process. As mentioned earlier, Gopher has made file access and retrieval a matter of navigating menus.

In addition to programs such as Gopher, most library services support menu-based access to databases, such as those in Figure 7.3. Client programs such as Archie, Gopher, Veronica, and Eudora are public-domain programs you can obtain by downloading them from networks. Perhaps the most powerful and friendly client yet is Mosaic, which is a mouse-driven hypertext interface (see discussion of hypertext later and in Chapter 8) to the World Wide Web (WWW). The WWW is a large set of thousands of especially powerful servers that are connected to the Internet. Mosaic lets you click on topics and navigate through the web, create your own set of servers that you can access simply by clicking on their names in your own personalized list, and automatically download audio, graphics, or video files by simply clicking on the file name. Mosaic is a powerful client that provides access to the most sophisticated set of servers in the world. It is definitely a harbinger of things to come in the CMC field.

## Conferencing Software

Computer conferencing can be managed by special-purpose conferencing software, such as EIES, Confer, Caucus, COM, VAXnotes, and CoSys. These are typically mainframe-based systems that support a variety of conferencing functions, such as synchronous and asynchronous correspondence, file transfer, and multiple sections and layers of conferences for large numbers of participants.

Since conferencing can also be supported on bulletin boards, keep in mind that setting up a bulletin board is relatively easy. As mentioned earlier, all you need is a dedicated PC, a phone line, bulletin board software that supports all of the connections with other computers that call in, and the patience to carefully read the documentation.

## Problem-Solving and Decision-Support Tools

CMC assumes that learners can naturally collaborate with each other, yet research shows that cooperative skills are undeveloped in most learners. Difficulties in collaborating are often exacerbated by CMC because learners often do not share physical space, nonverbal messages, or a common background. A potential solution to some of these problems is the use of decision-support systems. These are typically implemented on LANs to assist groups in negotiating, decision making, and communicating with each other. They are especially effective for facilitating brainstorming. Aiken (1992) found that decision-support systems implemented on a network produced greater student participation because of the anonymity afforded by the system. The system also improved group synergy by generating many more divergent applications of ideas. The use of such systems may significantly enhance the effects of CMC.

## Hypertext

One of the major difficulties encountered by users of computer conferences is keeping all of the ideas, issues, and positions straight. In a conference, numerous argument threads can develop, making it challenging to the reader and contributor to understand them all and contribute to the correct ones. Hypertext may be used to ease this problem.

Hypertext is a method for structuring text in a nonlinear, user-controllable form (see Chapter 8 for a more extensive discussion). Hypertext is chunked into nodes (information chunks of various sizes) that are linked to each other, allowing the user to navigate through the text in any sequence (Jonassen, 1989). Recently, hypertext is being used more as a means for structuring knowledge-construction environments than as media for disseminating information. For example, Dunlap and Jonassen (1992) developed a hypertext shell to facilitate argumentation of issues in an advanced seminar. The hypertext was inspired by the IBIS hypertext-based, collaborative problem-solving environment (Conklin and Begeman, 1987), which provides an argument structure including issue, position, and argument nodes that can be added or edited remotely through a networked computer system (see Figure 7.5). The hypertext supported a CMC seminar on comparative instructional design models, though a similarly structured conference could be run on any topic.

Each model included premises, theory base, applications, processes, and assumptions. Individuals in the class attached *issue* node to each of these content nodes. To each issue node, individuals could add personal *position* nodes, which might represent personal opinions, research perspectives, or positions presented by someone else in the literature. To each of these position nodes, individuals could link *argument* nodes, which would provide reasons for or against the position represented in the position node. The purpose of this collaborative hypertext was to model and scaffold the argumentation process in the conference. Collaboratively, students generated questions about the models, provided suggestions for improving or applying the models, and received feedback and comments from peers.

The results of imposing this type of formal argument structure onto the collaborative construction of a class text include more elaborate class discussions and better-argued class papers. Collaborative hypertexts are among the best methods for communicating the complexities, multiple

**Figure 7.5**
Argument model for hypertext

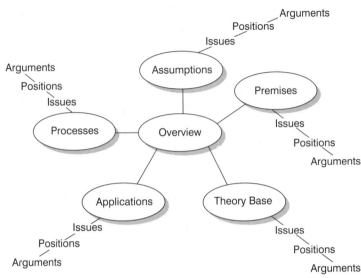

perspectives, and interconnectedness of knowledge in a content domain. They are not constrained by limitations on the size of the text fields in other Mindtools, such as semantic nets and databases. And the abilities to search text fields for specific words or phrases and to navigate through them affords them greater power and economy than other Mindtools.

# How to Use Computer-Mediated Communication in the Classroom

## Information Retrieval

Information retrieval from large numbers of complex, remote databases often presents problems for learners and teachers alike. Learners have difficulty selecting appropriate databases and forming queries in those databases. Teachers have difficulty managing large numbers of students in a telecommunications system using databases (Collis, 1992). After becoming familiar with the technology, the teacher must identify and locate all of the relevant databases that may support learning. This is no small task. The success of information retrieval through any means is always dependent on the availability of useful, relevant information. Teague, Teague, and Marchionini (1986) provide teachers with a number of suggestions for facilitating this process:

1. Be sure that you are comfortable with all aspects of the telecommunications system before engaging students in its use. If you are not, try to find the brighter, more computer-literate students to lead the way.
2. Conduct blackboard and paper simulations of the process before going online (or use simulation software).
3. Be sure that an uninterrupted phone line is available.
4. Demonstrate the actual searching process to students. Teach them information-seeking skills.
5. Organize students in pairs or small groups so they can assist each other while searching databases.
6. Remain present during searching to provide assistance.

## Computer Conferences

The facilitator or moderator of a computer conference plays a very important role in ensuring the meaningfulness of an electronic discussion, just as a teacher manages a classroom discussion. It is important that participants maintain a view of the structure of a discussion—that is, what are the issues and the positions on those issues—while avoiding definitive statements that may impede discussion. Teachers as conference moderators need to be coaches, not sources of knowledge. Several themes may emerge in a conference, with different aspects of the themes being discussed by different individuals. Several activities are important (Romiszowski & de Haas, 1989; Romiszowski & Jost, 1989):

1. Assure students that they can really communicate with the system. Motivating learners and overcoming phobias and anxieties may be the most important process. Welcome each new user to the conference.
2. Ensure that learners have access to the computer network through directly connected computers or computers with modems so they can log on frequently.
3. Provide active leadership. Start by playing host, welcoming participants to the conference and establishing a nonthreatening climate.
4. Periodically summarize the discussion and make sure that it does not drift off the theme or become too fragmented. Ask participants for clarification of their ideas, and resolve disputes or differences in interpretation.
5. Periodically prompt nonparticipants to contribute ideas or reactions to the conference and reinforce at least the initial contribu-

tions. You may want to send students private mail that provides feedback or other interpretations. Periodically throw out engaging questions or issues that can clarify ideas or become a new focus for discussion.

Eastmond and Ziegahn (1994) have developed a design model to support CMC courses. To them, it is important to apprise learners of the role of CMC in the course activities and requirements. In addition to staffing up such a course, including designer/developer, system administrator, and moderator/instructor, they recommend apprising learners in the syllabus about their

- required participation—in lieu of attendance
- CMC learning strategies—becoming interactive, dealing with multiple threads and perspectives
- effective online communications—recording notes in appropriate threads, keeping track of threads, and conveying messages in proper tone and length
- conference structure—including course area, personal area, and course map
- computer use, training, and support

Eastmond and Ziegahn go on to recommend a number of CMC instructional activities, such as

- instructor-led discussions to introduce the group, the topic, and themes
- brainstorming lists of ideas related to the topic
- a guest lecturer to lead discussion on a special topic
- short small-group discussions moderated by students
- individual presentations of term projects
- off-line activities, preferably consisting of real-world experiences
- face-to-face sessions with members of the group
- textbooks and media to support topics under discussion

We are only beginning to learn how to maximize the effectiveness of CMC learning experiences. In the next few years, these processes should become well researched and reliable.

## Fostering Collaboration with Computer-Mediated Communication

CMC is a naturally collaborative technology. It fosters collaborative meaning-making by providing multiple perspectives on any problem or idea.

The result of most CMC activities is the creation of large knowledge bases of perspectives. Making sense out of those perspectives may require the participation of the entire group.

**1. *Form the teams.*** CMC affords more flexibility in forming the groups than any other Mindtool. E-mail combines people based on need, common interest, and friendship. Bulletin boards or news groups attract members according to interest. Computer conferences may benefit from people with different backgrounds or perspectives. You may want to intentionally combine people with opposing points of view. The communication that results from different combinations of learners will vary according to the kinds of groups that are formed.

**2. *Clarify the group goal.*** This can be done from within the news group, conference, or bulletin board, although these types of CMC are usually formed to support a particular goal or purpose. That is, the purpose is defined by participation in the group. It may be necessary, at least initially, to structure the communication by suggesting topics or issues to be discussed. Inserting a controversial issue (e.g., "Abortions should be available on demand" or "The school year should be extended by 20 days") usually ignites discussion. The course itself should afford a meaningful context for the discussion, so avoid selecting a topic just to engage a discussion. For example, the topic "Political correctness poses one of the greatest threats to a democracy" will work in classes like sociology or political science but would probably be distracting and meaningless in biology or industrial arts.

**3. *Negotiate tasks and subtasks to be completed.*** Let the students know what role they are expected to play in the conversation. Are they to respond from their own perspective in order to be true to themselves and push the limits of their own knowledge, or should they play a role in the conversation? If the latter, are they supposed to take a conservative view or a liberal view? Many computer conferences are oriented by an instructional game or simulation that assigns roles. For example, Goodman (1992) describes a CMC simulation of the Arab-Israeli conflict in which students assume the role of negotiators or advisors for each country. You may also want to include requirements for a certain level of participation, especially with the more diffident members of the group.

**4. *Monitor individual and group performance.*** Most conference services provide a record of student logins or messages or correspondence left, so you have a comprehensive record of what and how much each individual has contributed. A personal message to those whose participation is low may be all that is needed. It will be interesting to see which students assume leadership roles in the discussions.

**5.** *Reconcile differences in interpretations or approaches to the goal.* The major purpose of CMC is to provide a forum for negotiating differences of opinion or interpretation regarding the content or task being learned. CMC is a less constrained mechanism for that negotiation. As a teacher, you simply need to ensure that participants do not get carried away, that the discussion remain intellectual and not acrimonious.

# Advantages of Computer-Mediated Communication as a Mindtool

- The primary goal of education, according to many theorists, is to socialize youth. Typically that process occurs only at a local level. Networked computers, however, are an even greater agent for the propagation and dissemination of social skills on a local, regional, national, and even international level (Margolies, 1991). In fact, those who perceive e-mail as important for their social life use it more.

- Hiltz (1986) found that CMC classroom interchanges produced more interaction and involved more exchanges between students than did face-to-face interchanges. This is probably because individuals have the ability to remain anonymous, so they reduce personal fears while enhancing academic efficacy (note that not all CMC applications afford anonymity). Hiltz also found that undergraduates felt they had better access to the instructor and that CMC courses were more interesting than traditional courses.

- CMC will likely enhance the effectiveness of collaborative efforts among learners, because it improves access to other group participants, eliminates social distinctions and barriers between those participants, contributes to a sense of informality, and fosters a stronger group identity (Pfaffenberger, 1986).

- CMC provides opportunities for professional growth through computer conferences and information access without having to travel to conferences. Intimate electronic dialogues can also be established and maintained.

- Berge and Collins (1993) discuss the independence of time afforded by CMC. Unlike face-to-face meetings, computer conferences are open and available 24 hours a day, 7 days a week. Time can also be allocated to reflecting on a message before responding, in order to develop one's arguments or position. Students may do their work when it is convenient or when they are most alert. In establishing CMC in your educational setting, it is essential to facilitate such convenient access.

- Students may argue and disagree without involving excessive conflict (Phillips & Santoro, 1989). This is especially helpful for introverted, shy, and reflective people.

- CMC facilitates collaborative learning. When working in groups through CMC, students accomplished more task objectives and participated more uniformly (Scott, 1993). Planning documents collaboratively enhances the writing of apprehensive and nonapprehensive writers (Mabrito, 1992). CMC is an effective means for teaching collaborative problem solving and other tasks.

- In comparison to a traditional classroom, where the teacher contributes up to 80% of the verbal exchange, online computer conferencing shows instructor contributions of only 10 to 15% of the message volume (Harasim, 1987; Winkelmans, 1988). Allowing learners to generate questions, summarize content, clarify points, and predict upcoming events is applicable to other educational tasks. When performed online, these types of activities can facilitate the discussion of various structural relationships within the subject matter.

# Limitations of Computer-Mediated Communication as a Mindtool

- Lefevre (1977) warned of the elitism and coercion that may result from controlling access to information through the networks. Since information is often equated with power, access to different computerized sources of information could initiate a class-oriented information society in which the information-rich become richer relative to the information-starved.

- The technical complexities of CMC and the resulting difficulties in connecting to the system and learning how to use new software are often very frustrating and anxiety-inducing. There can be high frontloading of technical skills in order to become a user. Networking issues are complex, and the jargon is inscrutable to the novice. Seek software that optimally combines user-friendliness and resources. And be patient and keep asking questions.

- Users must be somewhat skilled as communicators; that is, they need facility with the language. Unfortunately, not all learners have this facility.

- The primary mode of input is text, which means that users must be moderately skilled as typists. That is problematic for many, particularly since the text editors for many CMC clients and applications are comparatively primitive.

- The user interfaces in much of the software are unfriendly and difficult to use. The state of the art in software design is improving rapidly, however, so this should become less of a problem in the near future.

- The most common form of CMC is asynchronous, that is, when users are not online at the same time. This results in communication delays between sending messages and receiving replies. These delays vary with the state of the network (usage) and the frequency with which users check their e-mail. Conferencing or direct communication between individuals on different continents several time zones apart can appear to be delayed for hours or even days. The delays may reduce the impact of certain messages or feedback.

- Participation within groups of users varies. While full participation in electronic communication is as desirable as full participation in classroom discussions, technophobia or communications anxieties can prevent a number of individuals from participating fully in electronic communications. People can become "lurkers" when they post an idea and nobody responds or even acknowledges it, or when they are harshly or rudely treated.

- In group decision-making situations, computer-mediated decision making produced more polarized decisions than did face-to-face situations (Lea & Spears, 1991). Decision making takes longer and may result in the use of stronger, more inflammatory, and more personalized expressions (Siegel, Dubrovsky, Kiesler, & McGuire, 1986). Moreover, anonymity may increase rather than diffuse anxiety.

- CMC often amplifies social insecurities. These communication anxieties are especially common when communications are not acknowledged (Feenburg, 1987).

- The absence of social context cues can make discussion somewhat more difficult. Nonverbal communication is not available to help interpret the message.

- Hardware and communications lines and equipment are not 100% reliable, which may cause a loss of work or delays in communications. Such problems tend to frustrate users and may reduce participation.

## *Conclusion*

CMC is a different kind of Mindtool than the others described in this book. It is not a software tool that produces personal representations of knowledge. Rather, it is a medium for communicating with others to access information that has been contributed by others, to send personal messages to others, and to discuss and debate ideas with others. It is in this latter mode that CMC is most like a Mindtool. Meaning-making is largely a process of social negotiation. CMC affords learners the opportunity to negotiate meaning with individuals through e-mail or with groups of individuals through computer conferences. That negotiation process is supported by a vast array of information that can be retrieved from the network. This combination makes CMC the fastest growing and potentially the most powerful of all Mindtools.

## References

Aiken, M. W. (1992). Using a group decision support system as an instructional aid: An exploratory study. *International Journal of Instructional Media, 19*(4), 321–328.

Berge, Z. L., & Collins, M. (1993). Computer conferencing and online education. *Electronic Journal on Virtual Culture* [Online]. Available FTP: byrd.mu.wvnet.edu.

Bull, G., Harris, J., & Drucker, D. (1992). Building an electronic culture: The Academic Village at Virginia. In M. D. Waggoner (Ed.), *Empowering networks: Computer conferencing in education.* Englewood Cliffs, NJ: Educational Technology Publications.

Cohen, M., & Reil, M. (1989). The effect of distant audiences on student writing. *American Educational Research Journal, 26,* 143–159.

Collis, B. (1992). Supporting educational uses of telecommunications in the secondary school. Part II: Strategies for improved implementation. *International Journal of Instructional Media, 19*(2), 97–109.

Conklin, J., & Begeman, M. (1987). IBIS: A hypertext tool for team design deliberation. In *Proceedings of Hypertext '87.* Chapel Hill, NC: University of North Carolina, Computer Science Department.

Dunlap, J., & Jonassen, D. H. (1992, November). *Collaborative knowledge construction in an argument-based hypertext.* Paper presented at the annual meeting of the Association for the Development of Computer-Based Instructional Systems, Norfolk, VA.

Eastmond, D., & Ziegahn, L. (1994). Instructional design for the online classroom. In Z. L. Berge & M. Collins (Eds.), *Computer-mediated communication and the online classroom in distance education.* Cresskill, NJ: Hampton Press.

Feenburg, A. (1987). Computer conferencing and the humanities. *Instructional Science, 16,* 169–186.

Goodman, F. L. (1992). Instructional gaming through computer conferencing. In M. D. Waggoner (Ed.), *Empowering networks: Computer conferencing in education.* Englewood Cliffs, NJ: Educational Technology Publications.

Harasim, L. (1987). *Computer-mediated cooperation in education: Group learning networks.* Paper presented at the meeting of the Second Guelph Symposium on Computer Conferencing, University of Guelph, Ontario.

Harasim, L. M. (1990). Online education: An environment for collaboration and intellectual amplification. In L. M. Harasim (Ed.), *Online education: Perspectives on a new environment.* New York: Praeger.

Hiltz, S. R. (1986). The virtual classroom: Using computer-mediated communication for university teaching. *Journal of Communication, 36*(2), 95–104.

Howse, W. J. (1992, Spring). The Internet: Discoveries of a distance educator. *EDU Magazine,* p. 52.

Hudspeth, D. (1990). The electronic bulletin board: Appropriate technology. *Educational Technology, 30*(7), 40–43.

Jonassen, D. H. (1989). *Hypertext/hypermedia.* Englewood Cliffs, NJ: Educational Technology Publications.

Lea, M., & Spears, R. (1991). Computer-mediated communication, de-individuation and group decision making. *International Journal of Man-Machine Studies, 34,* 283–301.

Lefevre, B. (1977). The impact of electronic communication on town and regional planning. *Impact of Science on Society, 27*(2), 227–238.

Levin, J., Haesun, K., & Reil, M. (1990). Analyzing instructional interactions on electronic mail networks. In L. Harasim (Ed.), *Online education: Perspectives on a new environment.* New York: Praeger.

Mabrito, M. (1992). Computer-mediated communication and high apprehensive writers: Rethinking the collaborative process. *Bulletin of the Association for Business Communication, 55*(4), 26–29.

Margolies, R. (1991, January). The computer as social skills agent. *THE Journal,* pp. 70-71.

Merseth, K. K., Beals, D. E., & Cutler, A. B. (1992). *The beginning teacher computer network: Supporting new teachers electronically: An implementation guide for interested educators.* Cambridge, MA: Harvard University.

Palinscar, A. S., & Brown, A. L. (1984). Reciprocal teaching of comprehension fostering and monitoring activities. *Cognition and Instruction, 1*(2), 117–175.

Paulsen, M. F. (1994). An overview of CMC and the online classroom in distance education. In Z. L. Berge & M. Collins (Eds.), *Computer-mediated communication and the online classroom in distance education.* Cresskill, NJ: Hampton Press.

Pfaffenberger, B. (1986). Research networks, scientific communication, and the personal computer. *IEEE Transactions on Professional Communication, 29* (1), 30–33.

Phillips, G. M., & Santoro, G. M. (1989). Teaching group discussion via computer-mediated communication. *Communication Education, 38,* 151–161.

Reil, M. (1990). Cooperative learning across classrooms in electronic learning circles. *Instructional Science, 19,* 445–466.

Reil, M. (1993, April). *The writing connection: Global learning circles.* Paper presented at the annual meeting of the American Educational Research Association, Atlanta, GA.

Romiszowski, A. J., & de Haas, J. A. (1989). Computer-mediated communication for instruction: Using e-mail as a seminar. *Educational Technology, 29*(10), 7–14.

Romiszowski, A. J., & Jost, K. (1989, August). *Computer conferencing and the distant learner: Problems of structure and control.* Paper presented at the Conference on Distance Education, University of Wisconsin, Madison, WI.

Scott, D. M. (1993, January). *Teaching collaborative problem solving using computer-mediated communications.* Paper presented at the annual meeting of the Association for Educational Communications and Technology, New Orleans, LA.

Siegel, J., Dubrovsky, V., Kiesler, S., & McGuire, T. W. (1986). Group processes in computer-mediated communication. *Organizational Behavior and Human Decision Processes, 37,* 157–187.

Simón, C. (1992). Telematic support for in-service teacher training. In A. R. Kaye (Ed.), *Collaborative learning through computer conferencing.* Berlin: Springer-Verlag.

Teague, M., Teague, J., & Marchionini, G. (1986). The high tech road to research. *The Computing Teacher, 14*(3), 21–24.

Wells, R. (1992). *Computer-mediated communication for distance education: An international review of design, teaching, and institutional issues* (Research Monograph No. 6). University Park, PA: American Center for the Study of Distance Education, Pennsylvania State University.

Winklemans, T. (1988). *Educational computer conferencing: An application of analysis methodologies to a structured small group activity.* Unpublished master's thesis, University of Toronto, Toronto, Canada.

# 8

# Multimedia and Hypermedia:
## *Creativity Through Construction*

## What Are Multimedia and Hypermedia?

### Multimedia

Multimedia involves the integration of more than one medium into a form of communication. Multimedia such as slide/tape presentations, interactive video, and video productions have been available for a long time. Most commonly, though, this term now refers to the integration of media such as text, sound, graphics, animation, video, imaging, and spatial modeling into a computer system (von Wodtke, 1993). The concept has gained popularity recently with the advent of high-resolution monitors, sound and video compression cards, and increased RAM and processing speed for personal computers. The multimedia desktop computer (see Figure 8.2) is now able to capture sound and video, manipulate those sounds and images to achieve special effects, synthesize and produce sound and video, generate all sorts of graphics, including animation, and integrate them all into a single multimedia presentation. With a little experience, individuals can become their own artists, publishers, or video producers.

Multimedia presentations are more attention-getting and attention-holding because they are usually multimodal, that is, they stimulate more than one sense at a time. Many educators believe this is essential when working with today's video generation. There is little current research on learning effects from multimedia. Multiple-channel research from the past implies that when the channels provide complementary information, learning may increase. When the information in different channels is redundant, no improvement occurs. And when the information in different channels is

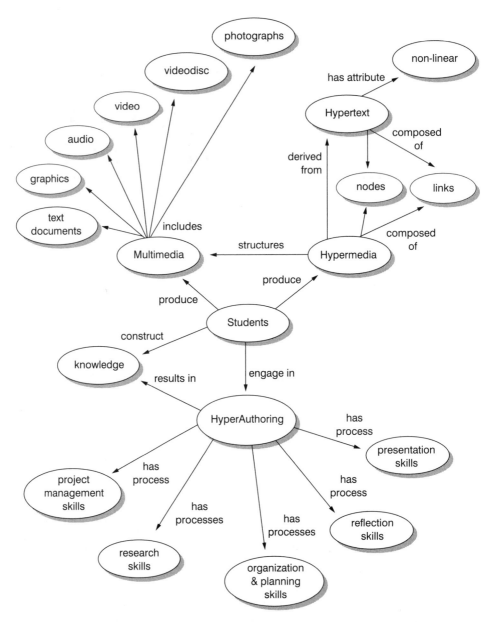

**Figure 8.1**
Multimedia and hypermedia as Mindtools

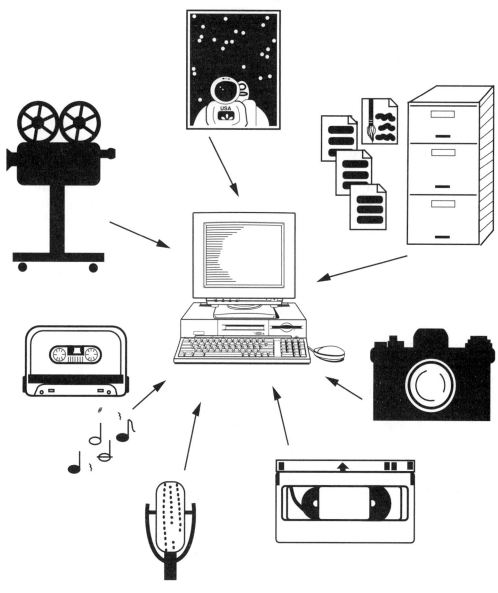

**Figure 8.2**
Multimedia in a box

inconsistent or distracting, learning decreases are likely to occur. These findings need to be verified with current multimedia products.

# Hypertext

Hypertext is based on the term *hyper,* meaning above, beyond, super, excessive—more than normal. Hypertext is beyond normal text. Normal text is linear, and is constructed to be read from beginning to end. The author uses a structure and a sequence to influence the reader's understanding of the topic. Hypertext refers to a nonsequential, nonlinear method for organizing and displaying text (Jonassen, 1989) that was designed to enable readers to access information from a text in ways that are most meaningful to them (Nelson, 1981). Hypertext is supertext because the reader has much greater control of what is read and the sequence in which it is read. It is based on the assumption that the organization the reader imposes on a text is more personally meaningful than that imposed by the author.

The most pervasive characteristic of hypertext is the *node,* which consists of chunks or fragments of text. The most common metaphor for a node is a card, so a node contains text on a card. Nodes are the basic unit of information storage in a hypertext. While reading a hypertext, you can access any node (card) in the hypertext, depending on what you are interested in reading. Nodes may also consist of larger bodies of text. Imagine a large hypertext on the history of the United States. Each node might consist of different documents or even books. While researching a particular theme, you could access whatever documents you thought were relevant. In many hypertext systems, the user can add to or change the information in a node or create his or her own nodes of information, so the hypertext can be a dynamic, growing knowledge base, representing new and different points of view.

The organization of a hypertext, that is, the interrelationships among the nodes, is defined by the *links* that connect them. Links in hypertext systems typically describe associations between the nodes that they connect. That is, while reading one node, you have links (usually identified as hot buttons or hot spots) that will take you to another node of information. At any node, you may have access to hundreds of other nodes, or only one or two. Links may consist of highlighted words, in which case you point at and click on the word to learn more about it. Having arrived at the new node describing that term, you may want to return to the node from which you came or go on to another node (Figure 8.3). The node structure and the link structure form a network of ideas in the knowledge base, the interrelated and interconnected group or system of ideas. These structures may be very rich.

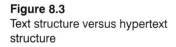

**Figure 8.3**
Text structure versus hypertext structure

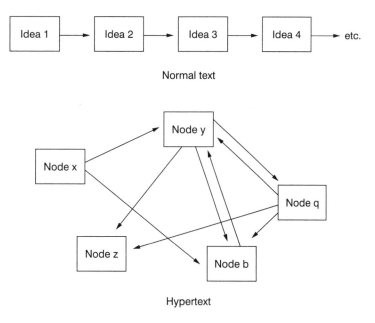

Hypertext systems permit users to determine the sequence in which to access information (browsing), to add to the information to make it more personally meaningful, or to build and structure their own knowledge base. Like most information systems, interaction is the most important attribute. Hypertext information systems afford interactivity by permitting more dynamic user control of the information in the knowledge base than do most other systems.

The organization or architecture of hypertexts is open. The same set of nodes can be organized in many different ways to reflect many different conceptual orientations or perspectives. The hypertext author may create a very tight structure, restricting access to information in ways that make it most easily understood, or the structure may be completely open, with immediate access to any node in the knowledge base. Large hypertext knowledge bases, such as the knowledge base on British literature developed by the Intermedia project, may consist of 5,000 or more nodes. Learners can access any of those nodes at any time or follow theme-oriented links to related information.

Hypertexts possess some or all of the following characteristics (Jonassen, 1989):

- nodes or chunks of information of varying sizes
- associative links between the nodes that enable the user to travel from one node to another
- a network of ideas formed by the link structure

- an organizational structure that describes the network of ideas (may reflect different models or conceptual structures)
- the ability to represent explicitly the structure of information in the structure of the hypertext
- dynamic control of information by the user; that is, a high level of inter-activity with the user, so the user decides where to go in the hypertext
- multi-user access to the information—many hypertexts are available to many users simultaneously

Although hypertext affords users many options, some significant problems have plagued hypertext users. The most commonly acknowledged problem in using hypertext is navigation. Hypertext documents often contain thousands of nodes, each with multiple links to other nodes, and it is easy for users to get lost in that morass of information. Users can easily become disoriented, losing track of the route they took or becoming unable to find their way out of the hypertext or to another topic of interest.

A related problem is how and when users access information in a hypertext. Although most hypertexts provide an array of options to the user, they typically do not provide suggestions for where the user should begin or proceed after beginning. This lack of direction can result in disorientation in the user.

Perhaps the greatest problem related to using hypertext to facilitate learning is how learners will integrate the information they acquire in the hypertext into their own knowledge structures (Jonassen, 1989). Once information has been acquired from a hypertext, it needs to reorganized by the learner to create new knowledge structures. It also must be applied and refined. Learners must synthesize new knowledge structures for all of the information contained in the hypertext. How will this be facilitated?

A solution to these problems is to think of hypertext not as a source of knowledge to learn *from,* but rather as a Mindtool to construct and learn *with* (see Chapter 1 for a discussion of this distinction). Learners may create their own hypertexts that reflect their own perspectives or understanding of ideas, or they may collaborate with other learners to develop a classroom hypertext knowledge base. The hypothesis of this book is that students learn more by constructing instructional materials than by studying them. Ultimately, we could think about eliminating textbooks in the classroom and enabling learners to research ideas and develop their own interpretations in a hypertext. A quick caveat, though. It is important to realize that novice hypertext and multimedia producers using the tools described in this chapter will not be able to begin producing sophisticated programs immediately. However, like all Mindtools, it is the process of engaging in knowledge representation that is of most value, not the product.

## Hypermedia

Hypermedia is simply the marriage of multimedia and hypertext. Hypermedia nodes may consist of different media forms. A node may be text, but it also may be a graphic image, a sound bite, an animation sequence, or a video clip. So rather than pointing to a hot button to retrieve a textual description of the Battle of Gettysburg, the learner may retrieve video clips from the movie, an animated sequence of the development of the battle, actual pictures taken at Gettysburg, or all of the above. Hypermedia makes information more interesting and richer (i.e., anchored to rich, sensory data).

# Examples of and Tools for Multimedia and Hypermedia Construction

## Designing an Information Kiosk for the Zoo

Beichner (1994) reports on a project in which highly motivated junior high school students worked cooperatively to seek out content materials from a wide variety of resources in order to create a touch-sensitive kiosk to be installed in the local zoo. Using HyperCard and an interface board to permit video display directly on the computer screen, students created a simple information hypermedia program for the kiosk. They worked with an on-screen audio recorder, a video tool to operate the videodisc player (see Figure 8.4), color painting and text tools, and a data-linking tool for connecting pieces of information. They used these tools to make hot spots on the kiosk screen. By touching these areas, zoo visitors could see and hear animals, look for more information, or even print out an information sheet, complete with a map of the zoo and student-generated questions and comments about the animal on the screen.

The multimedia production tools enabled students to grab a "snapshot," a video sequence, or an audio sequence from the videodisc and place it onto the screen being created; create text or colorful drawings; or capture images from a scanner or electronic camera. Anything placed on the information screen could be moved, resized, and deleted through the use of a single set of keystrokes.

To prepare the multimedia kiosk, students began by talking to zoo visitors and staff. Students became interested in the people who would be viewing their multimedia information screens. They quickly gained independence, and within a few weeks they demonstrated a strong desire to work on their own. Once they had mastered the software, roles changed rapidly. Students not only picked out what information and layout designs they would use, they also began showing other students and even their teachers how to best use the equipment and software. They began skipping study halls and lunch periods in order to work on their screens. Often the computer coordinator would arrive in the morning to find students who had come in early and were waiting for her to open the door.

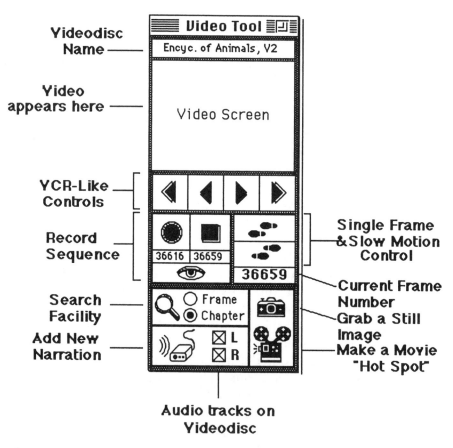

**Figure 8.4**
Multimedia editing tools

The reason for this enthusiasm was that students saw that the work they were doing had importance—it was a real-world problem. It was worthwhile for them to learn new material and uncover additional resources. By establishing an environment where creative thinking about the content material is combined with real-world assignments, students will learn content, enjoy the learning process, and recognize that they have created something worthwhile that serves their community.

## Learners as Multimedia Authors Using Mediatext

Participants in the Highly Interactive Computing Environments (Hi-CE) Group at the University of Michigan believe that, rather than using media to deliver instruction to learners, learners should use the media to generate their own instruction and, in so doing, learn more about the content. They believe that learners should be constructionists (see Chapter 1), creating multimedia documents containing text, graphics, sound, animation, and links to external technology devices such as videodisc players. When learners actively construct knowledge through multimedia, they acquire cognitive, metacognitive, and motivational advantages over those who merely attempt to absorb knowledge.

Hi-CE has developed a multimedia composition tool called Mediatext (Hays et al., 1993). Mediatext is to various media as word processors are to text (Hays et al., 1993). That is, a word processor is a tool for creating or generating text; Mediatext is a tool for creating and generating multimedia. It consists of the following components:

- a word processor for generating text (left-hand side of the window in Figure 8.5)
- MediaLinks, the icons in the right side of the screen in Figure 8.5 that link other media (videodisc, Quicktime movies, graphics, sound, etc.) to the document
- Media Margin, the space on the right side of the screen that contains the MediaLinks

Mediatext also has many media tools, including videodisc and compact disc tools, graphics and sound tools, animation tools, and a link tool that enables Mediatext documents to be linked to other documents, applications, or Mediatext documents.

The Hi-CE group has researched high school students creating Mediatext stories (Figure 8.5 illustrates an excerpt from a story written by my junior high school daughter), biographies, or instructional aids, as well as multimedia essays. Students have learned to use techniques such as mentioning, directives, titling, and juxtaposition to integrate their documents. They have found that as students' experiences with Mediatext increase, their documents become more integrated multimedia rather than consisting merely of annotated text. Students have been very enthusiastic about being constructionists, believing that they are learning more because they understand the ideas better.

---

It was a cold day at Loveland valley resort. The wind whipped across the valley like a roller coaster. The sky was a deep, crystal-clear blue. The snow sparkled like recently polished diamonds. The air was clean and fresh as it blew across the faces of the excited skiers. The metal on the chairs was as cold as the inside of a freezer as they grabbed it to steady their uphill flight. However, the cold did not dampen the spirits of the people. They were all eager to get on the slopes again.

About ten miles down the road, two skiers were driving in. Their names were Cody Brown and Todd Barber. They were both skilled skiers and had been skiing a fairly long time. As Cody and Todd got closer to the mountain, they noticed that it was a busy day, but there was one slope that no one was occupying. This was Psychopathics Gulch, a name which accurately described the type of run it was. As long as Cody and Todd had been skiing, they had never seen anyone on it. It was a dangerous run; people were often cautioned about it.

When Cody and Todd arrived they quickly bought tickets, then they hit the slopes. They were having a great day until around their tenth run. They were taking the lift to Parson's Bowl, which goes right above Psychopathic Gulch. The warm Colorado sun was soaking into their skin. The lift ride was about half way over when Cody decided to hang his poles on the side of the lift. As he was doing this, his pole suddenly

Clear Day on Slopes

Trail Map

Cody & Todd

Lift Ride

**Figure 8.5**
Mediatext story screen

## HyperAuthors

Lehrer (1993) reports the development and use of a tool, HyperAuthor, to engage eighth graders in designing history lessons. Knowledge, he believes, evolves from a process of design. It is not something to be transmitted from teacher to student, so students should design their own hypermedia compositions (what Lehrer calls a "HyperComposition"). The process requires learners to transform information into dimensional representations (see Chapter 5), determine what is and is not important, segment information into nodes, link the information segments by semantic relationships, and decide how to represent ideas. This is a highly motivating process because authorship results in ownership of the ideas in the presentation.

Lehrer developed HyperAuthor to facilitate these intellectual activities. Developed in SuperCard, HyperAuthor is a multimedia authoring environment that requires no programming skills. It features a Linkmaker for connecting nodes (cards), which requires the composer to identify the nature of the semantic relationship between the nodes being linked. HyperAuthor creates a user's guide and a point-of-view map to help users navigate through the knowledge base.

Students in the research group were high- and low-ability eighth graders developing hypermedia programs on the Civil War. They conducted library research and found pictures and video clips to exemplify many of the points they wanted to make. Students enjoyed assuming control of their learning and began to see history more as a process of interpretation than of memorization. In the process, they acquired knowledge "that was richer, better connected, and more applicable to subsequent learning and events" (Lehrer, 1993, p. 221). Research conducted by Carver, Lehrer, Connell, and Erickson (1992) showed that students worked harder, were more interested and involved, and collaborated and planned more.

Lehrer, Erickson, and Connell (in press) conducted another study on ninth-grade students developing hypermedia on World War I, lifestyles between 1870 and 1920, immigration, and imperialism. They found similar results: on-task behavior increased over time, and students perceived the benefits of the planning and transforming stages of development, such as taking notes, finding information, coordinating with other team members, writing interpretations, and designing the presentation. Figure 8.6 presents a montage of graphics that the learners created to illustrate ideas in their presentations, including charts to show the probability of

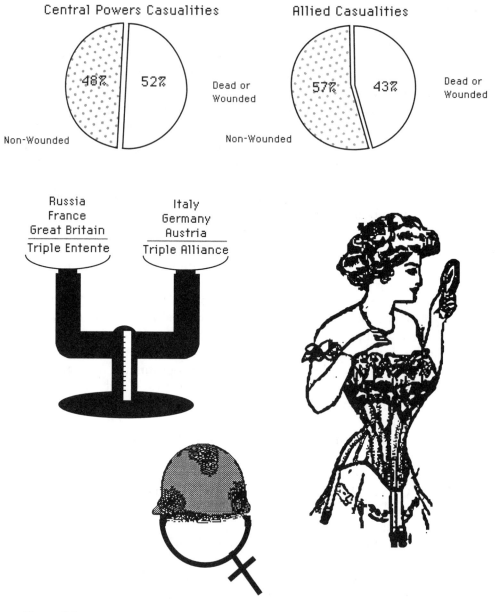

**Figure 8.6**
Icons used to illustrate ideas in HyperAuthor presentations

soldiers returning home safely, the balance of power among the competing countries, corsets illustrating contemporary versus past lifestyles of
women, and a helmet to illustrate the fight for women's rights. The results
of research on hypermedia design are clear. When learners become
designers, they engage readily and willingly in higher-order thinking.
What teacher would not favor these results?

# ACCESS Project

The ACCESS Project (American Culture in Context: Enrichment for Secondary Schools) focuses on subject matter commonly taught in high
school, such as U.S. history, American literature, and American Studies.
The project began in 1988 with teachers assembling a collection of textual, pictorial, audio, and video materials to supplement their courses.
Hypermedia was chosen because of its ability to represent diverse concepts and examples and use them to support abstract generalizations in a
complex web of conceptual relationships that characterize this type of
thinking. Its interactive capabilities were intended to help students make
such mental conceptual linkages for themselves. Initially, students used
and benefited from the materials for information retrieval (Spoehr, in
press; Spoehr, 1992; Spoehr & Shapiro, 1991). Those who made more
extensive use of the system's conceptual structure benefited more than the
ones who used the system like a linear, electronic book.

Spoehr and her colleagues found that hypermedia's effectiveness
depends on the extent to which students can internalize the important
conceptual structures in a subject matter as they browse. It thus became
clear that the more students grappled with conceptual organization, the
more likely it would be that hypermedia would benefit them. Students not
only used the teacher-created hypermedia materials but also created their
own hypermedia projects. Initial findings show that the process of building conceptual links for some subset of new material added to the system
by a student enhances the benefits of using hypermedia.

In order to make it easy for students to create hypermedia projects, the
ACCESS user interface includes a mouse-driven authoring tool palette,
which permits a student/author to rapidly carry out basic authoring activities. Many of the authoring "chores" (e.g., creating print buttons in
appropriate places) are done automatically by the authoring system. Students generally do several small authoring projects of increasing size and
complexity early in the school year in order to become familiar with the
authoring process. Then they generally take on one or more major
research projects, the results of which are presented in hypermedia form.

Students work individually or in pairs, and each member of a pair is obligated to make identifiable contributions to both the content and the technical aspects of the final hypermedia project. An important requirement of the project has been not only information collected by the students, but also some synthesis and analysis of it in an original essay.

One of the most important characteristics of any hypermedia product is its overall organization and structure. A few students (5–10%) typically underutilize the power of hypermedia and use a linear format (i.e., one overview card followed by a linear series of screens). The more interesting organizational types employed by students are the "star" and "tree" varieties. Nearly half of the student projects are stars, in which the entry point is an overview containing buttons to two or more subtopics, each of which appears as a linear sequence. A tree is similar to a star, except that one or more of the main branches off the initial overview are subdivided into further subtopics, which are then organized as linear sequences. In some cases the subtopics are further divided into sub-subtopics. Trees generally show a more sophisticated understanding of the topic than stars, and about a fourth of the student projects fall into the tree category. Figure 8.7 shows a relatively sophisticated tree representation for a student project on John Donne, with a sample screen from that project. In this example the student uses both sound (the student/author is heard reading Donne's poetry) and the interactive capability of hypermedia (the boldface text appears only when the user clicks on the light bulb button).

Hypermedia authors appeared to benefit from their computer-based experiences in many ways, all of which fall roughly into the category of superior knowledge representation and thinking skills. Project data (Spoehr, 1993) show that students who build and use hypermedia apparently develop a proficiency to organize knowledge about a subject in a more expert-like fashion; they represent multiple linkages between related ideas and organize clusters of concepts into meaningful clusters. Superior knowledge representations then support more complex arguments in written essays. And most importantly, the conceptual organization skills acquired through building hypermedia are robust enough to generalize to material students acquire from many other sources.

# Multimedia and Hypermedia Construction as Mindtools

Multimedia and hypermedia construction is predicated on the idea of "knowledge as design," which refocuses the educational process away

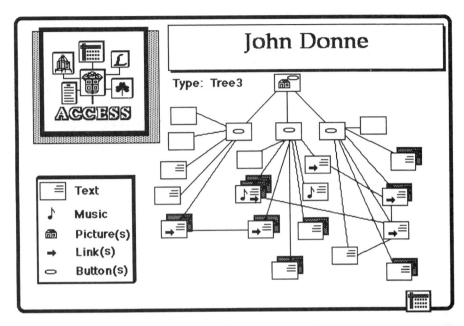

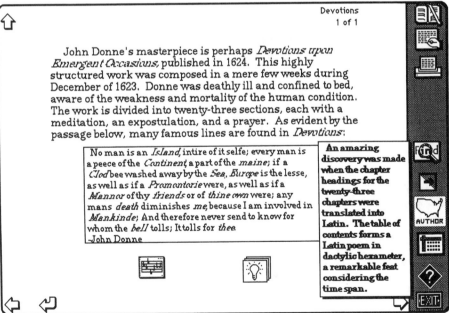

**Figure 8.7**
Sample student project from ACCESS Project

from one of knowledge as information and the teacher as transmitter of that knowledge (Perkins, 1986) to one of teachers and students as collaborators in the knowledge construction process. One way to promote this design process is to place learners in the role of instructional software designers (Harel & Papert, 1990). Rather than reading textbooks and solving textbook problems, students must define and constantly refine the nature of the problem and reconstruct their knowledge to fit that problem (Lehrer, 1993). Designing multimedia presentations is a complex process that engages many skills in learners. Carver et al. (1992) listed some of the major thinking skills that learners need to use as designers:

1. Project management skills
   - creating a timeline for the completion of the project
   - allocating resources and time to various segments of the project
   - assigning roles to team members
2. Research skills
   - determining the nature of the problem and how the research should be organized
   - posing thoughtful questions about the structure
   - searching for information using textual, electronic, and pictorial sources of information
   - developing new information with surveys, interviews, questionnaires, and other sources
   - analyzing and interpreting all of the information collected to find and interpret patterns
3. Organization and representation skills
   - deciding how to segment and sequence information to make it understandable
   - deciding how information will be represented (text, pictures, video)
   - deciding how the information will be organized (hierarchy, sequence) and linked
4. Presentation skills
   - mapping the design onto the presentation, implementing the ideas in multimedia
   - attracting and maintaining the interest of the audience
5. Reflection skills
   - evaluating the program and the process used to create it
   - revising the design of the program using feedback

## Evaluation of Multimedia and Hypermedia Construction as a Mindtool

**1.** *Computer-based.* Multimedia and hypermedia are computer-based phenomena. The integration of multimedia into a single display system relies on the computer; it cannot be created without computers.

**2.** *Readily available, general applications.* Multimedia are becoming the most common applications on computers. The multimedia tools listed later are available in every catalog and store selling computer products.

**3.** *Affordable.* Although multimedia can be extremely expensive to produce, some of the tools described earlier cost less than $100.

**4.** *Represent knowledge.* Multimedia provides the least constrained and most well-defined formalism for representing knowledge of all the Mindtools. Learners have much greater latitude and flexibility in representing what they learn, but they also have more power because multimedia are multimodal. Multimedia requires more creativity in the knowledge representation process.

**5.** *Applicable in different subject domains.* Any domain that can be taught can be represented in multimedia and hypermedia.

**6.** *Engage critical thinking.* These skills are described in the previous section and in the next section.

**7.** *Facilitate transfer of learning.* The planning, visualization, and design skills necessary to create multimedia (described in the previous section) can be applied to any complex project. The research shows that these skills carry over into other student projects.

**8.** *Simple, powerful formalism.* Communicating through multimedia refines communication skills that people have applied all of their lives. And multimedia relies on communication metaphors with which the students have become very familiar (video, music, etc.).

**9.** *(Reasonably) easy to learn.* Although multimedia can involve complex production processes that pose many new technological questions, students can learn to use some of the systems described later (e.g., Mediatext) in an hour or so. Experience has shown that young students readily grasp the processes and become proficient producers in a relatively short time.

## Critical, Creative, and Complex Thinking in Multimedia and Hypermedia Production

The most difficult and engaging part of the multimedia design and development process, as evidenced in Tables 8.1, 8.2, and 8.3, is organizing and designing the presentation. However, responsibilities do vary some. Researching the information that will go into the presentation involves critical thinking skills more than creative or complex thinking skills (Table 8.1). Organizing that information involves evaluating and analyzing skills, as the learners determine what information is useful and relevant for the presentation. Similarly, designing and organizing the presentation involves many critical thinking skills, especially analyzing. Learners must determine the purpose of the presentation and evaluate different approaches to organizing it. In addition to good negotiating skills, this step requires critical thinking. Note that managing the multimedia development project does not require many critical thinking skills.

Creative thinking is primarily involved in organizing and designing the presentation (Table 8.2). Selecting or designing multimedia resources such as graphics, animation, sound, and video involves elaborating on the plan and imagining and synthesizing how it should look. If this part of the process is not done well, the audience's attention will not be maintained. This is the part that learners usually enjoy the most. However,

**Table 8.1**
Critical thinking skills in multimedia design and development

|  | Researching Information | Organizing and Designing Presentation | Managing Project |
|---|---|---|---|
| **Evaluating** | | | |
| Assessing information | X | | |
| Determining criteria | X | X | |
| Prioritizing | X | X | X |
| Recognizing fallacies | X | X | |
| Verifying | X | | |
| **Analyzing** | | | |
| Recognizing patterns | | X | |
| Classifying | X | | |
| Identifying assumptions | X | X | |
| Identifying main ideas | X | X | |
| Finding sequences | X | X | |
| **Connecting** | | | |
| Comparing/contrasting | X | | |
| Logical thinking | | | |
| Inferring deductively | | X | |
| Inferring inductively | X | | |
| Identifying causal relationships | | | X |

retrieving information to go in the multimedia program also involves creative thinking skills for designing questionnaires and other data-gathering instruments. If students botch this part of the process, there will be little of meaning or importance to present.

Organizing and designing the presentation requires the most complex thinking skills (Table 8.3). However, project management also uses a number of problem-solving and decision-making skills. Ensuring that team members know what to do and that all the activities are scheduled and completed on time so that the presentation can come together is a complex thinking process that requires a lot of simultaneous thinking. Producers often have to be able to do several things at the same time. While simultaneous thinking is not as important in organizing and designing the presentation, a great many problems need to be solved. Deciding how to capture video, creating pictures and animations, and programming them into the presentation are examples of complex thinking activities.

## Related Mindtools

In a sense, multimedia is the amalgam of all other media, so it could be composed of any other communication form. In that case, any other

| Table 8.2 Creative thinking skills in multimedia design and development | Researching Information | Organizing and Designing Presentation | Managing Project |
|---|---|---|---|
| **Elaborating** | | | |
| Expanding | X | X | |
| Modifying | X | X | |
| Extending | | X | |
| Shifting categories | X | X | |
| Concretizing | | X | |
| **Synthesizing** | | | |
| Analogical thinking | | | |
| Summarizing | X | X | |
| Hypothesizing | | | |
| Planning | | | X |
| **Imagining** | | | |
| Fluency | | X | |
| Predicting | | X | X |
| Speculating | | X | |
| Visualizing | | X | |
| Intuition | | X | |

information sources, including databases, spreadsheets, semantic nets, and expert systems, could be included. In reality, however, multimedia makes scant use of most of these resources. Probably the most related Mindtool is the semantic network, which can be used as a structure for hypermedia knowledge bases. Jonassen (1990, 1991) describes how semantic nets can be modeled in the interface of multimedia and hypermedia systems, so that the expert's organization of ideas can be mapped onto the materials. Research has cast some doubt on the effectiveness of this approach, however (Jonassen & Wang, 1993).

Multimedia are somewhat related to computer programming also. Most of the multimedia authoring tools described in the next section have an associated scripting language that is used for achieving various effects. These programming languages are typically, though not always, object-oriented.

**Table 8.3**
Complex thinking skills in multimedia design and development

|  | Researching Information | Organizing and Designing Presentation | Managing Project |
|---|---|---|---|
| **Designing** | | | |
| Imagining a goal | | X | |
| Formulating a goal | | X | X |
| Inventing a product | | X | |
| Assessing a product | | X | |
| Revising the product | | X | X |
| **Problem Solving** | | | |
| Sensing the problem | | X | |
| Researching the problem | X | | |
| Formulating the problem | | X | X |
| Finding alternatives | | X | |
| Choosing the solution | | X | |
| Building acceptance | | | X |
| **Decision Making** | | | |
| Identifying an issue | X | X | X |
| Generating alternatives | X | X | X |
| Assessing the consequences | | | X |
| Making a choice | | X | |
| Evaluating the choices | | X | X |

# Software Tools for Constructing Multimedia and Hypermedia

There are three levels of tools for producing multimedia and hypermedia: commercial, high-end multimedia production packages; commercial hypermedia authoring systems; and special-purpose, school-based multimedia and hypermedia authoring systems. They vary in power and price.

## High-End Multimedia Production Packages

There are a number of powerful, expensive commercial software packages for producing multimedia programs. Programs such as Aldus Persuasion, Microsoft Powerpoint, Astound, and Cinemation for the Macintosh are powerful multimedia production and presentations systems that sell for less than $500. They import graphics and play Quicktime movies but have very limited animation capabilities. These systems are presentation systems for the most part. Advanced systems, such as Macromedia Director for the Macintosh and Authorware Professional for the Macintosh and for DOS machines running Windows, add full animation capabilities and higher levels of interactivity, all at a cost of up to $5,000. These systems are designed to produce glitzy programs and are not used as often in schools as they are by commercial producers.

## Commercial Hypermedia Authoring Systems

The most commonly used packages for producing hypermedia are a midrange class of tools, such as HyperCard and SuperCard for the Macintosh and Toolbook, Guide, and Linkway Live for DOS machines. Producer versions cost up to $500 but afford a great deal of flexibility in programming more complicated instructional hypermedia programs. In most cases, the price of this flexibility is having to learn an object-oriented scripting language in order to produce advanced interactivity. These programs import graphics and movies but have limited production capabilities. They produce card-oriented presentations. A number of school-based projects rely on Toolbook and HyperCard because of their flexibility, but they are not as easy to learn to use as the next class of multimedia and hypermedia tools.

## Special-Purpose, School-Based Multimedia and Hypermedia Authoring Systems

Some school-based multimedia production projects that were described in the Examples section of this chapter have resulted in the development of multimedia authoring systems. Products such as Mediatext and Hyper-Author have limited capabilities for importing multimedia resources, but they are designed to provide a friendly, easy-to-use authoring environment for students, and they are very inexpensive (less than $100). Commercial hypermedia authoring tools, such as HyperStudio, are HyperCard clones with a student-oriented interface. While HyperStudio is less powerful than HyperCard, it is easier to use and has been our choice for student multimedia construction.

# How to Construct Multimedia and Hypermedia in the Classroom

Lehrer (1993) has developed a very good framework for HyperComposition, consisting of four major processes:

1. Planning requires that students make decisions about
   - major goals of the knowledge base (who is the audience, what they should learn)
   - topics and content to be included in the knowledge base
   - relationships among the topics (how they will be linked)
   - interface design (what functions should be provided to the learner)
   - how the designers will collaborate to complete the task
2. Accessing, transforming, and translating information into knowledge, including
   - searching for and collecting relevant information
   - selecting and interpreting information sources
   - developing new interpretations and perspectives
   - allocating information to nodes and deciding how it will be represented, that is, in which medium (text, graphics, pictures, video, audio)
   - deciding on the nature of the links necessary to interconnect content and create links
3. Evaluating the knowledge base, including
   - assessing compromises in what was represented and how

- assessing the information coverage and its organization
- testing the browser
- trying it out with users and soliciting their feedback
4. Revising the knowledge base from the feedback, including
    - correcting any content errors that may have been reported
    - reorganizing and restructuring the knowledge base to make it more accessible or meaningful

This is a general process for building hypermedia programs. The role of the teacher should be to coach students in these different processes. Coaching is a less directive method of teaching, usually involving prompting or provoking the students with questions about the content and their treatment of it. You may suggest issues but should not recommend answers or treatments. Those are the students' responsibility. Lehrer (1993) suggests questions such as the following:

- How are you going to organize your presentation, and why?
- How are you going to decide on what to include and what to leave out?
- Can you draw a map of the flow of your program? Does it seem logical?
- Which stories do you want to include, and what do they represent?
- Which are the most important themes in describing your content? How did you determine that they were the most important?

Lehrer also suggests modeling certain processes, such as using notecards to represent nodes and connecting them with pieces of string.

## Fostering Collaboration with Multimedia and Hypermedia Construction

Because of the complexity of the process and the amount of research and background work required (e.g., finding visual and auditory material to include in the presentation), multimedia construction is probably the Mindtool that most requires collaboration. Many of these skills are likely to be novel to some or all of the learners, so collaboration is very important.

**1.** *Form the teams.* Although Lehrer (1993) found that even a group made up entirely of low-ability learners succeeded in multimedia authoring, heterogeneous groups of learners are likely to work the best. Groups should not be formed based on academic ability but rather on creativity, task orientation, and musical or visual talent. You may also group according to knowledge of the content being conveyed in the presentation.

**2.** *Clarify the group goal.* These tasks are defined in the planning process described in the previous section. Identifying the target audience and learning goals for the presentation, along with developing the content and treatment of the presentation, will probably be the most difficult part of the process.

**3.** *Negotiate tasks and subtasks to be completed.* Break down the required tasks according to the model presented in the last section (planning, accessing, evaluating, revising) and delegate them to different members of the group according to their preferences and strengths. Learners are likely to voice their preferences.

**4.** *Monitor individual and group performance.* Timelines and other project management methods (there are a number of computer-based tools that function much like Mindtools that can be used to facilitate this process) can be introduced to facilitate the planning and execution of the construction process. Students need to assume and practice leadership skills in order to ensure the project's completion. The monitoring process is usually aided by the intrinsic motivation that learners bring to this kind of task.

**5.** *Reconcile differences in interpretations or approaches to the goal.* Negotiating differences of opinion or interpretation in the content or the treatment to be used in the presentation requires a true collaborative spirit. Multimedia offers the option of representing ideas in several different ways, however, so multiple interpretations may be easily accommodated by offering everyone his or her "day in court."

# Advantages of Multimedia and Hypermedia as Mindtools

- Learners are much more mentally engaged by developing materials than by studying materials. The search for information is more meaningful when students have a meaningful purpose.
- Multimedia permits concrete representations of abstract ideas and enables multiple representations of ideas (Hays et al., 1993).
- Students constructing multimedia and hypermedia are actively engaged in creating representations of their own understanding by using their own modes of expression.
- Students are highly motivated by the activity because they have some ownership in the product.

- Building multimedia and hypermedia orients teachers and students away from the notion that knowledge is information and that the teacher's role is to transmit that information (Lehrer, 1993).
- Designing knowledge in the form of multimedia presentations promotes the development of critical theories of knowledge (not every design is successful) and critical thinking, such as defining the nature of the problem and executing a program to solve it (Lehrer, 1993).

# Limitations of Multimedia and Hypermedia as Mindtools

- Construction of multimedia and hypermedia is a time-consuming process.
- There are more significant hardware and software requirements for multimedia construction than for other Mindtools. In order to integrate audio, graphics, and video into presentations, a scanner, an audio/video capture card, a larger-than-normal color monitor, speakers, a video camera, and more sophisticated multimedia software are needed. The software tools are not terribly expensive, but the hardware can be. Usually only one or two multimedia production machines are needed per school, so this will limit the cost somewhat.

## *Conclusion*

The recent, phenomenal growth of multimedia has changed the face of computing. The most popular computers today are multimedia workstations, replete with large screens, stereo speakers, and high-density storage devices to accommodate memory-hungry multimedia programs. In educational computing circles, multimedia is the answer, but what is the question? Commercial software producers are frenetically racing to bring out multimedia products before the competition. It is very unlikely that this multimedia mania will substantively affect learning in schools unless and until students become the drivers. Most students today have grown up with multimedia, so delivering the same kind of instruction in multiple channels will not attract their attention. However, allowing students to become designers of multimedia will engage those students who become involved in new ways. Hypermedia provides a useful conceptual framework for designing multimedia materials. The combination of creativity and complexity required to author hypermedia in a form that is intrinsically motivating to students (multimedia) makes it probably the most compelling and potentially effective of all Mindtools. The richness of representational forms available in multimedia knowledge bases is greater than that in all other Mindtools. Future research will very probably document the effects of designing *with* multimedia, rather than learning *from* it.

## References

Beichner, R. J. (1994). Multimedia editing to promote science learning. *Journal of Educational Multimedia and Hypermedia, 3*(1), 55–70.

Carver, S. M., Lehrer, R., Connell, T., & Erickson, J. (1992). Learning by hypermedia design: Issues of assessment and implementation. *Educational Psychologist, 27*(3), 385–404.

Harel, I., & Papert, S. (1990). Software design as a learning environment. *Interactive Learning Environments, 1,* 1–32.

Hays, K. E., Weingard, P., Guzdial, M., Jackson, S., Boyle, R. A., & Soloway, E. (1993, June). *Students as multimedia authors.* Paper presented at the Ed Media conference, Orlando, FL.

Jonassen, D. H. (1989). *Hypertext/hypermedia.* Englewood Cliffs, NJ: Educational Technology Publications.

Jonassen, D. H. (1990). Semantic network elicitation: Tools for structuring of hypertext. In R. McAleese & C. Green (Eds.), *Hypertext: The state of the art.* London: Intellect.

Jonassen, D. H. (1991). Representing the expert's knowledge in hypertext. *Impact Assessment Bulletin, 9* (1), 93-105.

Jonassen, D. H. & Wang, S. (1993). Acquiring structural knowledge from semantically structured hypertext. *Journal of Computer-based Instruction, 20* (1), 1–8.

Lehrer, R. (1993). Authors of knowledge: Patterns of hypermedia design. In S. P. LaJoie & S. J. Derry (Eds.), *Computers as cognitive tools.* Hillsdale, NJ: Lawrence Erlbaum.

Lehrer, R., Erickson, J., & Connell, T. (in press). Learning by designing hypermedia documents. *Computers in Schools, 10.*

Nelson, T. (1981). *Literary machines.* Swarthmore, PA: Author.

Perkins, D. N. (1986). *Knowledge as design.* Hillsdale, NJ: Lawrence Erlbaum.

Spoehr, K. T. (1992, April). *Using hypermedia to clarify conceptual structures: Illustrations from history and literature.* Paper presented at the annual meeting of the American Educational Research Association, San Francisco, CA.

Spoehr, K. T. (1993, April). *Profiles of hypermedia authors: How students learn by doing.* Paper presented at the annual meeting of the American Educational Research Association, Atlanta, GA.

Spoehr, K. T. (in press). Enhancing the acquisition of conceptual structures through hypermedia. In K. McGilly (Ed.), *Classroom lessons: Integrating cognitive theory and classroom practice.* Cambridge, MA: Bradford Books.

Spoehr, K. T., & Shapiro, A. (1991, April). *Learning from hypermedia: Making sense of a multiply linked database.* Paper presented at the annual meeting of the American Educational Research Association, Chicago, IL.

von Wodtke, M. (1993). *Mind over media: Creative thinking skills for electronic media.* New York: McGraw-Hill.

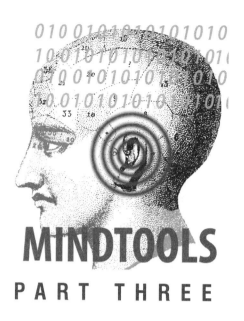

## MINDTOOLS

# Promoting Thinking with Mindtools: Learning *by* Computing

In Part 3 the emphasis shifts from learning *with* technology to learning by *engaging* technology. It includes the following chapters:

**Chapter 9**   Computer Programming: Reasoning with Computer Logic
**Chapter 10** Microworld Learning Environments: Immersion in Action

Computer programming and microworld learning environments are powerful tools for engaging learners in critical thinking and knowledge construction. However, because they do not meet all of the criteria for Mindtools set out in Chapter 1, I refer to them as *quasi-Mindtools*. They have the following characteristics:

1. They are computer-based tools that rely on the computational power of the computer.
2. They are readily available applications, though, in the case of microworlds, not as applicable to different content domains.
3. They are relatively affordable, though generally not as affordable or efficient as other Mindtools.

4. Programming can be used to represent knowledge; the primary purpose of microworlds is knowledge construction resulting from exploration rather than knowledge representation.
5. Programming methods can be applicable in different subject domains, although microworlds are designed to afford thinking in a confined domain of knowledge.
6. Both clearly engage critical thinking.
7. Both facilitate transfer of learning from the application to other types of problems and other domains.
8. Programming represents a powerful formalism, though it is not simple; microworlds are more exploratory environments and less of a formalism for representing knowledge.
9. Programming is not easy to learn; microworlds can be.

Although they are different in some respects from the Mindtools discussed in chapters 3 through 8, these quasi-Mindtools are powerful enough environments that they merit being addressed in this book. The structures of chapters 9 and 10 will be amended to reflect these differences.

# CHAPTER 9

# Computer Programming:
## *Reasoning with Computer Logic*

## What Is Computer Programming?

There are several levels of programs that control computers (see Figure 9.1). At the lowest level, many of the computer's electronic components (the ROM and EPROM chips) have hardwired programs that are encoded into the logic of the connections themselves. The programs that actually drive the computer describe memory locations and procedures for manipulating and moving zeroes and ones to and from those locations. These programs, often referred to as machine code, are written in binary (zeroes and ones) and hexadecimal (base 16).

Programmers use higher-level assembly language programs to activate these machine language programs. Assembly language programs are comprised of low-level commands to move information around the machine. Even higher-level programs are entered into the computer in the form of procedural languages, such as BASIC and Pascal. These languages are the ones most commonly taught to students.

Computer programming languages consist of sets of key words and commands that are interpreted or compiled by other assembly language programs in the programming language editors into machine code, which actually runs the computer. Combinations of commands define programming structures, that is, kinds of operations that computers can perform. Procedural languages have three major types of programming structures: list, repetition, and selection structures. *List structures* describe linear sequences of operations that are performed by the computer every time the list routine is invoked. *Repetition structures* (loops) are sets of operations that are repeated by the computer. The same set of operations may be

**Figure 9.1**
Levels of programs and languages

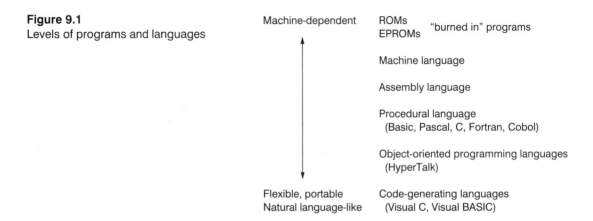

| Machine-dependent | ROMs EPROMs | "burned in" programs |
|---|---|---|
| | Machine language | |
| | Assembly language | |
| | Procedural language (Basic, Pascal, C, Fortran, Cobol) | |
| | Object-oriented programming languages (HyperTalk) | |
| Flexible, portable Natural language-like | Code-generating languages (Visual C, Visual BASIC) | |

repeated a specific number of times or until a certain condition exists or while a certain condition exists. Repetition structures are often embedded within each other, so that loops of operations run inside of other loops, which run inside other loops. *Selection structures* describe the causal, decision-making operations in a program. These statements are typically written in IF-THEN-ELSE format (i.e., if a specific conditions exists, then do one sequence of operations; if another condition exists, then do another sequence of operations; if neither condition exists, do something else). Decisions can be combined to provide complex options. There are many ways that these structures can be written and combined in order to solve computational problems.

## The Process of Programming

Selecting and sequencing programming commands to solve computational problems is a very complex process. Taylor (1991) defines five steps in the process of computer programming: problem definition, algorithm design, code writing, debugging, and documentation. According to Pea and Kurland (1984), programming consists of subtasks such as understanding the problem, designing and planning the program, coding the program, and comprehending and debugging the program.

When faced with a problem, the programmer must first decide if a computer program can help. If a program can be developed such that the effort saved by the program is substantially greater than the effort required to write and debug the program, the programmer must then clarify the nature of the problem. Just what kinds of outcomes are required, and what kinds of information are available? Next, the problem must be broken down into a sequence of more easily solvable subproblems. These subproblems are often broken down into even smaller sub-subproblems, thus enabling the programmer to plan the overall structure of the program and determine what programming structures are needed in order to process the information. Typically this consists of determining how to get information into the computer's working memory (input), how to massage or manipulate that information (process), and then how to report the product of the manipulations (output).

A large number of potential control structures may be selected. How they are sequenced will affect the way the program functions. At this point, programmers often flowchart these control structures or write what is called *pseudocode,* which is a more natural language version of what structures and processes need to be used, in the sequence they must be used. The pseudocode is later translated into specific programming statements. Because some structured languages, such as Pascal and Logo, require up-front definition of some of these elements, they require additional planning at this stage but generally require less debugging later.

Converting the pseudocode into computer language code requires using the correct commands and syntax. Accidental insertion of an unwarranted space, omission of a semicolon, or other seemingly minor mistakes can cause the program to fail. The thinking required to do this is rule-oriented and specific to the language the programmer is using. Languages like Logo are more popular beginning languages because they use more natural commands and much simpler syntax. Newer programming environments, such as Think Pascal and Think C, automatically format the code and flag syntax errors, making this implementation phase much easier.

Since most computer programs seldom work immediately after coding due to logical or syntactical errors, the most challenging part of programming is often the debugging process. Debugging involves locating the errors and figuring out why the program does not run or why it is providing the wrong information or conclusions. Again, if the program is well conceived and planned using a structured language, debugging should be easier.

The final process in programming is usually documenting the program, which may take the form of an external user's manual, online (embedded) documentation, user messages, and even training. Often, because of time pressure, this phase is omitted, thereby increasing the cost of subsequent efforts to revise the program. Providing information about the program in order to help users correctly run the program or to help future programmers in amending the program is a valuable part of the process and should be undertaken while the program is being conceived and written. Documentation may not help the program run, but it will help others run the program.

## Programming Languages

The programming languages that are most often taught in American schools are BASIC, Pascal, and Logo. A microcomputer version of the AI language Prolog is more often taught in European schools.

### BASIC

BASIC (Beginner's All-purpose Symbolic Instruction Code) accompanied the rapid growth of computing in the 1960s. It was developed at Dartmouth as a standard, introductory procedural programming language. BASIC is easy to use and very interactive because the computer "interprets" it; that is, when told to execute the program, the computer immediately executes each line of code. This makes testing and debugging easier than with compiled languages that convert the entire program into machine code before executing it.

The primary complaint about BASIC is its inherently unstructured nature. BASIC statements are written in the numerical sequence in which the program will be executed. Deviations from the linear sequence are controlled by GOTO statements, which refer to the line number of the statement to be executed. So, when told to GOTO 345, BASIC goes to and executes statement number 345. Unless a careful and very structured approach to writing BASIC code is used to generate modular code with defined procedures called superprocedures, the order of operations can become very confused through unrestricted use of GOTO statements, resulting in what is referred to as "spaghetti code." The following, very simple BASIC program shows a student interaction with the computer:

```
100 REM Distance Feedback Program
110 REM This program verifies that the learner can
properly calculate a distance.
130 REM This first section enters the problem informa-
tion.
150 PRINT "Enter the speedometer reading and the
elapsed time for the distance calculation."
160 INPUT Speedometer, Elapsed_time
170 PRINT "Enter the distance traveled."
180 INPUT Student_distance
200 REM This section evaluates the learner's response.
210 LET Correct_distance = Speedometer * Elapsed_time
```

```
240 IF Student_distance = Correct_distance THEN GOTO
280
250 PRINT "Your answer was incorrect."
260 GOTO 300
280 PRINT "You have calculated the distance cor-
rectly."
300 END
```

Newer versions of BASIC are more structured and powerful and so make it more difficult to create spaghetti code.

## Pascal

Compared to BASIC, Pascal is an inherently more structured programming language that requires programmers to identify at the beginning of the program all of the variables, procedures, and functions they intend to use in the program. The purpose of this requirement is to produce more organized, better structured programs. Pascal (named for the French mathematician and philosopher) was introduced in 1971 and since then has become the language most often taught first to computer science students.

Pascal, like Logo (described next), enables programmers to define subprograms, including functions and procedures, and then call them whenever they are needed. This feature avoids having to repeat sections of the code within the program. Unlike Logo, Pascal requires that the procedures and variables be identified by type at the beginning of the program. Another advantage of Pascal is the flexibility of its control structures, which are used to define subtasks or program modules. Repetition structures (e.g., REPEAT-UNTIL and WHILE-DO) and selection structures (e.g., IF-THEN-ELSE and CASE) are straightforward and easy to use. See Figure 9.2 for an example of a small Pascal program (it functions like the BASIC program above).

## Logo

Logo is a simplified language created at MIT to engage children in the construction of microworlds (discussed in Chapter 10). The part of the Logo language that is used most often consists of geometric commands that are sent to a turtle (a turtlelike object on the computer screen or a cybernetic turtle that motors along the floor) to draw objects on the screen or onto a piece of paper (under the cybernetic turtle). Using Pas-

```
program Distance Feedback (input,output);
{This program verifies that the learner can properly
calculate a distance.}

var
    speedometer:    integer;
    elapsed_time:    real;
    student_distance:    real;
    calc_distance:    real;

function distance(rate: integer; time: real): real;
{This function calculates a distance given a rate and time.}
begin
    distance := rate*time;
end;

procedure give_feedback(correct_distance: real; student_distance: real);
begin
    if correct_distance = student_distance
    then writeln('You have calculated the distance correctly.')
    else writeln('Your answer was incorrect.');
end;

begin {DistanceFeedback main program}
    writeln('Enter the speedometer reading and the elapsed time for the distance
calculation.');
    readln(speedometer, elapsed_time);
    writeln('Enter your distance calculation.');
    readln(student_distance);
    calc_distance := distance(speedometer, elapsed_time);
    give_feedback(calc_distance, student_distance);
end. {main program}
```

**Figure 9.2**
Pascal programming code

cal-like procedures, children teach the turtle to draw objects and then combine those procedures into larger procedures that draw more complex scenes containing those objects. The syntax of the language is simple enough to allow learners to explore and experiment with creating scenes (microworlds; see Chapter 10). The main ideas that are fostered by Logo are procedures, nesting procedures, and recursion (having a procedure call itself).

For example, in order to have the turtle draw a square, the learner could start by issuing the following commands:

```
FORWARD 50
RIGHT 90
FORWARD 50
RIGHT 90
FORWARD 50
RIGHT 90
FORWARD 50
```

Students learn that loops are easily accommodated in Logo using the REPEAT command, so the square can be drawn by

```
REPEAT 4 [FORWARD 50 RIGHT 90]
```

This sequence may be defined as a procedure "Box" and used in other procedures, such as the following:

```
TO WINDOW
REPEAT 4 [BOX LEFT 90]
```

The window procedure can be combined with other procedures to create more elaborate scenes, such as a house, which would consist of procedures such as WINDOW, DOOR, and ROOF. TREE procedures could be taught to the turtle to enhance the scene. Turtle graphics can also be used to solve more complex geometry problems.

In addition to turtle graphics, Logo contains a set of list (language)-processing commands that are equivalent to those in the AI language Lisp. Learners use these commands and the procedures acquired through turtle graphics to create poems or conversations with each other. Although Logo is syntactically much easier than BASIC or Pascal, it still requires the understanding of abstract concepts, such as variables, procedures, and recursion. If you plan to teach procedural computer programming as a Mindtool, Logo should probably be the language that you use, even with high school students. The other desirable option for using programming as a Mindtool is the object-oriented language, Prolog, which is fundamentally different from the procedural languages just described.

## Prolog

Prolog (*programming in *log*ic*) was developed in 1972 in Marseilles as an AI language for solving problems that involve objects and their relationships stated in terms of declarative logic. It is often used to write programs representing human knowledge structures. Prolog is interactive and conversational. Programming in Prolog consists of declaring facts about objects and their relationships, defining rules about those objects and relationships, and asking questions about those objects and relationships.

Micro-Prolog (Prolog for microcomputers) programs are made up of sentences that state objects and their relationships. These objects and relationships are added to the program individually, as in these examples:

```
add (Nancy likes Sluggo)
add (Vice_President is_head_of Senate)
add (Vice_President is_second_in_command)
add (assets have_value)
add (assets are_owned_by company)
```

or in lists, as in these examples:

```
(Delaware Rhode_Island Connecticut) member (states
mid_Atlantic_region thirteen_colonies)
(baseball basketball football) enjoyed_by (boys girls
couch_potatoes)
```

Prolog allows the user to ask true-false and search questions about the database you have developed, such as the following:

| | |
|---|---|
| `is (Sluggo likes Nancy)` | *No, because it wasn't added to the database.* |
| `which (x : x is_head_of Senate and x is second_in_command)` | *The Vice President, only if you added the attribute about second in command* |
| `is (Delaware Connecticut) member (mid-Atlantic_region)` | *Yes* |
| `is (assets are_owned_by IBM)` | *No, because Prolog doesn't yet know if IBM is a company* |

However, Prolog allows objects to inherit attributes from other variables. For example, if you

```
add (IBM is_a company)
```

then Prolog would infer that IBM owns assets; that is, IBM would inherit all of the stated attributes of a company, such as owning assets.

Prolog's power is afforded by its use of conditional, rule-based logic:

```
add (company legally_sells assets if assets have_value
and if assets are_owned_by company)
```

With these simple building blocks, Prolog can be used to develop complex databases of information. What makes Prolog especially useful as a Mindtool is its focus on knowledge representation. If you wish to teach programming as a Mindtool, especially with a focus on knowledge representation, then Prolog is perhaps the best.

In addition to its use as a Mindtool for school and university students, Prolog is used primarily as a database language, for natural language processing, and as a language for implementing expert systems. Because of these foci, Prolog is most like the other Mindtools described in this book, especially databases (Chapter 3), semantic networks (Chapter 5), and expert systems (Chapter 6). That is, Prolog focuses on the same kinds of relationships. In fact, semantic networks are often used to help Prolog programmers develop their programs.

## Other Languages

Other procedural languages (e.g., C and its derivatives) and AI languages (e.g., Lisp) are also taught to students, though certainly not with the degree of regularity as those just described. The trends in programming include a diminished interest in procedural languages like BASIC and Pascal and a translation of those and other procedural languages into object-oriented programming systems (OOPS). Rather than using procedures and functions as sequences of actions, OOPS think of them as reusable objects that can be combined like building blocks to construct a program. The program or the user sends messages to these objects, and the objects respond according to the message. The building block approach is especially important in defining screen objects such as scrollbars, windows, buttons, icons, and menus in window-type environments.

When the user points and clicks at an icon, the icon object responds, depending on its location and program.

Languages like Smalltalk were originally designed as OOPS environments; however, object-oriented versions of procedural languages like BASIC (Visual BASIC), Pascal, and C (Visual C) are preferred by programmers. OOPS languages can help to promote critical thinking as well as programming efficiency because they are very structured. Probably the most commonly used object-oriented language in schools is HyperTalk, the scripting language used with HyperCard, though object-oriented versions of most computer languages are now available.

Just as all computing environments are becoming more powerful, so too are programming environments, such as Visual BASIC and Visual C. These programming environments allow the user to input variables and identify programming structures, and the machine generates the code, all in the proper syntax. These environments are making programming easier and more productive. The issue for this book is the degree to which the enhanced production capability of these environments actually replaces the thinking that learners would master with less friendly programming environments. The issue is analogous to using calculators in math classes. Proponents argue that understanding the purposes of the algorithms and how they can be applied to solve problems is more important than learning to use the algorithm. I believe these environments can only enhance the likelihood that programming can be used as a Mindtool.

# Computer Programming as a Quasi-Mindtool

## Evaluation of Computer Programming as a Quasi-Mindtool

**1.** *Computer-based.* Although you can write pseudocode and programs without a computer, you obviously need one to execute them and test your thinking. Debugging cannot exist without a computer. Programming is an inherently computer-based process.

**2.** *Readily available, general applications.* There are numerous language systems—which include editors, interpreters or compilers, and debugging tools—available for every brand of personal computer on the market.

**3.** *Affordable.* Most language interpreters are relatively inexpensive, and they can be applied to a wide range of problems, thus making them less expensive.

**4.** *Represent knowledge.* List-processing and AI languages like Logo and Prolog are much better as knowledge representation tools. However, any language can be used for the purpose of representing knowledge, and all languages add a layer of intellectual complexity to the knowledge representation process, relative to other Mindtools.

**5.** *Applicable in different subject domains.* Since programming is necessary for creating applications such as Mindtools, and since Mindtools can represent different subjects, programming is at least equally capable of representing different domains.

**6.** *Engage critical thinking.* These skills are described later in this section of the chapter.

**7.** *Facilitate transfer of learning.* As the research described later shows, the transferability of most programming is questionable. If the task or activity to which you are hoping the programming skills transfer requires the same kind of logic that programming does, then transfer of learning is more likely. However, the gains in general reasoning from programming that have been claimed by many researchers are questionable.

**8.** *Simple, powerful formalism.* The power of computer languages has always been their flexibility of use. Although many languages were designed to perform a particular kind of operation, all languages can be used to solve a large range of problems. Many list-processing and AI languages are especially effective in teaching knowledge representation, which is a primary goal of Mindtools.

**9.** *(Reasonably) easy to learn.* This is the criterion that eliminates computer programming as a complete, effective Mindtool. Programming in most computer languages requires learning as many as 100 different commands, knowing when and how to embed those commands into programming structures, and, most problematic and time-consuming, learning a lot of syntax. After a semester-long Pascal course in high school, students made errors using virtually every Pascal construct (Sleeman, Putnam, Baxter, & Kuspa, 1986). Punctuation, spaces, order of operations, and a host of other syntactical requirements add hundreds of rules that must be learned and faithfully used before programs will run. Unlike regular languages, where the meaning of the writing can be determined despite misspellings, placement, and usage errors, computers are unforgiving. A single error can prevent a program from running, despite the fact that beginning programming students believe that computers have the reasoning power of humans in comprehending language (Sleeman et al., 1986). The cognitive overhead (the amount of mental effort required to use programming languages) mitigates learners' ability to use computer programming as an easy and effective means for solving problems or representing knowledge. After two years of programming instruction, many students have only rudimentary understanding of programming ideas (Kurland, Pea, Clement, & Mawbry, 1986). Until programming skills become automated (which requires years of experience to occur), more effort is required to program the computer than to represent the knowledge or solve the problem.

Note that this argument regarding the limitation of programming is mitigated by newer computer programming environments, such as Think Pascal and Think C, which have syntax error detection and correction routines built in. These routines identify syntax errors when they are made, thereby reducing the cognitive load on and responsibilities of the learner. They also automatically format the code by indenting where necessary. Newer programming languages such as Visual BASIC and Visual C provide even more sophisticated code-generating routines, so the programmer need only identify the program structure and the variables, and the environment is able to generate the necessary programming code. These languages are especially effective for producing user interfaces by automating the creation of dialogue boxes, windows, and so on. These types of environments represent major steps in simplifying the programming process, allowing the programmer to act as a designer who focuses on the problem-solving task more than on writing code. However, to what extent does this replacement affect the thinking the programmer is required to do? These environments definitely enhance code generation, but do they support critical thinking?

## Computer Programming and Learning

Computer programming is not the primary application of computers in schools. In fact, only 14% of computer access time is normally spent on computer programming, with computer applications and computer-assisted instruction comprising 84% of the time (Beaver, 1989). Nonetheless, computer programming has been taught for many years in schools. Initially, programming was offered as a specialty course for students in accelerated math and science programs. Later, educators and researchers began to believe that learning to program a computer engaged students in critical thinking, so it was a useful thinking strategy for all students to learn. For the past decade or more, a significant amount of research on programming has been conducted in schools. This research has addressed primarily two issues: the cognitive (thinking) requirements of learning to program, and the transferable learning effects that come from learning to program. I shall briefly review some of this research, because it is important to investigate the validity of programming as a Mindtool.

## Cognitive Requirements of Computer Programming

Programming is a complex task, not a simple one. It involves many aspects of problem solving, such as problem decomposition, selecting appropriate information, assigning variables, identifying plausible solutions, applying programming structures, and debugging code. The cognitive skills required to perform these various tasks are also complex and have been investigated in the research.

* Cafolla (1987–88) found that the strongest predictors of learning to program were verbal reasoning, level of cognitive development, and mathematical reasoning.
* Among high school students learning to program in Logo, analogical reasoning ability is strongly related to the ability to write subprocedures (Clement, Kurland, Mawbry, & Pea, 1986).
* McCoy (1990) showed that programming requires five skills: general strategy, planning, logical thinking, variables, and debugging.
* Field-independent learners perform better than field-dependent learners in computer programming classes; that is, they are more analytical thinkers (see Jonassen & Grabowski, 1993, for more detail).
* Field-independence, logical reasoning, and direction-following skills were found to be most highly correlated with the most programming skills among college students (Foreman, 1988).
* Fourth graders were far less able to understand and use variables, because of the level of abstraction, the dynamic nature of the values of variables, the degree of complexity in using variables, and the level of reasoning required (Nachmias, 1986). This means that computer programming may be introduced at the upper elementary level but that abstract concepts in programming must wait until later.
* Fischer (1986) found that, among undergraduates, programming skill in a course was highly correlated to formal operational reasoning, especially the classification of abstract concepts, the identification of control structures, and the use of structured programming methods.
* Chin and Zecker (1985) found that programming ability was not, as expected, related to math ability, but rather that internal locus of control (the belief that one is in control of events in one's life) was a much better predictor.

- On the other hand, Nowaczyk (1983) found that math and English course performance, previous computer experience, and logic and algebraic word problem performance were significantly correlated to programming performance among college students.

Computer programming has long been associated with mathematics. It has often been assumed that skilled mathematicians make competent programmers because the same kinds of logical reasoning are required. This is partially true; however, programming computers is more directly related to analytical reasoning. Being able to break down problems and search for and select relevant information and solutions to those problems are most important for learners. Many people, including scientists, engineers, and mathematicians, are analytic, while many others are not. Most people can learn to function more analytically, but it is not easy. Programming is difficult because it requires a type of thinking that learners are not often called upon to perform.

## Cognitive Outcomes of Computer Programming

Most of the educational research on computer programming has assessed how much the logical reasoning required to program computers generalizes or transfers to nonprogramming problems. The assumption of most of this research is that the analytic thinking required to program will naturally make learners better problem solvers in other settings. Although learning to program has been shown to have a variety of effects on learners' thinking in different settings, the research findings are inconsistent.

- After one year of working with Logo, fifth and sixth graders performed better on Logo-related problem solving, general problem solving, and spatial reasoning ability, such as mental rotation of geometric figures (Miller, Kelly, & Kelly, 1988).
- Although Harel and Papert (1991) showed that planning was a significant activity that students were required to engage in and reflect on, Pea and Kurland (1984) found that Logo programmers were no better at planning skills than control-group students.
- Students who studied BASIC for six weeks performed better in mathematical thinking skills, including programming ability, generalization, and understanding variables, than the control group (Oprea, 1988).
- Liao and Bright (1991) conducted a meta-analysis of research on the effects of computer programming on cognitive outcomes. They found that a large majority of studies concluded that students who learned to

program scored higher on various cognitive tests than those who did not, although the differences were not large. This was especially true for students who took shorter programming courses rather than longer ones, and for those who learned Logo rather than BASIC or Pascal.

- Among fourth and fifth graders, no differences in the ability to visualize and draw designs resulted from learning to program (Williamson & Ginther, 1992).
- Ahmed (1992) reviewed 21 studies and found that half of the studies showed some positive effects of learning to program and half did not.
- Clements and Gullo (1984) found that learning to program in Logo improved six-year-olds' reflectivity, divergent thinking, and metacognitive ability, compared to a group receiving computer-assisted instruction.
- After studying programming for a year, programming experience did not transfer to other domains with similar properties (Kurland et al., 1986).
- Swan and Black (1990) found that explicitly teaching problem-solving strategies and applying them to solving problems in Logo was more effective than providing only Logo programming practice, teaching the strategies with concrete manipulables, or providing traditional problem-solving instruction.
- Three studies conducted by Jansson (1987) found that students' conditional reasoning tasks did not improve following instruction in programming.
- Clements (1985) conducted a thorough review of Logo research. He concluded that almost all children can learn to program in Logo, and that Logo is especially effective in encouraging prosocial behavior, positive self-image, and positive attitudes toward learning. Among his other findings were that the cognitive gains from Logo apply only to Logo-related learning; that programming does facilitate some problem-solving behaviors; and that Logo may facilitate the development of some cognitive skills such as classifying, seriating, and conserving.

Thinking is always somewhat dependent on the nature of the problem or the content. Programming requires learners to think deeply. However, that level of thinking does not necessarily transfer to other content or problems as much as content-dependent problem-solving skills do. The transfer of programming logic could probably be greatly enhanced by direct instruction that models how to apply programming skills to other problems rather than teaching the language and only later applying it to solving problems. Sometimes programming can improve the ability to perform on some critical thinking tests; however, the gains may not be worth the effort required to learn to program.

## Critical, Creative, and Complex Thinking in Computer Programming

Computer programming is probably among the most engaging and difficult of all of the Mindtools in terms of critical thinking. A competent programmer needs to know and be able to use hundreds of rules, so a large number of critical, creative, and complex thinking skills are required. Tables 9.1, 9.2, and 9.3 identify the skills required to define the problem, design the algorithm (select and sequence the necessary programming structures), write program code to fill in those structures, and debug the code when it doesn't work. The skills in each table that are marked by an "×" are those that are employed by each process, based on an information-processing analysis of the tasks.

There are probably more critical and complex thinking skills required to program computers than creative ones. This is because programming is a very analytical process that makes heavy use of logical thinking and prob-

**Table 9.1**
Critical thinking skills in computer programming

|  | Defining Problem | Designing Algorithm | Coding | Debugging |
|---|---|---|---|---|
| **Evaluating** | | | | |
| Assessing information | X | | | X |
| Determining criteria | X | X | | |
| Prioritizing | X | X | | |
| Recognizing fallacies | | | | X |
| Verifying | | | X | X |
| **Analyzing** | | | | |
| Recognizing patterns | | X | | X |
| Classifying | | | X | |
| Identifying assumptions | X | X | | |
| Identifying main ideas | X | | | |
| Finding sequences | | X | X | X |
| **Connecting** | | | | |
| Comparing/contrasting | | | | X |
| Logical thinking | X | X | | |
| Inferring deductively | | X | X | |
| Inferring inductively | X | | | X |
| Identifying causal relationships | | | | X |

lem solving. Isolating and defining the problem to be solved is primarily a process of evaluating what is known and what needs to be known. Assumptions and ideas must be identified, requiring logical and inductive thinking. Designing the algorithm is the challenging part of the process. The programmer must determine criteria, recognize patterns, and generate sequences of activities, which requires logical and deductive thinking (see Table 9.1). Coding programs is a more rule-bound activity, while debugging engages the most critical thinking skills, especially recognizing fallacies. Debugging is the part of the programming process that requires the most critical thinking and therefore is typically considered the most difficult.

Creative thinking is mostly required during the algorithm design process (see Table 9.2). Reconceptualizing and restating the problem in terms of programming structures requires great insight into the language and involves expanding, modifying, and reconceptualizing principles of the language to fit the situation. The process is often visualized using flowcharting. Note the number of imagining skills that are used in the programming process. Debugging makes significant use of those imagining skills as well.

**Table 9.2**
Creative thinking skills in computer programming

|  | Defining Problem | Designing Algorithm | Coding | Debugging |
|---|---|---|---|---|
| **Elaborating** | | | | |
| Expanding | X | X | | |
| Modifying | | X | | |
| Extending | | | | |
| Shifting categories | | X | X | |
| Concretizing | | X | | |
| **Synthesizing** | | | | |
| Analogical thinking | | X | X | |
| Summarizing | | | X | |
| Hypothesizing | X | | | X |
| Planning | X | | | |
| **Imagining** | | | | |
| Fluency | | | X | |
| Predicting | | X | | X |
| Speculating | X | | | X |
| Visualizing | | X | | |
| Intuition | X | | | X |

Complex thinking skills are the ones most frequently used in computer programming (see Table 9.3). Defining the problem and designing the algorithm both make heavy use of designing, problem-solving, and decision-making skills. Debugging is also a problem-solving process. Because computer programs are so complex, the need for complex thinking is probably greater for programming than for any other Mindtool.

# How to Use Computer Programming in the Classroom

Learning how to program in a computer language requires a separate book for each language and so is beyond the scope of this book. A few suggestions can be made, though. Lockard (1985/86) recommends that structured programming (implicit in languages like Pascal and Logo) be taught. Structured programming makes use of principles such as top-down design (identify main tasks, main subtasks for each task, and subtasks for each subtask), modularity (developing functions and procedures

**Table 9.3**
Complex thinking skills by computer programming requirements

|  | Defining Problem | Designing Algorithm | Coding | Debugging |
|---|---|---|---|---|
| **Designing** |  |  |  |  |
| Imagining a goal | X | X |  |  |
| Formulating a goal | X | X |  |  |
| Inventing a product |  | X | X |  |
| Assessing a product |  |  | X | X |
| Revising the product |  |  |  | X |
| **Problem Solving** |  |  |  |  |
| Sensing the problem | X |  |  |  |
| Researching the problem | X |  |  |  |
| Formulating the problem | X |  |  | X |
| Finding alternatives | X | X |  | X |
| Choosing the solution | X | X |  | X |
| Building acceptance |  |  |  | X |
| **Decision Making** |  |  |  |  |
| Identifying an issue | X |  |  |  |
| Generating alternatives | X | X | X | X |
| Assessing the consequences |  |  | X | X |
| Making a choice |  | X | X |  |
| Evaluating the choices |  | X |  | X |

as independent modules), and using a limited number of building blocks (list, repetition, and decision structures).

Generally, I recommend that teaching students to program makes heavy use of meaningful, real-world problems from the beginning. Programming should be taught as a problem-solving tool rather than as a subject. The most difficult part of programming is figuring out how to apply the rules you learn to the problems you encounter, so teaching the skills in the context of solving real problems will make those skills more transferable. Make sure that you explicitly teach problem-solving skills (e.g., problem decomposition, generating hypotheses, and gathering evidence to support those hypotheses) and coach students in reflecting on their applicability in other domains. Apply top-down programming principles to decomposing meaningful real-world problems in English first, then in a pseudolanguage, and finally in whatever computer programming language you are using.

The most difficult task for most teachers will be coaching students to hypothesize and test ideas rather than giving them answers. In the computer literacy age of the early 1980s, too many students experienced programming by keyboarding canned programs into the computer's memory, unable to understand or debug problems or generalize their use to any other situation, and certainly unable to write their own programs to solve problems. Clearly, these learners were not thinking critically. Programming was not taught as a Mindtool.

## Fostering Collaboration Through Computer Programming

The reasons for learning computer programming collaboratively are the same as those for using Mindtools collaboratively. The cognitive skills required to program and the cognitive outcomes from programming are likely to be novel to most learners, so several heads are likely to be better than one. Accepting multiple perspectives on any problem or idea may seem less important for programming, since the problems and the solutions offered by most programming languages are more circumscribed. However, there are usually many ways to solve problems using any language, and some of those ways are always more elegant than others.

Most Mindtools, like most programming projects, result in the creation of large knowledge bases of information. In corporate settings, most programming projects are collaborative, simply because of the enormity of the programming demands, which often produce thousands of lines of code. These projects are typically plagued most by the inability of the teams of programmers to communicate and collaborate on solving the problem. So, learning to program collaboratively may benefit many sorts of people. The following are some suggestions regarding the process of collaboratively learning and using programming as a Mindtool.

**1. *Form the teams.*** It is probably best to use groups of two or three students to integrate them all in the group's activities and to avoid losing some learners. Given the mix of creative and complex thinking required to write programs, heterogeneous groups of learners are appropriate. Also, since software engineers tend to be very analytical and often experience difficulty in communicating with nonengineers, analytics should be paired with globals. This arrangement will make communication difficult, so a lot of coaching from you will be required.

**2. *Clarify the group goal.*** Problem definition is perhaps the most complex part of programming. The group is likely to spend less effort discussing the content domain being represented and more effort on the methods. One of the most consistent principles of computer programming is that a little bit of effort in planning will save a lot of effort later in debugging. Stress the understanding of how ideas are represented in different forms (English, pseudocode, and programming code).

**3. *Negotiate tasks and subtasks to be completed.*** Because the tasks vary so much in terms of the required thinking, you may not wish to break down the required tasks and delegate them to different members of the group. If the groups delegate, most learners will miss important parts of the process. If you choose to separate and delegate, do so by problem; that is, let smaller groups work on different problems or parts of a larger problem so that everyone can experience all of the parts of the process. Clear delegation of functional requirements is a more efficient means of completing programming projects, though not necessarily the most productive for learning by all.

**4. *Monitor individual and group performance.*** Carefully negotiating the expectations of each learner and a timeline for completing the various activities is essential for most programming projects.

**5. *Reconcile differences in interpretations or approaches to the goal.*** During the group settings, learners must negotiate differences of opinion or interpretation in the content or in the nature of the task. Encourage experimentation with different programming approaches. Very structured approaches to programming will help this process.

# Advantages of Computer Programming as Quasi-Mindtools

Under certain circumstances, learning to program may enhance problem-solving and spatial reasoning abilities. These outcomes will not necessarily result from every programming project.

• Programming languages are often bundled with computers when purchased or are otherwise available inexpensively.
• Computer programs may be used to solve a wide range of problems. Programming skills are applicable to many situations and content domains.
• Programming skills are marketable, especially if the language is commonly used.

# Limitations of Computer Programming as Quasi-Mindtools

• Learning to program, even in a simple language like Logo, is time-consuming, requiring months of practice before adequate skills are developed.
• Gains in critical thinking that may result from learning to program may not justify the amount of effort required.

## *Conclusion*

Learning computer programming requires a considerable intellectual investment and calls on skills that are more difficult for some learners. However, once learners gain proficiency in programming, it can become the most versatile and flexible knowledge representation tool available. All of the other Mindtools have constrained formalisms. Programming allows the user to represent and integrate a range of ideas. Each of the other Mindtools was created using programming, so programming allows the learner to perform the knowledge representation activities that most Mindtools do at a lower level. Programming requires a lot of critical thinking and so can function as a Mindtool. It is more likely to be used as a Mindtool if it is taught more as a problem-solving tool than as an academic subject to be mastered.

### References

Ahmed, A. M. (1992). *Learning to program and its transference to student's cognition.* (Eric Document Reproduction Service No. ED 352261)

Beaver, J. E. (1989, February). *How are successful elementary schools allocating their instructional computing time?* Paper presented at the annual meeting of the Eastern Educational Research Association, Savannah, GA. (ERIC Document Reproduction Service No. ED 305912)

Cafolla, R. (1987–88). Piagetian formal operations and other cognitive correlates of achievement in computer programming. *Journal of Educational Psychology, 16*(1), 45–57.

Chin, J. P., & Zecker, S. G. (1985). *Personality and cognitive factors influencing computer programming performance.* Paper presented at the annual meeting of the Eastern Educational Research Association, Boston, MA. (ERIC Document Reproduction Service No. ED 261666)

Clement, C. A., Kurland, D. M., Mawbry, R., & Pea, R. D. (1986). Analogical reasoning and computer programming. *Journal of Educational Computing Research, 2*(4), 473–485.

Clements, D. H. (1985). Research in Logo in education: Is the turtle slow but steady or not even in the race? *Computers in the Schools, 2*(2–3), 55–71.

Clements, D. H., & Gullo, D. F. (1984). Effects of computer programming on young children's cognition. *Journal of Educational Psychology, 76*, 1051–1058.

Fischer, G. B. (1986). *Computer programming: A formal operational task.* Paper presented at the annual symposium of Piaget Society, Philadelphia, PA. (ERIC Document Reproduction Service No. ED 275316)

Foreman, K. H. D. (1988). Cognitive style, cognitive ability, and the acquisition of initial computer programming competence. In M. Simonson (Ed.), *Proceedings of selected research papers presented at the annual meeting of the Association for Educational Communications and Technology.* Washington, DC: Association for Educational Communication and Technology.

Harel, I. & Papert, S. (1991). *Constructionism.* Norwood, NJ: Ablex.

Jansson, L. C. (1987). Computer programming and logical reasoning. *School Science and Mathematics, 87*(5), 371–379.

Jonassen, D. H., & Grabowski, B. L. (1993). *Handbook of individual differences, learning, and instruction.* Hillsdale, NJ: Lawrence Erlbaum Associates.

Kurland, D. M., Pea, R. D., Clement, C., & Mawbry, R. (1986). A study of the development of programming ability and thinking skills in high school students. *Journal of Educational Computing Research, 2*(4), 429–455.

Liao, Y. K. C., & Bright, G. W. (1991). Effects of computer programming on cognitive outcomes: A meta-analysis. *Journal of Educational Computing Research, 7* (3), 251–268.

Lockard, J. (1985/86). Computer programming in the schools: What should be taught? *Computers in the Schools, 2*(4), 105–114.

McCoy, L. P. (1990). Literature related to problem solving in mathematics and in computer programming. *School Science and Mathematics, 90*(1), 48–60.

Miller, R. B., Kelly, G. N., & Kelly, J. T. (1988). Effects of Logo computer programming experience on problem solving and spatial relations ability. *Contemporary Educational Psychology, 13*, 348–357.

Nachmias, R. (1986, April). *Variables—An obstacle to children learning computer programming.* Paper presented at the annual meeting of the American Educational Research Association, San Francisco, CA. (ERIC Document Reproduction Service No. ED 290459)

Nowaczyk, R. H. (1983, March). *Cognitive skills needed in computer programming.* Paper presented at the annual meeting of the Southeastern Psychological Association, Atlanta GA. (ERIC Document Reproduction Service No. ED 236466)

Oprea, J. M. (1988). Computer programming and mathematical thinking. *Journal of Mathematical Behavior, 7,* 15–19.

Pea, R. D., & Kurland, D. M. (1984). On the cognitive effects of learning computer programming. *New Ideas in Psychology, 2*(2), 137–168.

Sleeman, D., Putnam, R. T., Baxter, J., & Kuspa, L. (1986). Pascal and high school students: A study of errors. *Journal of Educational Computing Research, 2*(1), 6–10.

Swan, K., & Black, J. B. (1990, April). *Logo programming, problem solving, and knowledge-based instruction.* Paper presented at the annual meeting of the American Educational Research Association, Boston, MA. (ERIC Document Reproduction Service No. 349 968)

Taylor, K. A. (1991). *An annotated bibliography of current literature dealing with the effective teaching of computer programming.* (ERIC Document Reproduction Service No. 338217)

Williamson, J. D., & Ginther, D. W. (1992). Knowledge representation and cognitive outcomes of teaching Logo to children. *Journal of Computing in Childhood Education, 3,* 303–322.

# 10

# Microworld Learning Environments:
## *Immersion in Action*

. . . . . . . . . . . . . . . . . . . . . . . . . . . . . . . . . . . . . . . . . . . . . . . . . . . . . . . . . . . .

## What Are Microworlds?

### Logo-Based Microworlds

The term *microworld* was coined by Seymour Papert in *Mindstorms: Children, Computers, and Powerful Ideas* (1980) as part of his work on the development of Logo at MIT. He believed that Logo was a simple formalism for creating microworlds, which are constrained problem spaces that resemble existing problems in the real world. The problems in microworlds are generated by learners because the problems that can be created by the microworld are inherently interesting (experimenting to "see if I can do that"). Logo enables learners to use simple commands to direct the turtle (see Chapter 9) to create their own personal, visual worlds. Having posed a problem, learners test hypotheses for solving it.

Logo, Papert argued, is an ideal environment for creating microworlds. Learners enter commands to manipulate a turtle on the screen in an effort to create more elaborate renderings, thus becoming familiar with "powerful ideas" underlying the turtle's operations, ideas such as variables, procedures, and recursion. The computer should be an "object to think with," according to Papert.

Lawler (1984) provides simple examples of such microworlds. One, the POLYSPI (for poly-spiral) procedure, requires learners to use variables in a procedure to create a spiral. By manipulating the values of the variables, the spiral changes form. Another, the beach microworld, uses the turtle to draw a beach scene, replete with bird, boat, house, kid, man, sun, and many other objects. The beach is a visual model for testing hypotheses about the placement and movement of objects in a scene. Because the ideas and methods are simple and grounded in a visual reality, they become useful to learners in their experimentation.

Thompson and Wang (1988) used Logo to create a microworld where learners could explore concepts by plotting points in a Cartesian coordinate system. Students created pictures (as in the beach microworld) by placing objects in the picture using $x$ and $y$ coordinates. Students in the microworld treatment not only outperformed a control group on a posttest of coordinate problems, but, more importantly, they performed substantially better on a test of transfer of the ideas to real-world coordinate problems. The key here is creating an environment in which students can explore the ideas being learned.

Not all of the research and experience with Logo has been positive. There are at least two significant limitations of Logo-based microworlds:

**1.** Logo microworlds typically represent very constrained and circumscribed problems that engage a limited set of skills. The procedures used to create Logo microworlds and the skills they require are not very generalizable. They are powerful, but learners cannot practice a range of exploratory skills, which is an important criterion for Mindtools.

**2.** The generalizability of Logo microworlds can certainly be enhanced if learners create their own microworlds using Logo rather than using those created by a teacher, but that entails that students learn Logo. Although Logo is a syntactically simple language, it still requires several months of practice to develop skills sufficient for easily creating microworlds. The requirements of learning the language impede its utility for experimentation (see discussion of programming in Chapter 9).

The idea of microworlds as problem-exploration spaces is indeed powerful. I believe that many other microworld environments have been created that offer the exploratory advantages of Logo without the requirement of learning a programming language. Those environments are the subject of this chapter.

## Generic Microworlds

Notwithstanding my concerns about Logo, the concept of microworlds remains a "powerful idea," in Papert's words. Microworlds have been created in a diverse number of learning environments and have proven extremely effective in engaging learners in higher-order thinking such as hypothesis testing and speculating. Microworlds can assume many forms in different knowledge domains; however, they are primarily exploratory learning environments, discovery spaces, and constrained simulations of real-world phenomena. "Microworlds present students with a simple model of a part of the world" (Hanna, 1986, p. 197) and replicate the functionality needed to explore phenomena in those parts of the world. That is, they provide learners with the observation and manipulation tools necessary for exploring and testing objects in that part of the world.

> *The ideal associated with this approach is the feeling of "direct engagement," the feeling that the computer is invisible, not even there; but rather, what is present is the world we are exploring, be that world music, art, words, business, mathematics, literature or whatever your imagination and task provide you. (Draper & Norman, 1986, p. 3)*

According to Dreyer (1984), microworlds usually contain simple examples of complex natural phenomena. They support exploration of complex phenomena through activities such as games, creation of art, and communication, and allow the underlying concepts for exploring natural phenomena to be defined by the learner using characteristics of the microworld.

Microworlds are not necessarily computer-based. They can exist in the classroom, the kitchen, or anywhere. And they are relative to the learner's age and interests. When I was a child, a chemistry set and later a crude darkroom became microworlds that occupied much of my time. A cabinet full of pots and pans can be an engaging microworld for a toddler to learn about measurement, shape, hardness, gravity, and other concepts.

Burton, Brown, and Fischer (1984) use skiing instruction as a pretext for developing a model for designing increasingly complex, skill-based "microworlds." They believe that a microworld is a controlled real-world learning environment where a student is able to try out new skills and knowledge. It is important to their definition of microworlds that skills be practiced in the real environment with skills "isomorphic in [their] most important components to the final form of the skill" (p. 143).

In microworlds, instruction proceeds from simple to complex skills. Knowledge, skills, and attitudes are integrated through problem-solving activities, and instruction is situated in rich, meaningful settings. There are only a few factors involved in microworld design. For example, with skiing, complexity is learner-controlled by manipulating the equipment (e.g., the length of the skis), the task (e.g., gliding downhill, making easy turns, making more difficult turns), and the environment (e.g., a gentle slope feeding into an uphill slope, a steep slope, moguls). Initially, these decisions are coached to ensure that the learner has challenging but attainable goals and practices an appropriate set of necessary subskills.

Microworlds are exploration environments that exploit the interest and curiosity of the learner, so they must contain phenomena that learners are interested in. They incorporate instructional strategies such as modeling, coaching, reflecting, exploring, and encouraging the learner to debug his or her knowledge rather than apply principles attained during direct instruction. But they also rely on the learner. Self-regulated learning is an important component of microworld use. Learners need to identify their own goals and use the microworld to satisfy those goals.

Microworlds are based on powerful ideas. Powerful ideas are major building blocks in children's mental models, so they should be foundational for microworlds as well. Powerful ideas have powerful criteria (Lawler, 1984). If microworlds are based on powerful ideas, they should have the following characteristics:

- *simple,* so they can be understood
- *general,* so they apply to many areas of life
- *useful,* so the ideas are important to learners in the world
- *syntonic* (resonant with one's experience), so learners can relate them to prior knowledge and experience

Most important, microworlds are experiential. Learners learn by doing, instead of just watching or listening to a description of how something works. Because of this, microworlds tend to be intrinsically more motivating than traditional descriptions of activities.

## Examples of Microworld Learning Environments

The following examples of microworlds are representative of the kinds of environments that I refer to as microworlds—easy-to-learn and easy-to-manipulate environments that enable learners to experiment with ideas in a content domain. There are many other fine examples of microworlds, such as Boxer (diSessa & Abelson, 1986), Writing Partner (Salomon, 1993), ThinkerTools (White, 1993), and Stella (Steed, 1992; Richmond, Peterson, & Vescuso, 1987), that are not described in this chapter. If this chapter convinces you of the value of microworlds, you can search for, evaluate, and select learning environments with these characteristics to use with your students.

# Interactive Physics

Interactive Physics is a research environment for exploring topics in Newtonian mechanics, such as momentum, force, and acceleration. It consists
of a number of demonstrations, such as Car Crash (students' favorite; see
Figure 10.1), Falling Object, and Projectile Motion, and many experiments, such as Particle Dynamics, Rotational Dynamics (see Figure 10.2),
Equilibrium, Motion in a Plane, and Collisions. More importantly, it provides objects and tools that enable learners to design their own experiments to model Newtonian phenomena.

Each experiment and demonstration is a physics microworld that simu-
lates a physical phenomenon, allowing the learner to easily manipulate
several attributes of the world, such as gravity, air resistance, elasticity of
bodies, and various surface parameters. Students can also choose the
aspects of the microworld they want to attend to by showing grids, rulers,
vectors, axes, centers of mass, and mass names. They can turn on a
tracker, which shows the motion of objects. They can also select meters,

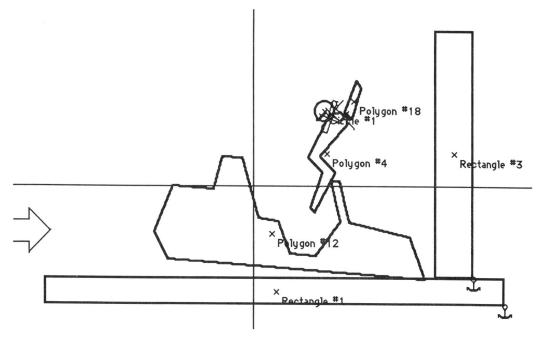

**Figure 10.1**
Car Crash demonstration in Interactive Physics

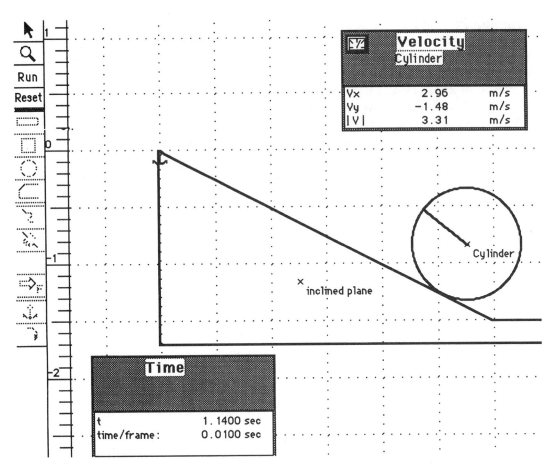

**Figure 10.2**
Rotational Dynamics experiment in Interactive Physics

such as velocity, acceleration, momentum, various forces (friction, gravity, air), and rotation, in order to measure the effects of changes in the variables they designate. Interactive Physics is an excellent example of what I refer to as a microworld, because the experiments are simple to use and syntonic. They are also very helpful to the teacher, because it would require thousands of dollars of equipment and many hours of work to set up the actual physics experiments contained in this environment.

## Bubble Dialogue

Although most microworlds support science learning, others support different forms of knowledge construction. Based on Vygotsky's notion of "zone of proximal development" in the social process of learning, the

Learning Development and Hypermedia Research Group at Ulster University (McMahon & O'Neill, 1993) have developed an environment called Bubble Dialogue that provides a "zone of engagement in learning." Bubble Dialogue supports the skills of role-playing, dialogue creation, and reflective analysis of the dialogue. Literate users of all ages assume the roles of screen characters. As shown in Figure 10.3, each page of the dialogue has four icons, representing one speech and one thought bubble per character. While creating dialogue, learners can switch into review mode and evaluate the sequence of the dialogue, add explanatory notes about the characters or their feelings, edit the content of any of the speech or thought bubbles, and add dialogue where none existed before.

These features engage and enhance student reflections on the dialogue. Initially, learners express their personal views of the world in the dialogue, but gradually they begin to assume different perspectives in both public and private speech. We make meaning through social interaction, but so much of our language use is hidden from us in the private thoughts and conversations of others. Bubble Dialogue provides a dialogue space that

**Figure 10.3**
Speech and thought bubbles in a Bubble Dialogue

allows learners to see and hear their own dialogue, thus promoting reflection, reconstruction, and decontextualization of language. These processes enable learners to internalize as personal meaning that which is within their zone of proximal development, which is where the transition from social to personal knowing takes place. The dialogue and the interactions it reflects become zones of engagement for learners.

The nature of the discourse among students is set by the context included in the Prologue and the opening speech. The kinds of interactions that take place in the bubbles and in the conversation leading to their creation depend on the number of learners and the role the teacher assumes in the learning process. The most direct role is for the teacher to assume one character and a student the other. The student may be asked to play the role of the expert while the teacher assumes the role of learner. A single learner may play both roles, or learners can assume both of the roles. Learners may collaborate to create dialogue. This is most interesting when the teacher assumes one role and the learners collaborate on the other.

What makes Bubble Dialogue attractive to learners? The learners identify strongly with the characters they create. However, there is a concomitant distancing of the person from the character because one is playing a role. The learner does not have to *become* that character. The learner can also revise or reconstruct the characters using the graphics tools provided by HyperCard. Often, when learners collaborate to create dialogue for a character, they end up competing to control the character.

Bubble Dialogue is also attractive because of its versatility. Learners can create dialogue between any characters in any context. They use the Bubble Maker program to create characters or choose them from a graphics library, paste them into a comic strip frame, write a Prologue establishing the context for the story, and fill in the speech and thought bubbles to create a dialogue. Teachers can get learners started by creating the context and the first speech bubble and then allowing learners to complete the dialogue.

Bubble Dialogue is a powerful but very simple microworld that mediates the internal and external dialogue necessary for making sense of the world. It is also general, applicable to many areas of life. It is syntonic, with learners applying their experiences and understandings to the creation of meaning. Bubble Dialogue allows learners to experiment with social roles and use their underlying concepts for exploring natural phenomena.

## Geometric Supposer

One of the best-known microworlds is Geometric Supposer, a tool for making and testing conjectures in geometry through constructing and manipulating geometric objects and exploring the relationships within and between these objects (Schwartz & Yerushalmy, 1987). Geometric Supposer allows students to choose a primitive shape, such as a triangle, and construct it by defining points, segments, parallels or perpendiculars, bisectors, or angles (see Figure 10.4) (Yerushalmy & Houde, 1986). The program plots and remembers each manipulation and can apply it to similar figures. For example, if the students conjecture that "a median drawn from the vertex of any triangle to the opposite side bisects the angle" (p. 419), they can test it easily by asking Geometric Supposer to measure the angles or by applying the relationship to several other triangles. The student will learn immediately that the conjecture is not true. Constructing

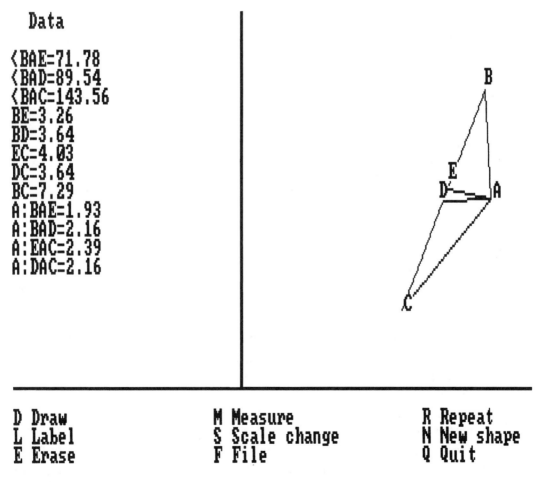

**Figure 10.4**
Investigating a triangle with Geometric Supposer

these test examples manually would require more effort than students are likely to generate, but the computational power of the computer makes this testing very easy.

Geometry instruction is traditionally based on the application of theorems to prove that certain relationships exist among objects. This top-down approach requires analytic reasoning, which a majority of students find difficult. Geometric Supposer supports the learning of geometry by enabling the student to inductively prove these relationships by manipulating the components of geometric objects and observing the results. Rather than having the student apply someone else's logic, Geometric Supposer makes explicit the relationships between visual properties and the numerical properties of the objects (Yerushalmy, 1990). Rather than using the computer to provide conclusive results, the computer calculates the results of students' experiments. The research results with Geometric Supposer have been consistently positive.

# Microworlds as Quasi-Mindtools

## Evaluation of Microworlds as Mindtools

**1. *Computer-based.*** The computational abilities of the computer make most microworlds possible. The computations in microworlds, such as Interactive Physics and Geometric Supposer, are embedded in the program. It is the computer's ability to make and display the products of computations quickly that makes these kinds of microworlds fun.

**2. *Readily available, general applications.*** Microworlds usually can be acquired from their publishers or through software catalogs. They are not always available to run on more than one kind of computer. For example, Geometric Supposer is available for Apple IIs and Macintoshes, as well as DOS computers, while Bubble Dialogue is for the Macintosh only.

**3. *Affordable.*** Most microworlds are reasonably priced. However, they are specific to a one content domain, so they do not have the versatility offered by many other Mindtools.

**4. *Represent knowledge.*** Unlike other Mindtools, more of the knowledge in microworlds is represented by the environment itself. The purpose of microworlds is not so much to represent knowledge as to test it.

**5. *Applicable in different subject domains.*** This is the major limitation of microworlds. They do what they do quite well, and, although some of the knowledge and skills that are gained from working with a microworld may transfer to other domains, microworlds themselves cannot provide opportunities to explore those domains. Microworld environments are usually designed to depict only a single kind of content domain. So, even though they support the development of a range of skills in one domain, they typically cannot be used in others.

6. *Engage critical thinking.* These skills are described in the next section.

7. *Facilitate transfer of learning.* Within a knowledge domain, the major advantage of exploration and discovery of principles and concepts is their transferability to other problems. Research has shown that the kinds of thinking engendered by microworlds definitely transfer within a knowledge domain. Given the content dependence of the skills used, however, it is unknown whether the skills engaged by microworlds would transfer to another domain. But that is not their purpose.

8. *Simple, powerful formalism.* As described in the beginning of this chapter, a simple, powerful formalism is virtually the definition of microworlds.

9. *(Reasonably) easy to learn.* Most microworlds require only an orientation to the objects contained in them and instruction in how they can be manipulated. The intellectual investment should be in how the microworld can be used, not in how to use it.

## Critical, Creative, and Complex Thinking in Microworld Use

The purpose of microworlds is to engage learners in hypothesis generation and testing, skills that naturally entail a large number of critical, creative, and complex thinking skills. However, the critical thinking skills engaged by microworlds are somewhat specific to the microworld. Tables 10.1, 10.2, and 10.3, identify the critical, creative, and complex skills involved in using Interactive Physics, Bubble Dialogue, and Geometric Supposer. Other microworlds would engage different sets of skills. The skills in each table that are marked by an "×" are those that are employed by each process, based on an information-processing analysis of the tasks.

Experimenting with phenomena requires many critical thinking skills (see Table 10.1), such as assessing what is known, recognizing problems, identifying causal relationships, and generating hypotheses (inferring deductively). All of the microworlds engage combinations of evaluating, analyzing, and connecting skills. The most important evaluating skills that Interactive Physics engages are assessing information and determining criteria. Its major requirements are connecting skills, such as logical thinking and inferring, as well as identifying causal relationships. Bubble Dialogue engages more analyzing skills because of its emphasis on analyzing the patterns and assumptions of the dialogue created by the other characters in order to produce a meaningful response. Geometric Supposer potentially engages almost every critical thinking skill in order to evaluate figures, analyze them for their attributes, and reason logically in order to generate and test hypotheses.

More creative thinking skills are engaged by Bubble Dialogue and Geometric Supposer than by the very analytic, experimental environment of Interactive Physics (see Table 10.2). Bubble Dialogue primarily requires learners to elaborate on the conversation by expanding, modifying, extending, or controlling it. Geometric Supposer engages synthesizing and imagining skills in order to generate and test hypotheses. For that reason, both Interactive Physics and Geometric Supposer are rich in imagining skills.

Complex thinking skills are those necessary for planning and carrying out experiments, so Interactive Physics and Geometric Supposer are rich in these skills, while Bubble Dialogue engages very few of them (see Table

**Table 10.1**
Critical thinking skills in Microworld use

|  | Interactive Physics | Bubble Dialogue | Geometric Supposer |
|---|:---:|:---:|:---:|
| **Evaluating** | | | |
| Assessing information | X | X | X |
| Determining criteria | X | | X |
| Prioritizing | | X | |
| Recognizing fallacies | X | | X |
| Verifying | X | | X |
| **Analyzing** | | | |
| Recognizing patterns | X | X | X |
| Classifying | X | X | X |
| Identifying assumptions | X | X | X |
| Identifying main ideas | | X | |
| Finding sequences | | X | X |
| **Connecting** | | | |
| Comparing/contrasting | | X | X |
| Logical thinking | X | | X |
| Inferring deductively | X | X | X |
| Inferring inductively | X | | X |
| Identifying causal relationships | X | | X |

**Table 10.2**
Creative thinking skills in
Microworld use

| | Interactive Physics | Bubble Dialogue | Geometric Supposer |
|---|---|---|---|
| **Elaborating** | | | |
| Expanding | | X | |
| Modifying | | X | |
| Extending | X | X | X |
| Shifting categories | | X | X |
| Concretizing | X | X | X |
| **Synthesizing** | | | |
| Analogical thinking | | X | X |
| Summarizing | | X | |
| Hypothesizing | X | | X |
| Planning | X | X | X |
| **Imagining** | | | |
| Fluency | | X | |
| Predicting | X | | X |
| Speculating | X | | X |
| Visualizing | X | | X |
| Intuition | X | X | X |

10.3). None of the environments engages designing skills to any significant degree, since the environments are very circumscribed and already designed. That is, there is less emphasis on originating ideas or representation in microworlds. Geometric Supposer does enable learners to create a variety of shapes. However, since microworlds are exploratory environments, they are more likely to engage problem-solving and decision-making skills.

# How to Use Microworlds in the Classroom

Because microworlds vary so much in both the content they convey and the skills they facilitate, it is difficult to provide prescriptions for how to support their use. The following are a few general principles for using microworlds to foster self-regulated learning:

**1.** Computer-based microworlds support self-regulated learning. This means that the teacher cannot always set specific goals or objectives for instruction but should encourage the learners to set goals for themselves. Requiring students to articulate these goals is very important to their intellectual development.

**Table 10.3**
Complex thinking skills in Microworld use

| | Interactive Physics | Bubble Dialogue | Geometric Supposer |
|---|---|---|---|
| **Designing** | | | |
| Imagining a goal | | | X |
| Formulating a goal | | | X |
| Inventing a product | | X | X |
| Assessing a product | | | |
| Revising the product | | | |
| **Problem Solving** | | | |
| Sensing the problem | X | | X |
| Researching the problem | X | | X |
| Formulating the problem | X | | X |
| Finding alternatives | X | X | X |
| Choosing the solution | X | | X |
| Building acceptance | | X | |
| **Decision Making** | | | |
| Identifying an issue | X | X | X |
| Generating alternatives | X | | X |
| Assessing the consequences | X | | X |
| Making a choice | X | | X |
| Evaluating the choices | X | | X |

**2.** Microworlds best serve any curriculum as self-directed problem-solving practice. Most microworlds are problem-solving spaces, permitting learners to generate their own hypotheses about ideas within the content domain being studied. This form of problem-solving practice is more likely to produce transfer of learning than more traditional problem sets.

**3.** In a related concern, incidental learning should be accepted and encouraged when using microworld learning environments. Incidental learning consists of the unintended, serendipitous learning that occurs when learners find something interesting. Schools normally impose strict agendas on learning and therefore de-emphasize incidental learning in order to "cover the curriculum." Incidental learning is not rewarded. Since learners need to set their own goals rather than those set by the teacher or the curriculum, much learning from microworlds may be perceived as incidental. Allow learners to diverge from their own goals in order to explore new, interesting ideas.

**4.** Encourage students to compare the objects in the microworld with objects and actions they are already familiar with. Regularly ask them if they can think of things in the real world that behave as those in the microworld do. This is what Papert means by syntonic learning, and it is very important to the learning outcomes in microworlds, since microworlds are designed to model events in the real world.

**5.** When learners get bogged down and are unable to generate problems, goals, and hypotheses, you should first model how to generate hypotheses and later coach them by prompting hypothesis-generating behaviors. "What do you think will happen if . . . ?" This may be especially important in encouraging students to observe carefully the results of their actions in the environment and to modify their thinking in order to generate alternative hypotheses about the objects in the environment.

**6.** Encourage students to collaborate in mixed groups of two or three. Which collaborative arrangements work best will depend on the nature of the learning environment and the skills it requires.

**7.** Ask students to report their findings in each microworld to the class. This will increase their awareness of all possible solutions to various problems.

## Advantages of Microworlds as Quasi-Mindtools

Since microworlds vary in content and skills, so do their advantages. However, there are some generally accepted advantages of all microworlds.

- They contain understandable examples of complex natural phenomena and provide environments for representing those phenomena.
- They support exploration of phenomena through activities and provide the tools for facilitating that exploration.
- They allow the underlying concepts for exploring natural phenomena to be defined by the learner using characteristics of the microworld; they provide the tools for defining their world (e.g., speech and thought balloons in Bubble Dialogue).
- They support learning, from simple to complex skills.
- They integrate knowledge, skills, and attitudes through problem-solving activities.
- They provide instruction that is situated in rich, meaningful settings and are thus more motivating than traditional learning activities.
- They support self-regulated learning, where learners identify their own goals and use the microworld to satisfy those goals.
- They are based on powerful ideas, which are major building blocks in students' mental models.

- They provide for experiential learning, so learners learn by doing, instead of just watching or listening to a description of how something works.

# Limitations of Microworlds as Quasi-Mindtools

There are few real limitations or disadvantages of microworlds.

- They are single-purpose, organized to explore a single content domain, and not adaptable to other purposes.
- They call on skills that students likely do not possess and must acquire, so their openness can be frustrating at first.

## Conclusion

Microworlds are quasi-Mindtools that engage learners in hypothesis testing and mental model building. This chapter diverges most from the others in the book in that it describes constrained, predefined, exploratory learning environments for engaging learners in problem solving rather than tools for constructing knowledge representations. Microworlds are predefined discovery spaces that present constrained simulations of real-world phenomena, but they do not necessarily limit the learner to prescribed problems. Most microworlds, such as those described in this chapter, enable learners to construct and define their own problems to solve. The underlying notions of microworlds are representations of complex, real-world phenomena that facilitate exploration of those "micro" worlds and hypothesis testing about the components of that world. Allowing the learner to redefine the phenomena and the tools for exploring natural phenomena makes microworlds even more powerful Mindtools. Though many learners will not readily accept the responsibility for defining their own learning, the rewards of doing so will justify the effort required to coax, coach, and cajole learners into becoming explorers and knowledge constructors.

### References

Burton, R. R., Brown, J. S., & Fischer, G. (1984). Skiing as a model of instruction. In B. Rogoff & J. Lave (Eds.), *Everyday cognition: Its development in social context.* Cambridge, MA: Harvard University Press.

diSessa, A., & Abelson, H. (1986). BOXER: A reconstructible computational medium. *Communications of the ACM, 29*(9), 859–868.

Draper, S. W., & Norman, D. (1986). Introduction. In D. A. Norman & S. W. Draper (Eds.), *User-centered system design.* Hillsdale, NJ: Lawrence Erlbaum Associates.

Dreyer, P. H. (1984). Cognitive development and computers: Why Logo might just be revolutionary. In M. Douglas (Ed.), *Claremont Reading Conference.* Claremont, CA: Claremont Reading Conference.

Hanna, J. (1986). Learning environment criteria. In R. Ennals, R. Gwyn, & L. Zdravchev (Eds.), *Information technology and education: The changing school.* Chichester, UK: Ellis Horwood.

Lawler, B. (1984). Designing computer-based microworlds. In M. Yazdani (Ed.), *New horizons in educational computing.* Chichester, UK: Ellis Horwood.

McMahon, H., & O'Neill, W. (1993). Computer-mediated zones of engagement in learning. In T. M. Duffy, J. Lowyck, & D. H. Jonassen (Eds.), *Designing environments for constructive learning.* Heidelberg, FRG: Springer-Verlag.

Papert, S. (1980). *Mindstorms: Children, computers, and powerful ideas.* New York: Basic Books.

Richmond, B., Peterson, S., & Vescuso, P. (1987). *An academic user's guide to Stella.* Lyme, NH: High Performance Systems.

Salomon, G. (1993). On the nature of pedagogic computer tools: The case of the writing partner. In S. P. LaJoie & S. J. Derry (Eds.), *Computers as cognitive tools.* Hillsdale, NJ: Lawrence Erlbaum Associates.

Schwartz, J. L., & Yerushalmy, M. (1987). The Geometric Supposer: Using microcomputers to restore invention to the learning of mathematics. In D. N. Perkins, J. Lockhead, & J. C. Bishop (Eds.), *Thinking: The second international conference.* Hillsdale, NJ: Lawrence Erlbaum Associates.

Steed, M. (1992). Stella, a simulation construction kit: Cognitive process and educational implications. *Journal of Computers in Science and Mathematics Teaching, 11*(1), 39–52.

Thompson, A. D., & Wang, H. M. (1988). Effects of a Logo microworld on student ability to transfer a concept. *Journal of Educational Computing Research, 4*(3), 335–347.

White, B. Y. (1993). ThinkerTools: Causal models, conceptual change, and science education. *Cognition and Instruction, 10*(1), 1–100.

Yerushalmy, M. (1990). Using empirical information in geometry: Students' and designers' expectations. *Journal of Computers in Mathematics and Science Teaching, 9*(3), 23–33.

Yerushalmy, M., & Houde, R. A. (1986). The Geometric Supposer: Promoting thinking and learning. *Mathematics Teacher, 79,* 418–422.

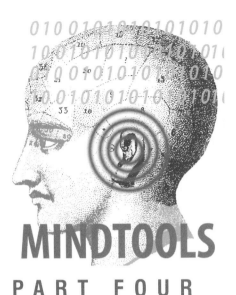

# MINDTOOLS

Implementing Mindtools:
Implementing Mindtools:
Problems and Potentials

····································································

Part 4 describes the problems involved in implementing Mindtools in the classroom. These problems and concerns are discussed in the following chapters:

Many technology-based innovations have failed because they were not properly implemented, and the intellectual and social challenges Mindtools present make them potential victims of a similar fate. The two chapters in Part 4 relate the responsibilities that you, the teacher, must accept if you choose to use Mindtools. These responsibilities are not insignificant. Mindtools represent a new approach to instruction and learning in which teachers must relinquish some of their intellectual authority and learners must assume more responsibility for making their own meaning. That will not be easy for today's learners, who are used to simply repeating what they are told.

There is also the very difficult problem of assessing learners' higher-order thinking and individual knowledge construction. Although these problems represent impediments to successful implementation of Mindtools, they can be overcome. The rewards of any effort, especially one that leads to meaningful learning, should justify confronting these difficulties.

# The Challenges of Teaching with Mindtools:
## *Supporting Mindfulness and Self-Regulation*

## The Role of Mindtools in Society

In recent years, national reports have documented a diminution in the ability and willingness to think among American students. Declining test scores are but symptoms of a malady in our schools. From Chapter 1, we know that educators are concerned about the future abilities of learners. What is needed in education at all levels is a revolution—not just a change in methodology, but a fundamental revolution in spirit. This revolution will be marked by children who are energized by the personal growth that results from mastering something new rather than complaining about having to complete another assignment or grilling the teacher about the contents of the next test; by teachers who are invigorated by the intellectual challenges of their students and who model, coach, and facilitate thinking rather than telling students what is on the next test; and by educational systems that seek to prepare learners for adapting to their changing environments by being lifelong learners, systems that revile mindless memorization of meaningless trivia. This is a tall order, and, although Mindtools alone will not be the cause or even the catalyst for the social change necessary for reclaiming an emphasis on learning in schools, they can be the tools of reform.

I do not pretend that Mindtools are the only means to engage students in meaningful thinking. There are other computers tools and many more ways to engage learners in thinking that do not even require a computer. However, if you believe that education is a process that should, at least some of the time, engage students in higher-order thinking, and if you believe that computers can and should assist that process, then Mindtools can help.

I hope there is no misinterpretation of the goals of using Mindtools. The goals are vigorous. They are challenging. They will work only if students and teachers agree that thinking hard is a meaningful goal unto itself.

# Constructive Roles for Learners

Why are learners often unable to think, to learn, to solve problems, and to reach their learning potential? Salomon and Globerson (1987) suggest three reasons. First, learners have not acquired a repertoire of learning strategies for successfully accomplishing different kinds of learning tasks. Too often, they apply a "brute force" memorization strategy, and when that does not work they lack alternative strategies to employ. This is especially problematic with Mindtools, for which memorization strategies simply will not work.

Second, learners are poorly motivated. I believe that the most pandemic, yet most insidious, cause for underachievement in schools is lower expectations on the part of teachers, which reduces expectations of students and parents, which further erodes the expectations of teachers and the entire educational system. Salomon and Globerson also refer to factors such as learned helplessness, poor perceived self-efficacy, and improper attribution of success or failure. In the United States, people too frequently litigate personal responsibility. Students ask for help before investing significant mental effort in solving problems. They have learned to be helpless, and they believe that it is not their fault.

Third, students tend to rely only on vague perceptions and global, quick-fix solutions to problems rather than thinking about and analyzing them—that is, engaging in effortful reasoning. When students are not motivated to perform, their initial strategy is to misapply their misconceptions rather than decompose the problem, analyze assumptions, elaborate on the information, and use other critical thinking skills.

Mindtools will work most successfully in a venue of educational reform where learners are perceived as constructors of ideas and defenders of those constructions. Learners must approach learning mindfully, and they must realize and execute personal intentions to learn and think and to regulate those processes. Their productions must be taken seriously by educators, and their efforts must be rewarded by the educational system, their parents, and society in general. Mindtools can support both mindfulness and self-regulation, but they may not be able to cause them, although there are examples of that occurring (recall the students in Chapter 8 giving up their recesses and study halls to develop the multimedia program for the zoo). Mindfulness and self-regulation must become a natural part of the learner's repertoire.

## Mindful Learning

Mindfulness is the "volitional, metacognitively guided employment of non-automatic, usually effort demanding processes" (Salomon & Globerson, 1987, p. 625). Mindfulness is required for meaningful learning, learning that is applicable to similar situations and transferable to dissimilar situations. Mindful learning, according to Salomon and Globerson, is characterized by the following activities:

- suppressing initial responses and reflecting on aspects of problems
- gathering, examining, and personalizing information about problems
- generating and selecting alternative strategies
- making connections to existing knowledge and building new structures
- expending effort on learning
- concentrating
- reflecting on how a task was performed

The goal of education should be to engage learners in mindful learning. This is not a level of activity that learners are inured to, but they certainly are capable of it. What is necessary is to provide them with a relevant purpose for thinking and the tools to guide the process. Salomon (1985) urges the use of computers not to drill "low-road" learning (drill and practice, leading to automatic responses) but rather to foster "high-road" learning (thinking-intensive, situation-dependent, mindful processing). High-road learning, he argues, depends on learners' mindfulness, which is dependent in part on the learning materials used. Mindfulness can be promoted by using the computer as a Mindtool, as an intellectual partner in the learning process (as described in Chapter 1). Ultimately, however, mindfulness is dependent on the students and their willingness and interest in learning.

## Self-Regulated Learners

The goal of many educational reforms over the years has been the development of self-regulation skills in learners. Rather than functioning passively in classrooms, learners should be able to determine their goals for learning, plan for learning, prepare themselves to learn, engage in learning activities, monitor what and how they best learn, regulate the learning activities in light of that monitoring, and maintain motivation and a purpose for learning. While these activities seems intrinsically appropriate learning skills, they contrast sharply with most classroom routines, where teachers determine what the students will learn (or apply a mandated curriculum), seek the students' attention, deliver everything the students need to do or know, quiz them to be sure they are completing assignments, and assess whether they understand what they were told.

According to Simons (1993), self-regulated learners

- maintain an orientation to learning goals and activities
- plan learning activities to fulfill those goals
- select goals in light of personal ability, prior knowledge, and interest
- intrinsically motivate their own performance (self-motivation)
- access relevant prior knowledge to apply to new learning
- apply strategies for getting started
- attribute successes and failures to personal effort

The key to self-regulation among learners is intentionality. Students must accept and even embrace the intention to learn and to perform. Those intentions are the purpose around which they can regulate their activity. Instruction needs to help learners first to articulate what those goals and intentions are and then to reflect on how well they have been achieved. This is the essence of self-regulation. Mindtools require learners to articulate such a purpose, so their primary goal, as knowledge representation tools, is to engage learners in reflecting on what they know.

Students normally do not approach learning mindfully, and few consistently exhibit self-regulation of that learning. Most have never been required to, so they do not know how. Most, if not all, of their learning careers have been directed by teachers, so making the transition to learner control and self-regulation will not be easy for them. In most cases, your efforts to help them become more mindful and self-regulatory will be frustrated by their lack of ability, experience, and tenacity. You will need to ease the transition by providing guidance and encouragement. Persevere, for there are no more noble goals of education. And use all of the tools—including Mindtools—at your disposal to assist you in the process.

## Constructive Roles for Teachers

The success of Mindtools will depend largely on you, the teacher. It is important that you accept and adopt not only the use of Mindtools, but also their underlying constructivist theory, at least to some degree. Your role as the teacher must change from purveyor of knowledge to instigator, promoter, coach, helper, model, and guide of knowledge construction. Experience with implementing Mindtools has shown that this is difficult, that teachers are simply used to showing students how to do things and providing them with the answers they seek. We have often seen students' semantic nets, databases, and expert systems appear virtually identical, because the teacher (however well intentioned) directly taught the content and organization of the knowledge bases created by students. It will be difficult for you to observe the frustration experienced and expressed by your students while they try to think for themselves without intervening with the answer being sought.

## How Teachers Can Foster the Integration of Mindtools: Learners as Cognitive Apprentices

In order for Mindtools to engage learners in critical thinking (as described in Chapter 2), teachers must adopt a new model of teaching. Direct instruction, with teachers as purveyors of knowledge and students as recipients, will not work. The contemporary model of instruction that best supports the use of Mindtools is *cognitive apprenticeship* (Collins, 1991; Collins, Brown, & Newman, 1989), a formalization and revision of the oldest form of instruction in the world. It emerged from apprenticeship learning, where apprentices acquired skills through observation of crafts-people and through extended practice of the skills used. The acquisition of useful, real-world skills was situated in a real-world context, such as the stable, the tailor shop, or the accountancy office. The emphasis was on learning to do something meaningful.

The industrial revolution ushered in an era in which machines largely replaced human labor and the need to pass on skills through apprentice-ship. Formal education (schools) replaced apprenticeships for many, but schools, which were not needed to teach these learners how to *do* any-thing, began to simply dispense knowledge that was supposed to make students more worldly and better developed intellectually. Compared with apprenticeships, there was no clear purpose for acquiring the knowledge. The most common method of teaching that emerged was the sponge method (Schank & Jona, 1991), in which students absorbed the knowl-edge dispensed by the teacher and were wrung out during examinations.

The present revolution in learning theory development, known as situ-ated learning, claims that what students are forced to learn is not very meaningful to them because there is no opportunity for them to use it for any relevant or meaningful purpose. Cognitive apprenticeships are part of this revolution. Rather than seeing students as recipients of knowledge, the cognitive apprenticeship model suggests that students should become apprentice learners, that schools should function as apprenticeships in learning how to learn, and that teachers should model, coach, and scaffold learners to help them articulate their knowledge and reflect on what they know.

## Modeling

Modeling involves performing mental tasks in front of students so that they can observe the kinds of thinking they need to use in order to solve problems and develop their own knowledge. This means not only modeling the performance, but also modeling the thinking processes overtly. A good example of this is Schoenfeld's (1985) model of math teaching, in which he challenges students to bring him problems he cannot solve. While trying to solve them, he articulates how he goes about solving the problems, what strategies he uses, and what mental models are required for understanding the problems.

To use this strategy, start with simple problems and work up to more complex, demanding problems. Perhaps the most important part of this strategy is reflecting on the process you use, examining the dilemmas that you face and the thought processes that you use to conquer them. Sometimes the strategy will fail, and you will not be able to solve the problem, perhaps because there is no solution. But knowing that the teacher also struggles occasionally assures the students that they are not the only ones who experience difficulty.

## Coaching

Coaching is a technique of cognitive apprenticeship in which the instructor observes students as they try to complete tasks and provides hints, help, and feedback as needed to get them to think like an experienced performer. Coaching is similar in many ways to Socratic dialogue, because the teacher must diagnose how students are thinking and provide guidance when they are experiencing difficulties in order to help them correct their thinking. It is best to provide only as much help as is needed to enable students to accomplish the task.

Coaching most often assumes the form of questions, prompting learners to think about aspects of the problem that they have not considered. Such prompts should be faded as soon as possible. *Fading* is a technique in which the instructor gradually withdraws the coaching prompts and transfers full control of the performance to the learner. Coaching also prompts learners to articulate what they know and to reflect on what they know and do not know.

## Articulation

Articulation refers to methods that teachers use to get students to consciously describe how they are thinking. According to Collins (1991), articulation makes tacit knowledge explicit and more available to be used in performing other tasks. It also helps students see how other students are thinking about problems or ideas; that is, it provides students with alternative perspectives on the knowledge being gained. Articulation most often assumes the form of questions that require students to think about how they are understanding the content. For example, "Think of an analogy for this process. Factoring equations is like . . . " Another articulation method is the think-aloud protocol, where learners think aloud as they solve problems or perform tasks.

## Reflection

Reflection refers to strategies that encourage learners to compare their thinking with that of other learners and the teacher or other skilled performer. There are several methods for facilitating reflection. Students can imitate other performers, articulating how their performance differs. Another method is the "instant replay" or "postmortem" of a learning or problem-solving process, or a more involved, abstracted replay of the performance where the essential features of the solution process are highlighted. According to Collins (1991), reflection is an important strategy because what the student does becomes the object of instruction, and students can compare their performance with others' performances.

## Scaffolding

Scaffolding is a cognitive apprenticeship technique in which the instructor performs or supports the performance of parts of a task that the learner is not yet able to perform. When students are stuck, suggesting a solution or performing that step for them *before* they give up will help them complete the task and gain the confidence to try other problems. The student and teacher work cooperatively to solve the problem together. It is important that the teacher encourage students to assume as much of the responsibility for completing the process as they are able to, and scaffolding should be faded as soon as possible. Having received just enough help to solve a problem, it is very likely that learners will need less help in solving the next problem.

Lehrer (in press) talks about scaffolding the construction of hypermedia programs (see Chapter 8 for more discussion) in several ways. He scaffolds complex activities by modeling the cognitive processes required, such as summarizing and planning. He scaffolds task or skill performance by asking leading questions and asking students to justify their choices. Scaffolding also takes the form of alternative assessments that encourage cooperation among learners and deeper forms of thinking. Finally, he scaffolds performance through the use of computer tools, thereby facilitating the process of creating and linking multimedia chunks of information.

The premise of this book is that Mindtools scaffold thinking. Mindtools scaffold articulation of and reflection on what learners know and how they organize and interrelate that knowledge. Mindtools are articulation tools. As discussed in Chapter 1, they provide students with formalisms for representing what they know; that is, they help learners articulate what they know in different ways. Mindtools are also reflection tools. They are tools for scaffolding performance of complex thinking tasks. When used with other apprenticeship strategies, such as coaching and modeling, Mindtools can provide the foundation for supporting learners in cognitive apprenticeships.

# Challenges to Teachers

For a number of reasons, using Mindtools may be challenging for teachers. I state the following assumptions about the commitment necessary for teachers to effectively use Mindtools, not as a threat but as a challenge. If you cannot accept the following premises, it is unlikely that you will be successful in effectively integrating Mindtools in your classes. If you don't, even the process of reflecting on your values vis-à-vis these assumptions will be enlightening. Effective learning and thinking requires that we all are able to reflect on what we are and are not able and willing to do.

## Teacher Skills

Effectively integrating Mindtools into the educational process requires that teachers be able to use the Mindtools. Computers, like other technologies, have too often been used in schools as electronic baby-sitters. Plug the kids into a film, video, or computer game and they at least present the illusion of engagement, and who knows, they may just learn something. Television allows learners to remain passive, uncommitted, mindless, and unregulated. That strategy will not work with Mindtools.

Computer Mindtools require learner engagement. Not all students will spontaneously adopt their use. As discussed before, mindful learning requires intellectual, not just physical, engagement. This will not happen unless you are also engaged in the students' constructions. You cannot model, coach, and scaffold what you do not know, so you too must become at least moderately skilled with the tools. This does not mean that you have to be "the authority" on the functioning of each tool. As Schoenfeld (1985) has shown, it is OK to admit that you do not know everything. It is also useful to model the process of searching through documentation to discover what you do not know. But you should know how to use the tools well enough to facilitate their use by your students. This will show your commitment to the goals of Mindtools. If you communicate that you are not committed, then it is unlikely that your students will be either.

## Teacher Commitment

Mindtools require that you, the teacher, work harder at teaching when using computers, rather than relying on the computer to sustain the learning activity. It is intellectually more demanding to apprentice your students than to dispense knowledge. You cannot "plug the kids into Mindtools" and expect them to work without your support. Strategies such as modeling and coaching require that you take risks and admit that you do not know everything, but that you show that you do know how to go about discovering what you do not know and using that new knowledge to solve meaningful problems. The reward will justify the risks.

## Teacher Authority

Constructivism (discussed in Chapter 1) argues that we each construct meaning for the objects and events that surround us by interpreting our perceptions of them in terms of our past experiences, beliefs, and biases. To some degree, we all mentally represent our own personal reality. Each reality is somewhat different, because each individual's experiences and resulting perceptions are different. This does not mean that each and every representation is equal. Experts are experts because their experiences have helped them to develop richer, better-integrated, more useful representations of their part of the world. What it does mean is that the meaning an individual constructs in any domain is meaningful for that person. It also argues, as does cognitive apprenticeship, that more meaning is constructed while engaged in doing something than from hearing or reading about something.

The implications of constructivism for teaching are clear. For constructivist methods to work, teachers must relinquish some of their authority. Some argue that schools intentionally retard the development of creative, critical, independent thinking because it would result in some loss of power for the educational system, which dictates what and how things should be known. For Mindtools to be used most effectively, you must be willing to relinquish some of your authority as teacher, both your power-related authority and your intellectual authority.

There are many ways to perceive and understand most knowledge domains. You must become more willing to accept different perspectives and interpretations of the world and perhaps to allow students to challenge your perspective while supporting theirs. You are not the ultimate arbiter of meaning. You must be willing and able to develop and use multiple assessment methods and criteria (discussed in Chapter 12) that permit students to express ideas in terms that are more meaningful to them, not necessarily as the textbook or the curriculum states them. The rewards will be obvious. When students have some ownership of ideas, they are more willing to generate and use them. The purpose of schools should be to educate, to "educe," which means to evoke, extract, or elicit something that is latent, that is, to draw out what learners know. That means that you cannot tell students what they should know; instead, your role should be to help them articulate what they know and come to know it better. Mindtools are computer tools for educing knowledge.

## Administrative Support

Finally, Mindtools, like most innovations, will not work without administrative support. In most schools, the principal controls the intellectual tempo of the school. So, first and foremost, you need an administrative staff with a philosophy that begins with meaningful expectations for learning. Committed teachers are not enough if the administration is not committed to change and to student knowledge construction and critical thinking. The entire school culture has to believe that students can and will, given the opportunity, think meaningfully.

Second, you need computers. Most schools have only one computer for every 20 students, so each student, on the average, is able to use it at best for only one twentieth of the time he or she is in school. I firmly believe that if computers are to become effective tools, then students must have constant access to them. Imagine asking carpenters to build your house but allowing them to use their saws and hammers for only 25 minutes per day. The rest of the time they have to talk about building a house, listen to lectures, and take multiple-choice tests on home construction. This does not necessarily mean that there ought to be a computer on every desk, since collaborative use of Mindtools has been shown to be effective. The administration must support thinking with equipment and with expectations that critical thinking is an important outcome.

Third, you need logistical support for using Mindtools, especially in terms of scheduling. Mindtools require engagement, and engagement cannot always reach fruition in 50-minute periods. Our experience has shown that flexible scheduling and interdisciplinary teaching arrangements greatly facilitate the use of Mindtools. Students need blocks of time to get involved and negotiate meaning among themselves. If your administration insists that your students move when the bells ring, then it will be more difficult to engage students and to use Mindtools.

## Conclusion

Mindtools pose a number of problems for schooling. Successfully implementing Mindtools assumes that the school staff and the society in which the school exists must respect and encourage critical thinking and personal knowledge construction as meaningful goals. It assumes that learners should spend their time in school mindfully engaged in thinking and learning (articulating what they know and reflecting on its personal and societal relevance) and that they should learn to regulate their own learning habits. Successfully implementing Mindtools also assumes that the role of teachers should change from purveyor to coach and that teachers must be skilled and committed to the goals of critical thinking and to Mindtools. Finally, successfully implementing Mindtools in schools requires that the administration and the support system that it provides should also be committed to these goals and do everything they can to facilitate higher-order thinking and meaning-making among learners.

### References

Collins, A. (1991). Cognitive apprenticeship and instructional technology. In L. Idol & B. F. Jones (Eds.), *Educational values and cognitive instruction: Implications for reform*. Hillsdale, NJ: Lawrence Erlbaum Associates.
Collins, A., Brown, J. S., & Newman, S. E. (1989). Cognitive apprenticeship: Teaching the crafts of reading, writing, and mathematics. In L. B. Resnick (Ed.), *Knowing, learning, and instruction: Essays in honor of Robert Glaser*. Hillsdale, NJ: Lawrence Erlbaum Associates.

Lehrer, R. (in press). Learning by designing hypermedia documents. *Computers in the Schools, 10.*

Salomon, G. (1985, April). *Information technologies: What you see is not (always) what you get.* Paper presented at the annual meeting of the American Educational Research Association, Chicago, IL. (ERIC Document Reproduction Service No. ED 265 872)

Salomon, G., & Globerson, T. (1987). Skill may not be enough: The role of mindfulness in learning and transfer. *International Journal of Educational Research, 11*(6), 623–637.

Schank, R. C., & Jona, M. Y. (1991). Empowering the student: New perspectives on the design of teaching systems. *The Journal of the Learning Sciences, 1*(1), 7–35.

Schoenfeld, A. H. (1985). *Mathematical problem solving.* New York: Academic Press.

Simons, P. R. J. (1993). Constructive learning: The role of the learner. In T. M. Duffy, J. Lowyck, & D. H. Jonassen (Eds.), *Designing environments for constructive learning.* Heidelberg, Germany: Springer-Verlag.

# CHAPTER 12

# Assessing Learning Outcomes from Mindtools:
## *Reap What You Sow*

## Assessment and Learning: Problems Posed by Mindtools

Imagine that you encounter, in your work as a teacher, principal, professor, or other professional, a complex and vexing problem you need to solve. Would you lock yourself in a sterile, fluorescent-lit room with 30 to 300 other people, sit at an uncomfortable desk, avoid communicating with anyone else or asking their advice, remove all of the tools that you normally use (computer, telephone, fax, calculator, etc.), remove all of your reference sources, and, armed only with a ballpoint pen, solve the problem using only multiple-choice responses? You cannot leave until the problem is solved or until the period is over (whichever comes first). This scenario sounds silly, yet it describes the very conditions under which we normally ask students to describe what they know.

What is taught and what is learned in most educational institutions is driven by what we measure. The tests, projects, and examinations we require of students determine what they study and attempt to learn. Though we may say that our goal is for learners to become critical, independent thinkers, if the only way we assess their thinking is through multiple-choice, recall examinations administered in settings such as the one described above, we are communicating a clearer expectation of how we want them to think than all of the mission statements and educational objectives produced by school districts can ever convey. Most students are able to think critically enough to realize that we are not serious about the lofty goals included in the curriculum guides and that their primary responsibility is to memorize the material.

The implication is clear. If you subscribe to the purposes for using Mindtools—engaging critical, creative, and complex thinking—then you are obligated to assess *those* kinds of constructive outcomes and not reproductive learning. If you integrate Mindtools into your instruction but then assess the learning outcomes with recall measures, your students will learn quickly that the Mindtools do not count and that, instead of thinking critically, they need to employ their well-rehearsed strategies for memorizing the content. As the title of the chapter suggests, if you sow the seeds of critical thinking, you should harvest critical thoughts and not reproductive learning.

## Purposes of Assessment and Evaluation

Traditional assessment methods, especially those based on objective forms of examination, tend to

- decontextualize the learning being evaluated
- focus on reproductive learning outcomes
- remove supports that are part of meaningful situations in the real world
- remove prompts that are part of meaningful situations in the real world
- make the evaluation process as stressful as possible
- make the evaluation process as artificial as possible

Clearly, these attributes belie the assumptions and methods of Mindtools. If this is the case, how do we evaluate the effects of learning with Mindtools? The most difficult problem in using constructivist tools rather than lectures and drill-and-practice strategies is evaluating the learning outcomes. I have argued throughout this book that these tools support individual meaning-making, but how do we best assess what meaning has been made and what quality and utility that meaning may have? We should be able to quickly agree that criterion-referenced testing, with questions tied to specific instructional objectives, is inappropriate. With Mindtools, the learner is responsible for constructing personal knowledge. That kind of knowledge needs to be flexible, not inert or reductive; stable, so that it is retained and interpreted consistently; generalizable to new situations and contexts; and reflected in problem-solving outcomes that require near and far transfer of learning.

Evaluating learning outcomes from Mindtools and constructivist environments, according to Jonassen (1992), ought to

- be negotiated between learners and teachers or learners and learners (articulation of learning intentions is a fundamental precept of constructivism)

- be based on authentic tasks—those that have real-world relevance and utility, that integrate those tasks across the curriculum, that provide appropriate levels of complexity, and that allow students to select appropriate levels of difficulty or involvement
- require knowledge construction, not reproduction, thereby actively engaging learners in building personal representations of experiences and the knowledge structures to organize them
- occur in real-world contexts that are just as rich and complex as those used during instruction
- use real-world, context-dependent criteria—those criteria that emerge from the context being presented are the most relevant
- represent multiple perspectives and criteria, reflecting and accepting different perspectives in the evaluation process referenced by a domain of possible outcomes, rather than learning being referenced by a single behavior
- employ a multimodal portfolio, describing either different student interpretations of the assignment or different stages in its development, since each of those perspectives, modes, or dimensions of learning is best represented in different products
- be based on socially negotiated meaning, usually in the form of contracts

These principles argue that in order for the assessment process to be meaningful, it should employ the same methods and activities that are afforded by the tools. As discussed in Chapter 1, the most basic components of constructivist learning are context, collaboration, and construction.

## Assessment in Context

If we attempt to embed learning in authentic, real-world contexts, then assessment and evaluation of learning should require the completion of authentic tasks that are also embedded in some reasonably authentic context. As educators we should be interested in assessing students' ability to handle problem solving with authentic problems; that is, we should engage students while serving cognitive apprenticeships (described in Chapter 11), not at some arbitrarily appointed time. The assessment should be focused on the outcomes of a cognitive apprenticeship, namely articulation and reflection. The assessment methods we select should require learners to articulate what *they* know, not what we told them. Assessment should also require learners to reflect on how they came to know what they know. Assessing the cognitive outcomes of using Mindtools should examine how well learners have articulated and reflected on what they know.

### Assessment during Collaboration

If the learning tasks engaged by Mindtools and constructivist learning environments involve collaboration, as most real-world tasks do, then why should learners be evaluated independently? If the skills they are trying to acquire are best performed collaboratively, then removing collaboration during evaluation violates the most basic of assessment premises, that the conditions, performances, and criteria for the assessment ought to replicate those stated in the learning goals and employed during instruction.

### Assessment of Knowledge Construction

Finally, since constructivist tools and environments engage learners in knowledge construction, assessment activities should also require knowledge construction by the learners and not the regurgitation of ideas previously delivered to them. Genuine intellectual performance is inherently personalized, so the meanings students derive from knowledge construction experiences are inherently more personal and idiosyncratic. Common knowledge need not always be the goal of education. If learning is more like "contextual insight" and "good judgment" than it is like inert knowledge, we need to rethink our reliance on traditional assessment activities and methodology (Wiggins, 1993). Among the changes that are necessary are a redirection of assessment toward self-assessment by learners, and alternative forms of assessment that provide learners the opportunity to express what they know in the best way. These principles are diametrically opposed to traditional conceptions of assessment. Let me explain.

Assessment is normally used as a means of gathering the information necessary to evaluate student performance. Evaluation implies that students' performances are compared with a standard of performance, and a judgment about the quality of their performance is based on their level of performance relative to that standard. Most schools employ a normative standard for evaluating student performance; that is, each student's performance is compared relative to the performance of other students. Grades are normally assigned on this basis, and society passes judgment on individuals based on these comparisons.

The purpose of assessment and evaluation in constructive learning situations and with Mindtools is not to provide society with the information it needs to judge the individual, but rather to provide learners with feedback that will enable them to comprehend how much they have learned in order to better direct their learning. That is, the most important kind of assessment is self-assessment, in which learners assess what they know (articulation) and how able they are to learn a particular skill or subject (reflection) in order to compare their base knowledge with what they need to acquire in order to meet their learning goals. Learners must also be able to self-assess their own knowledge growth. Finally, learners must also be aware of how they build their knowledge structures. Laveault (1986) argues for "adaptability" in the learner. He says that adaptability "accounts for four characteristics of adult intellectual evaluation: flexibility, stability, generalizability, and organizability of operations" (p. 2). These are the primary goals of constructivist learning and should become the foci of assessing learning with Mindtools.

The most important concern in selecting constructive assessment methods, therefore, is the ability of these activities to measure students' progress based on their accomplishments rather than their aptitudes. We should be concerned first with how students can perform when given an authentic task, and then with how they are able to regulate their own learning performance, rather than measuring each student's aptitude and achievement on indirect measures of intelligence. Assessment activities therefore should facilitate self-assessment, articulation, and reflection.

# What to Assess

This is the most difficult problem posed by Mindtools. Conceptually, instructional systems recommend criterion-referenced assessment, which means measuring what you have stated in your objectives for instruction. In each of the Mindtools chapters of this book, I have analyzed the critical, creative, and complex thinking that I believe are engaged by using each of the Mindtools. So the most logical way to assess those outcomes would be to administer tests designed to assess critical, creative, and complex thinking. You could administer those tests at the beginning of the school year and again at the end. Gains in test scores should be attributable, at least in part, to using Mindtools. However, there are a number of problems with this method, not the least of which is that those tests do not yet exist. The Iowa educators who developed the model of critical thinking used in this book to compare Mindtools' outcomes lacked the time and resources needed to construct measures for assessing critical thinking. In addition to the lack of specific critical thinking tests, other measurement problems are raised by Mindtools.

## Limitations of Existing Measures

1. *Critical thinking is difficult to assess.* As evidenced in the preceding chapters, critical thinking is a complex skill, and (as discussed in Chapter

2) there is no universal agreement on what critical thinking means. Existing tests of critical thinking therefore may not be useful. There are a number of critical thinking assessment tools, such as the Watson-Glaser test and the Cornell Test of Critical Thinking, but they are not tied specifically to the outcomes of Mindtools, and there are questions about their validity and reliability. Norris (1989) contends that true critical thinking involves not only the ability to think critically but also the disposition to do so, and that it is unreasonable to attempt to measure judgment about when and how to think critically with a multiple-choice test. Furthermore, there is no evidence on what test takers actually consider when taking these kinds of tests. Are they actually thinking critically? These are generic measures of thinking ability that research has shown to be too insensitive to the kinds of thinking engaged by Mindtools (Wang & Jonassen, 1993).

**2.** *Critical thinking is context-dependent.* That is, solving problems and functioning in different subjects (e.g., math, science, social studies) and in different real-world contexts requires different critical thinking skills. Thinking critically to solve an engineering problem in a factory requires different thinking than solving a political problem at a city council meeting. So, different measures of critical thinking would need to be developed for each context in which Mindtools were used. There is no such thing, according to many psychologists, as generic critical thinking skills. Even transferring critical thinking within a subject domain is difficult to assess, because if transfer of learning fails to occur, you never know whether learners are unable to transfer critical thinking or simply lack subject-specific knowledge to be transferred (Norris, 1989). Although Mindtools are generalizable to different domains, their effects are likely to vary in different domains, so assessment in each domain also has to be different. Assessment should be based on the nature of the problems in the domain that is being studied.

**3.** *Critical thinking skills are stable and not easily altered.* Much of the research in the instructional systems field is predicated on the magical effects of very short treatments. Half-hour instructional treatments are expected to alter thinking patterns that have taken a decade or more to establish. Changes in critical thinking are more evolutionary. You cannot expect to see significant changes in how someone thinks after constructing a single knowledge base. Any detectable changes in critical thinking would be more subtle and occur over longer periods of time.

The implication of the foregoing discussion is that learning with constructivist tools such as Mindtools cannot occur in traditional ways. Objective tests (e.g., multiple choice) are not sensitive enough to assess meaning-making in learners. Alternative methods of assessment are necessary.

## Products to Assess

Collins (1990) proposes three kinds of evaluation measures to measure learning and thinking: diagnosis, summary statistics, and portfolios. *Diagnosis* is the kind of continuous self-assessment described before. It uses several sources of data, including learners' self-perceptions. *Summary statistics* about performance, like batting averages in baseball, keep track of learners' performances on different tasks. *Portfolios* consist of a variety of learner-generated products that can be used for summary statistics and for diagnosis. Portfolios may consist of writing samples, multimedia knowledge bases, or other compositions that reflect a learner's knowledge. Their most important attribute is that they reflect real-world performance, not a contrived set of artificial activities. They also require learners to use a variety of intellectual skills.

The most appropriate products to include in a portfolio to be assessed are the Mindtool products themselves. It is therefore necessary for learners to use a variety of Mindtools and not rely on one kind of activity for assessment. For each area being studied, students should construct two or more knowledge bases, using a combination of databases, spreadsheets, semantic networks, expert systems, computer-mediated communication, and multimedia and hypermedia knowledge bases. The intellectual effort that students invest in the knowledge bases they create with these tools will be obvious to the teachers who help them.

## Alternative Assessments

Mindtools may not be rich enough or varied enough to capture students' understanding of a content domain. The most important principle of constructivist assessment appears to be requiring a variety of activities to be included in any portfolio for assessment. The assessment activities described on page 276 have been suggested by various authors from diverse perspectives, including Cross and Angelo (1988). They represent products that can be included in an assessment portfolio. They are offered as an initial list of possible activities that can be used as cognitive apprenticeship outcomes.

Whichever assessment activity is used, the process of selection must be overt and shared with everyone involved. Through the process of sharing their learning goals, outcomes, and methods of assessment, students are afforded the opportunity to formalize their intentions. Thus a spirit of support and cooperation among all stakeholders in the learning process is created. The opportunity for students to suggest and choose the methods of evaluation will increase both their commitment to and their motivation for the activity, in addition to allowing them the opportunity to formalize their thoughts and ideas used in selecting and developing these assessment methods.

## Learning Logs or Self-Studies of Engaged Learning Time

Students estimate, monitor, document, and reflect on how effectively they use academic learning time. Focusing on an assignment, class session, or activity, they estimate the amount of engaged learning time that will be devoted to the task and monitor the actual time usage, stopping every 10 to 15 minutes to note how many of those minutes were actually spent engaged in active learning and what the nature of the learning activity was (Cross & Angelo, 1988).

## Student Rankings of Course Objectives

Ranking course objectives provides both the teacher and students with an opportunity for a comparative match between the students' current learning goals and the goals of the course. Having the students rank and estimate the difficulty of achieving selected course goals and objectives will provide valuable insight into the activities that might facilitate learning for those students (Cross & Angelo, 1988).

## Think-Aloud

Think-aloud protocols can be used in a variety of constructivist settings. By modeling think-aloud protocols, the instructor can demonstrate an effective tool for identifying individual steps and potential faults in a problem-solving process. An even more effective use of think-aloud protocols occurs in collaborative groups. One student, while engaged in a problem-solving activity, uses think-aloud procedures to describe to the others in the group how he or she is solving the problem. Later the group can discuss the results and effectively prepare a procedural description of a problem-solving method, highlighting both problem-solving and metacognitive monitoring strategies.

## Documented Problem-Set Solutions

Students document the steps taken in solving problems in order to "show and tell" their work. This encourages them to focus on, classify, and evaluate the steps and strategies they used to solve a problem. Teachers can elicit two types of valuable information: (1) patterns of skill acquisition, and (2) use and levels or types of metacognitive monitoring strategies the student recalls during a problem-solving activity. This technique provides specific information about the student's success in solving domain-specific problems and general information about the student's approaches to broader problem-solving tasks (Cross & Angelo, 1988).

For example, a student working alone or in a collaborative group solves a series of age-appropriate math problems and notes the individual strategies used to complete the task. The student would then be instructed to create a written document or working diagram sharing the methods and procedures that he or she found most effective for tackling various types of problems, thereby creating a user-oriented problem-solving guide.

## Focused Autobiographical Sketches of Students as Learners

The focused autobiographical sketch is a shorter, more specific version of the commonly used autobiographical essay. In this task, students are directed to write a one- to three-page autobiographical sketch focusing on a single past learning experience. The experience should be relevant to the particular course or session in which this assessment technique is used (Cross & Angelo, 1988). For example, it might be suggested that before beginning a new task or content area, students reflect on their last experience with that content or material. The resulting autobiographical sketch should include references to feelings of success, level of understanding, and current attitudes toward the material. This will suggest a variety of topics for discussion among students and between students and teacher on the prospect of success during the upcoming similar learning task, including attributions for success and strategies for improving chances for success.

## Stump the Teacher

Students generate questions for the teacher in an effort to find one that the teacher cannot answer. This method has been used successfully by Schoenfeld (1985) in math teaching. In order to find unanswerable questions, learners must reflect on what they know in order to speculate about what the teacher may not know.

## Cognitive Interview

This technique is an outgrowth of applied memory research and offers several powerful mnemonics that have been shown to increase the number of things remembered (Bekerian & Dennett, 1993). During the cognitive interview, students are asked to restate or re-create the surrounding context connected to a learning event. This includes emotional and internal states of the learner, physical surroundings, and the context in which the subject matter was presented. Using the cognitive interview techniques, the interviewer will suggest that the interviewee restate the context or recall events in a different order, or may challenge the student to change perspectives.

## Essays

Writing demonstrates both comprehension and composition skills, including inventing, revising, elaborating, defending, and stating one's ideas to fit the purpose and the audience. In addition, it demonstrates students' knowledge of context-specific language and the correct situational usage of syntax and grammar (Feuer & Fulton, 1993). For writing to be used effectively, it should be focused on a real-world problem or event, so writing about current, controversial topics is likely to produce the best arguments. Also, the writing task should be directed at a specific target audience that is commonly associated with such a task (e.g., letter to the editor of the local paper) and should be written from the perspective of a professional or expert.

## Directed Paraphrasing

Students paraphrase a reading or a lecture, using their own words, for a specific audience and purpose, and within a specific page-length or speaking-time limit (Cross & Angelo, 1988). To replicate an authentic paraphrasing activity, the student will be responsible for writing a summary of a specific topic for a designated elected official. Often written for politicians, this type of document is limited to a single page of one-paragraph summaries of the current arguments, perspectives, and various concerns on a single subject up for vote or debate.

## Analytical Memos

Students produce a short, structured writing assignment that develops an effective argument of a specific purpose, toward a predefined audience and from a professional perspective. This activity requires the ability to collect adequate supportive information, build an effective argument, and draft a persuasive paper. The memos may be used as a continuing dialogue between students, within collaborative groups, or between student and instructor. The feedback provided during this ongoing dialogue would be the most effective part of this exercise (Cross & Angelo, 1988).

In an interesting variation of the analytical memo, the teacher would create and facilitate an ongoing dialogue between two or more collaborative teams by posting or printing an editorial page containing the writing of each group. Each collaborative team would represent opposing opinions on a single topic. Their editorial contributions would refer to other comments, rewriting and restating their original ideas and rebutting an opposing team's arguments.

## Classification/Decision Matrix

Students create two-dimensional matrices and list on the left side of each matrix all the items, objects, or concepts to be classified within a specific context. Across the top of each matrix they list the features they determine are important in the classification of objects within this domain. They then begin to categorize the items according to the presence or absence of a defining feature. As the matrix builds, students will often find it necessary to expand the matrix to include more features as an attempt to further classify the items or objects. Given enough time and experience, they will begin to eliminate some feature columns as redundant or include them in higher-order classification schemes. The combination and reconstruction of these defining features is both more efficient and common to the process observed in the development of expertise. This activity replicates the thinking required for creating databases, so it probably would not be best used as an alternative assessment for the effects of building a knowledge-oriented database (see Chapter 3).

Creating and using a decision matrix requires students to evaluate lists of alternative outcomes or activities against a set of selection criteria that constrains the situation or environment in which the decision must be made (Schnitzer, 1993). Classification matrices can be created for any question or decision. An effective implementation of this technique would begin with the student creating classification matrices for decisions he or she currently faces, such as activities to pursue, classes to choose, or gifts to buy. Gradually, as students become accustomed to the technique, it may be developed and used to classify content material. The classification matrix can also be used as an effective tool for developing a hypothesis regarding the most probable outcome of a classroom experiment.

## Diaries and Journals

Reflections on events, as perceived by the learner, are valuable sources of information about what learners know and, especially, what they find interesting and important. If the diary is to be used for evaluation purposes, however, it is necessary to inform learners that their ideas will be seen by another person. These might effectively be shared in a computer conference (see Chapter 7). Dialogue journals are also useful for facilitating social negotiation among teachers and students. A dialogue journal is an ongoing written communication in the form of a dialogue between two or more people. The teacher or students initiate the dialogue, commonly with a question or statement. The students follow up with their thoughts or ideas, which may then be shared with others involved in the process. Written comments are added by each reader of the journal, thereby serving as a written record. Dialogue journals can be accomplished effectively using computer-mediated communication methods described in Chapter 7.

## Exhibits

Exhibits are designed as comprehensive demonstrations of skills or competence. These often require the student to produce a demonstration or live performance in class or before other audiences. This can take the form of a competition between individual students or groups or may be initiated as a collaborative project (Feuer & Fulton, 1993). The poster sessions common to many conferences and seminars serve as a good example of the use of exhibits as an assessment activity.

## Experiments

Experiments are used to test how well a student understands scientific concepts and can carry out scientific processes. Increased emphasis on hands-on laboratory work allows the measure of these skills directly rather than through paper-and-pencil tasks (Feuer & Fulton, 1993). Science education has traditionally taken advantage of the effective use of classroom experiments and laboratories. These can be facilitated through different experimental microworlds (see Chapter 10). Experiments should not be limited to science, however. Every area of study has the potential to exploit experimentation in the effort to provide each student the opportunity to test his or her cognitive representation against objective reality.

## Concept Maps

Through the construction of any number of structural representations of knowledge, the student is able to share a diagram that includes both conceptual/declarative knowledge and the more complex structural information by which this knowledge is organized. These diagrams allow the student working alone or collaboratively to illustrate his or her perception of the relationships and associations among objects, items, concepts, and ideas. Jonassen, Beissner, and Yacci (1993) provide a detailed account of various methods of representing structural knowledge, such as concept maps, Pathfinder nets, ordered trees, and pattern notes. The semantic nets described in Chapter 5 also provide the means for generating concept maps.

## Oral Debates

Unlike most of the previous assessment opportunities, oral debate provides the experience of quickly formulating one's thoughts and responses. This form of oral discourse should always be situated in an authentic experience in which the goals and outcomes of the discussion seem to have an effect. Argumentation is another effective use of the oral debate. The learner is in the position of presenting and defending a perspective from the content area.

## Dramatic or Musical Performances

Within the fine arts, students have always been evaluated on their ability to perform the particular art or skill being studied before a live and often critical audience. These performances often serve as a culminating act to the end of a period of study and indicate the transition toward new goals and objectives. This type of stage assessment can also be found in the martial arts.

## Invented Dialogue

When students invent a dialogue fulfilling a specific scenario, they synthesize their knowledge of both sides of an issue, personalities, and historical periods to form a carefully structured illustrative conversation. This invented dialogue may be created by carefully selecting and weaving together reasonable quotations that fit the character of the speakers. It may be constructed alone or in collaborative groups, based on an individual's knowledge of a character's point of view, personality, and opinions (Cross & Angelo, 1988). For example, in the study of history or sociology, students can invent dialogues between famous historical figures. A dialogue may also be invented about fictitious individuals and focus more directly on the situational conditions of the event.

# Criteria for Evaluating Learning Outcomes from Mindtools

If you use any of the portfolio items just described for assessing your learners, in addition to the Mindtools products that they have developed, you will next face the vexing question of how to evaluate them. The personal nature of the responses will not lend itself to the traditional template approach to comparing a learner's response to a standard response. Students' responses will also be affected by the quality of the activity. Authentic activities are most likely to produce the best results.

Each of the products described earlier can be evaluated using the following criteria. The process will not yield a single numerical value that describes the learner's understanding, but it will very likely produce more certainty on your part about what the learners know.

- *originality*—Do the products represent the student's original thoughts, or are they copied from sources or other students?
- *complexity*—How many ideas are represented, and are those ideas richly interconnected? How useful would that knowledge be in solving problems?
- *coherence*—Are the relationships that are expressed in the product meaningful and appropriate, and are they consistently used?
- *inference*—Are the students able to make hypotheses and conjectures based on the information in their products?
- *predictability*—Are the students able to solve the kinds of problems faced by citizens, consumers, and professionals in the field?
- *contextual relevance*—Do the learners' responses reflect representations of the contexts encountered in a field of study or in the real "tests" of life?
- *resource/tool use*—Do the students make effective use of the resources and tools that were made available during the activity and those commonly available in the real world?

- *repertoire of knowledge*—Did the students' responses call on a repertoire of knowledge and judgment in different forms, that is, a mix of declarative, structural, and procedural knowledge?

Although these criteria are necessarily somewhat vague, they should serve as guidelines for assessing what students know and have learned. The concept of "objective evaluation" is an oxymoron. The purpose of evaluation is to make a value judgment about students' performance, and that is something that can never be completely objectified. However, as I have argued in this book, if what you ask students to do is meaningful, the chances are much greater that their responses will also be meaningful.

## Conclusion

The premise of this chapter is simple. If you teach learners how to think critically and provide them with the tools they need to do so, you are clearly corresponding an intention and desire to have them think critically, so you are obligated to assess the expectations that you communicate and not something else. Assessing the critical thinking and higher-order learning outcomes that Mindtools engage is difficult. It will require you to make different assumptions about assessment, to employ a variety of methods of assessment in a portfolio, to relinquish some of your authority as teacher by allowing students the opportunity to negotiate their goals and intentions, and to use multiple criteria when evaluating the outcomes of student learning. In doing so, you will allow your students to construct more flexible, meaningful, stable, and transferable knowledge than if you dictate the goals and products of assessment. If you accept these challenges, then the only major problem you will encounter is selling the importance of these methods to parents and the community, who are generally more interested in drawing numerical comparisons between students than in understanding what children are learning. What they seek is accountability, but what they do not understand is that in order to be accountable, individuals need a personal stake or investment in determining the goals for which they are to be held accountable. Convincing parents of that will be an important challenge.

## References

Bekerian, D. A., & Dennett, J. L. (1993). The cognitive interview technique: Reviving the issue. *Applied Cognitive Psychology, 7*(4), 275–297.
Collins, A. (1990). Reformulating testing to measure learning and thinking. In N. Fredericksen, R. Glaser, A. Lesgold, & M. G. Shafto (Eds.), *Diagnostic monitoring of skill and knowledge acquisition.* Hillsdale, NJ: Lawrence Erlbaum Associates.

Cross, P., & Angelo, T. (1988). *Classroom assessment techniques: A handbook for faculty.* San Francisco: Jossey Bass.

Feuer, M. J., & Fulton, M. (1993). Better tests and testing practices: Options for policy makers. *Phi Delta Kappan, 74*(7), 530–533.

Jonassen, D. H. (1992). Evaluating constructivistic learning. In T. M. Duffy & D. H. Jonassen (Eds.), *Constructivism and the technology of instruction: A conversation.* Hillsdale, NJ: Lawrence Erlbaum Associates.

Jonassen, D. H., Beissner, K., & Yacci, M. A. (1993). *Structural knowledge: Techniques for conveying, assessing, and acquiring structural knowledge.* Hillsdale, NJ: Lawrence Erlbaum Associates.

Laveault, D. (1986, April). *The evaluation of adult intelligence: A new constructivism.* Paper presented at the meeting of American Educational Research Association, San Francisco.

Norris, S. P. (1989). Can we test validly for critical thinking? *Educational Researcher, 18*(9), 21-26.

Schnitzer, S. (1993). Designing an authentic assessment. *Educational Leadership, 50*(7), 32–35.

Schoenfeld, A. H. (1985). *Mathematical problem solving.* New York: Academic Press.

Wang, S., & Jonassen, D. H. (1993, April). *Using computer-based concept mapping to foster critical thinking.* Paper presented at the annual meeting of the American Educational Research Association, Atlanta, GA.

Wiggins, G. (1993). Assessment: Authenticity, context, and validity. *Phi Delta Kappan, 75*(3), 200–214.

# Index